WRITING AND LEARNING IN CROSS-NATIONAL PERSPECTIVE

Writing and Learning in Cross-National Perspective

Transitions from Secondary to Higher Education

Edited by

DAVID FOSTER
Drake University

DAVID R. RUSSELL
Iowa State University

 National Council of Teachers of English
1111 W. Kenyon Road, Urbana, Illinois 61801-1096

 Lawrence Erlbaum Associates, Inc.
10 Industrial Avenue, Mahwah, New Jersey 07430

The seven figures depicting structures of the educational systems discussed in this book have been reprinted from T. Neville Postlethwaite, editor, *International Encyclopedia of National Systems of Education*, Copyright 1995, pp. 207, 333, 347, 498, 893, 1026, 1035, with permission from Elsevier Science.

Staff Editor: Bonny Graham
Interior Design: Jenny Jensen Greenleaf
Cover Design: Pat Mayer

NCTE Stock Number: 59192-3050

Lawrence Erlbaum Associates, Inc. ISBN 0-8058-4485-6

Library of Congress Cataloging-in-Publication Data

Writing and learning in cross-national perspective : transitions from secondary to higher education / edited by David Foster, David R. Russell.
    p. cm.
Includes bibliographical references and index.
   ISBN 0-8141-5919-2 (pbk.)
   1. Rhetoric. I. Foster, David, 1938 Aug. 17– II. Russell, David R., 1951–
  P301 .W737 2002
  808' .042—dc21

48906397

2002001023

To Suzy and Joyce
and to the memories of Gene Russell
and Irving and Dorothy Foster

Contents

ACKNOWLEDGMENTS

Work on this book was supported by grants from the British Council, the Drake University Research Fund, the Drake University Center for the Humanities, the dean of the Drake University College of Arts and Sciences, the German-American Fulbright Commission, the British Institute, the John S. Knight Institute for Writing in the Disciplines at Cornell University, and the Iowa State University Science, Technology, and Society Program.

We want to thank Michael Greer, formerly with the National Council of Teachers of English, for his support of the project in its early stages, Zarina Hock for her support in its later stage, the panel of anonymous reviewers for their helpful comments, and Kurt Austin and Bonny Graham for their expertise, patience, and good spirits in seeing the project through to completion.

We received support and encouragement for this project from many people in the United States and other countries. It is impossible to name them all, but we would especially like to thank Gerhard Bach, Deborah Brandt, Batong Gu, Bruce Horner, Otto Kruse, Lienhard Legenhausen, Joseph Lenz, Min-Zhan Lu, Winfried Marotzki, Gary Olson, the late Alan Purves, Julius Redding, Goodman Shezi, and the Group for Research in Applied English Studies, Iowa State University.

We are also grateful to the faculty and students of Drake University and Iowa State University for stimulation and encouragement as this project developed.

Rearticulating Articulation

DAVID R. RUSSELL AND DAVID FOSTER

In most national education systems, students' writing development plays an important—though often unacknowledged—role in the crucial transition from secondary school to university. There is a great deal at stake, for both individual students and the societies involved, in how and how well students write. In most nations, whether students can enter and remain in higher education—and thus move into positions of greater responsibility and status in society—depends in large part on whether and how they have developed their writing. Thus, writing development is bound up with questions of equity in access to higher education and to powerful roles in society. And in a larger sense, written communication is essential to the successful continuation and future development of important institutions—professional, governmental, industrial, commercial, and nonprofit—that increasingly depend on specialized written communication in a global environment.

Writing and Learning in Cross-National Perspective presents research studies from six nations on academic writing development in the "mother tongue," or, rather, in the dominant language of schooling (each of these nations has significant numbers of students—a majority in South Africa and Kenya—who do not speak the dominant language of schooling as their mother tongue). The chapters focus on:

◆ **China.** Xiao-ming Li analyzes the writing of secondary students in Chinese classrooms in terms of the struggle between ancient traditions of exam writing and the demands of modernization. She then presents results of a survey of university students that was designed to reveal their perceptions of their secondary school experience in light of university writing demands.

- **England.** Mary Scott looks at the mutual misperceptions of students and teachers in the discipline of English literature as students move from secondary school assumptions about literary criticism in a humanist tradition to university literature courses that critique those assumptions in a domain of contested theory. She carefully analyzes the ways students negotiate their own "interests" with those of the changing discipline through their texts.

- **France.** Christiane Donahue examines student writing in the transition from secondary to higher education in France's very centralized system, where the demands of early specialization and the ideology of egalitarian access collide in the writing-based examination system. She finds that secondary school students in general learn to write a few genres very well and make a smooth transition to the similar university writing—but with clear costs.

- **Germany.** David Foster presents data from interviews with students and faculty from institutions on both sides of the old East-West divide in order to consider the different kinds of authority students must develop as writers when they make the transition from the relatively more nurturing environment of secondary school *Gymnasien* to the pressures of seminar pedagogy in higher education.

- **Kenya.** Mary N. Muchiri looks at the special problems of developing student writing in a multilingual, multicultural education system still dealing with the legacy of colonialism. She sees writing development in terms of a deep contradiction between indigenous values of community solidarity and the demands of a higher education system structured on notions of Western individualism and commerce.

- **South Africa.** Suellen Shay and Rob Moore describe three students from different social and educational backgrounds writing in a university history course on colonialism, within the context of a newly integrated university undergoing dramatic reforms. The authors see students struggling to create meaningful agency through the writing tasks of new curricula designed in a time of rapid social and political transition.

We conceived this collection to give cross-national perspective to issues of writing development, issues that many nations face with the growth of higher education worldwide. We invited contributors who have done significant research in their own nations but who are also familiar with other education systems, mainly that of the United States. Individual chapters use a variety of empirical research methods, qualitative and quantitative. These include surveys; interviews with students, teachers, and university faculty; discourse analysis of student texts and official documents on curriculum, teaching, and assessment; classroom observation; and analysis of historical studies. We chose contributors to represent a range of national systems—large and small, Western and non-Western, English-speaking and non-English-speaking. Several of the nations represented here have a robust tradition of research on writing, which the authors draw on for their studies. Had space permitted, other nations might also have been chosen, such as Australia, which has seen a great deal of innovative research into writing in the secondary education to higher education transition.

Indeed, researchers around the world have addressed the problem of articulating secondary/higher education writing within the context of their individual national systems. Yet there has been little cross-national dialogue on these issues. This is understandable. Research in mother-tongue writing development in secondary and higher education—what is called in North America "composition"—is very much local in origin, responsive to particular cultural and institutional needs.

While composition studies have flourished in U.S. education, for example, these studies have tended to focus on issues related to the special status of general writing courses and programs in U.S. schools and universities. U.S. composition studies have paid little attention to insights that might emerge from cross-national comparisons of writing development and pedagogy, given that general college composition courses largely do not exist outside the United States. This collection is a step toward filling this gap by making a variety of non-U.S. perspectives available to U.S. readers, and to others around the world, who are looking to rearticulate the articulation between secondary and higher education writing development.

Although there has been some important cross-national research on writing, that research has shown the limits of direct cross-national comparisons of student writing. In the 1980s, the International Association for the Evaluation of Educational

Achievement (IEA) sponsored a major project comparing student performance on a range of writing tasks in fourteen countries (Purves et al.). This ambitious effort to compare student writing cross-nationally was in one significant respect a "failure," the project director says, because "what was thought to have been comparable . . . has proved impossible to achieve" (199).[1]

At the outset, the IEA project team assumed that writing was "a general cognitive capacity or activity" that could be studied apart from culture and ideology—what Brian Street calls the autonomous view of literacy. Instead they discovered that it was impossible to find useful comparisons in ostensibly similar statistical findings among participating educational systems. Although the writing tasks in the study were designed to be similar in each system measured, the researchers found it difficult to assess results in any standard or uniform way. Because of the national and local variations in teaching and evaluative practices, even "common qualities of handling content . . . and style" in writing samples had "national or local characteristics" (Purves et al. 199). As a result, the editor concludes, "the construct that we call written composition must be seen in a cultural context and not considered a general cognitive capacity or activity. Even the consensus on goals and aims of writing instruction masks a variation both in ideology of teachers and in instructional practices" (199).

This central lesson of the IEA study is the starting point for this collection. If cultural-historical differences prevent direct comparisons, then in order to learn from other nations we must look closely at the cultural-historical factors in each nation that shape writing development. By understanding the differences, we may be able to rethink our own national and local institutions, and perhaps find common issues that can help teachers, researchers, and policymakers rearticulate writing development in their own institutions and nations, informing further research, curriculum development, faculty development, and educational policy debates. That is what we attempt in this collection.

Of course, this makes generalizations difficult and deceptive. Studies and comparisons provide no firm lessons, much less one best way to develop students' academic writing. Not only is each national system different, but also each nation exhibits profound differences in writing development. Likewise, different regions within a nation show differences, as Foster points out in his comparison of schools and universities in the eastern and western sectors of Germany. In every nation, institutions display differences in status, mission, and goals. And within every institution, disciplinary differences also shape writing development. Thus, the studies in this volume do not pretend to make systematic comparisons, nor do we in this introduction.

Although systematic comparisons of the type attempted in the IEA study seem fruitless at this stage, we nevertheless believe that informal and admittedly unsystematic comparisons are useful. This collection should give readers new perspectives for understanding their own practices as teachers and writers. Our comparisons are tentative and offered as heuristics for rearticulating national and local practices, not for drawing conclusions about "best practice" or ranking the quality of learning and teaching in various systems. We hope readers will also want to make their own comparisons and judgments based on their situations and experience.

In this spirit of exploration and understanding, we suggest that all of the systems face some basic issues. Though the chapters focus on a variety of issues, levels, and disciplines, each examines functions common to all systems: instruction, evaluation, and placement at the secondary level; how students make the transition as writers from the secondary to the university level; and how they meet the challenges of academic writing in the university. These discussions offer various "lenses" for viewing one's own national and local practices in light of others' practices.

In this introductory chapter, we outline ten common themes that surface again and again in these studies and others. These themes are useful in examining the role of writing in the transition to higher education from a cross-national perspective. The first five themes take up issues affecting writing development in the context of an entire education system, and we use the U.S. system as a reference point because it is the only system that has widespread university-level general writing courses. We hope that U.S. readers will see how radically different other systems are in their response to similar issues.

- The point at which students specialize into disciplinary majors, and the effects of early and late specialization on writing development
- The effects of educational traditions and ideology
- The degree of centralization/decentralization and its effects on efforts to develop students' writing
- The roles that writing plays in tracking and selection, particularly examination writing
- Attitudes and orientations toward writing

The last five themes take up specific issues of teaching and learning in classrooms in relation to assessment and professional access:

- Identity and authority in making the transition to disciplinary conversations
- Problems students have handling intertextuality: citation, synthesis, and plagiarism
- Assessment, especially gatekeeping and the consequences of examinations for pedagogy and writing development
- Language policy and traditions
- Teaching—whether it is done explicitly or implicitly

We then conclude by posing questions that the cross-national perspective of these essays raise for teachers, researchers, and policymakers, in order to help them find ways of rearticulating the secondary-higher education transition in terms of writing development.

The Roles of Writing: Local, Systemic, and Cultural Issues

As Muchiri, Mulamba, Myers, and Ndoloi have argued, writing development is, like all academic work, situated within complex national, regional, and local environments. And although academic work is increasingly international in scope, with "journals, conferences, publishers and research projects" all "linked by e-mail, photocopies, faxes and airlines," Muchiri et al. suggest that "this apparent globalization is deceptive." After all, "everyday academic work is still overwhelmingly determined by national settings. The funding, the geography, the politics, the national ideology determine daily concerns like hours, class size, assessment, careers. And access to that global network of contacts is by no means equally apportioned" (Muchiri et al. 194).

All of these local factors produce traditions of writing development and pedagogy that seem transparent or even inevitable, second nature for students and teachers in their respective systems. As the IEA study points out, the terms educators in various countries use to describe practices are often the same (e.g., essay, composition, clarity, argument), but "the nuances and values given those terms are a part of the national culture that makes such sharing superficial at best" (Purves et al. 200):

> Students adapt to and become members of a rhetorical community that shares a number of assumptions and beliefs, only some of which are explicit: the kinds of writing valued, the approach to the activity of composition that is desired, the relative importance of convention and individualism, the models of text and text practices that are considered appropriate in the school. (200)

As already noted, the most striking difference between writing development in the U.S. educational system and writing development in most other national systems is the prevalence in U.S. universities of general writing courses. This ubiquitous tradition in the United States—perhaps the only curricular common denominator in what is otherwise a sprawling and diverse higher education system—strikes many teachers in other nations as strange. Similarly, U.S. educators are often surprised that students in other nations learn to write without general composition courses. U.S. readers of this volume will find it irresistible to compare the singular U.S. reliance on general writing instruction courses with the widely differentiated settings for students' development as writers found in other systems. Several factors have influenced this important systemic difference—factors that affect different countries and systems in different ways. Understanding the differences makes it possible to see more clearly the ecology of general writing instruction and its impact on its unique U.S. habitat, and by contrast to understand better how other systems develop writing differently. The following factors are most important in thinking about these differences generally.

Time of Specialization

In the United States, students specialize (choose a major) very late compared to students in other nations. Students in many countries (such as France and England) specialize as early as age sixteen or seventeen, in the second two years of secondary school. U.S. students are admitted to a university rather than, as in most of the systems discussed in this collection, to a department. U.S. students aren't expected to choose a profession until late in their higher education—or even until graduate school or entering the workforce. Late specialization provides a longer period of general or liberal education and a curricular space for general composition courses that can teach a wider variety of genres than those of one specialty (e.g., informal personal essays). Early specialization, by contrast, allows for greater focus on the genres of one or a few disciplines, which brings students more quickly into a deeper engagement with the discourse of a field. There is no clear space for general composition courses, and any formal university writing instruction (many systems have little or none) must come from within the disciplines or in special student support units (similar to U.S. writing centers). Late specialization is costly to society, keeping millions of students in higher education longer than in other nations. (The United States spends far more per capita on higher education than any other nation, partly due to what has been called "the composition industry.") But late specialization also provides the possibility of a broader education and certainly more time for making choices. It is interesting to note that some higher education systems are beginning to move toward wider access and later specialization, as the United States did almost a century ago. As they do, they are hearing calls for instituting general composition courses, or at least institution-wide writing support units, which we will discuss when we focus on recent changes in education systems.

Ideology and Educational Traditions

Traditions and ideologies play a huge role in writing development. In the late nineteenth century in the United States (and somewhat later in Europe), technological developments spurred by corporate capitalism produced rapid professionalization that was accomplished through credentialing in the new modern higher education systems. Individual accomplishment was seen as the product of individual merit rather than of parentage or social class (see Ohmann for a critique). But this meritocratic ideology played out differently in different education systems. The U.S. tradition of egalitarian individualism, for example, has for over a century viewed formal education as a route to social advancement, and the U.S. system has moved toward wider and wider access, with more and more chances for individuals to enter and remain in a very decentralized education system—and receive formal writing instruction designed, in theory, to make new chances possible (Russell, *Writing*). By contrast, France has tended toward an egalitarian view that works to provide, in theory, an identical education for all in a very centralized system, but with few second chances (though democratic pressures have in recent decades increased enrollments in secondary and higher education). Students are tracked relatively early and there is an emphasis on examination writing. In Kenya a deep cultural tradition of *harambee*, or communal pulling together to meet others' needs, coexists in deep contradiction with an individualistic, meritocratic ideology of Western higher education that was imposed during colonial rule, with significant implications for writing development in terms of the social processes students use for writing—and in the constraints of Western notions of individual authorship and plagiarism, as Mary Muchiri argues in Chapter 5. Indeed, in all of the systems described in this volume, traditions and ideologies are constantly contested in the ways students write and learn to write.

The Size and Shape of Systems: Centralized or Dispersed

The United States has a huge and extremely decentralized system of education, both secondary and postsecondary, public and private (see Figure 1). Enrollments in secondary and higher education achieved levels by the 1930s that most other industrialized nations did not reach until the 1970s, and the United States still enrolls a far higher percentage of students in higher education than other nations (Day and Curry).

The U.S. primary and secondary educational system is organized by local districts within each state. The postsecondary system is equally decentralized but in a different way, with local, state, and regional public institutions coexisting with a wide range of local, regional, and national private institutions.

This system is sprawling and complex, with some 3,535 higher education institutions of amazing variety: prestigious, highly selective private research universities; small private colleges; and government-funded institutions. There is no centralized control, apart from voluntary accrediting organizations, or direct funding at the national level. State and local government institutions account for only 17 percent of institutions but enroll 80 percent of students, from huge state research universities to a large number of two-year colleges, mainly public, with no graduate programs and low or no tuition.

Other nations generally have smaller systems (China excepted), and all have more centralized control, with a far smaller private higher education sector. In other nations, the national government controls admission to higher education and funds it, unlike the United States, where individual institutions or local and state governments control admissions and funding. Students in other nations generally pay much less than U.S. students, with the government footing most of the bill. This leads other nations to focus on specific disciplines, often in specialized institutions, and therefore generally to focus on discipline-specific writing development. There is less perceived need for an introduction to university writing, whereas in the United States, the general writing courses fit into a general education component of higher education.

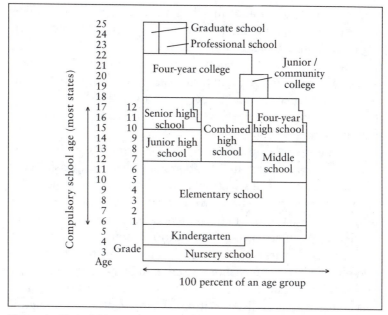

Figure 1. *United States of America: Structure of the formal education system.*

Tracking and Selection

Because most U.S. students specialize (and are selected for specialized training) later, curricular requirements are broad and educational choices remain continuously available—at least officially—as students move through secondary school into university or even graduate school. Students do not need to be selected on the basis of their ability to write (or speak) the discourse of a discipline or disciplines when they enter higher education. Machine-scored examinations of general "ability" or, less common, tests of general "writing ability" are the norm. In secondary schools, students are typically sorted into tracks or "ability groups." These tracks sort students "destined" for higher education (and for more selective postsecondary education). Though all students take courses in roughly the same subjects, the content of the required subjects, as well as expectations of students, varies widely by tracks, and social sorting (and preparation for higher education) is accomplished without formal assessments of writing beyond those in individual classrooms. Extended writing is not required on the most widely used nationwide U.S. college entrance (or "aptitude") examinations, though many institutions and professions are beginning to demand written examinations because students' writing is perceived to be inadequate. Thus, the stakes for writing development are comparatively low in the United States.

By contrast, European educational systems (which are largely the models for African and Asian systems) have emphasized earlier specialization and selection, and the ways students write in a discipline (or two or three) are crucial. Accordingly, examinations in other nations emphasize extended written (or oral) performance, and there is very little multiple-choice testing. Students must typically write examinations in a discipline to enter the second phase of secondary school, to enter higher education, to continue in higher education, and to receive an undergraduate degree. The stakes for specialized writing development are very high in these systems.

Again, there are complex trade-offs. U.S. students lack the intensive, specialized experience in disciplinary writing that European students get in academic-track secondary school as they prepare for the extended writing required in examinations (and the courses that prepare them for those exams). But students in other nations rarely have a university writing course to help them make the transition to writing the specialized discourse of the disciplines and professions—or the opportunity to write in a wider range of genres with fewer stakes attached.

Orientations toward Writing Development

Throughout the essays that follow, we can see many attitudes or orientations toward writing being contested and negotiated, tacitly and explicitly, in the various national systems and institutional programs described. Drawing on Lea and Street's categories ("Writing"), we can distinguish three general orientations: study skills, academic socialization, and academic literacies. The study skills orientation treats writing as a single, generalizable set of skills learned once and for all, usually at an early age. Though this orientation focuses on writing, it separates writing from the social, disciplinary, and personal dimensions so crucial to success, as twenty years of writing research have shown. And it too often carries a remedial stigma (often with ethnic or class overtones) for students who do not learn the "code" early. This has been the dominant orientation in the United States for the last century, though it has been greatly contested for the last thirty years by U.S. composition, and it operates in complex ways in many other nations as well.

The academic socialization orientation sees writing development as a tacit aspect of an apprenticeship in a discipline or social practice: writing is an embedded element of disciplinary learning. Although this view takes account of the social and disciplinary dimensions of writing, it tends to make writing disappear as an object of attention for teachers, students, and policymakers. One sees this orientation most strikingly in European systems, though it is common among professors across the curriculum in the United States. In this view, there is no need to teach writing per se, either in a disciplinary course or a separate writing course, because in learning the content students are learning to write—almost automatically, it is assumed. From their first semesters at university (or later secondary school), they are required to write the analyses and interpretations, reports, seminar papers, and examinations that will mark their progress in their fields of study, and writing appears to be an ability they come by as a matter of "course."

Despite such expectations, however, students in European systems do not necessarily move readily and smoothly into the discourse of their disciplines. The studies in this book indicate that they struggle with exams and papers in their disciplines just as U.S. students struggle in courses across the curriculum. U.S. students, by contrast, do have general writing instruction before (and sometimes during) their encounters with discipline-specific discourse in their major fields, but this direct instruction may have little to do with students' personal learning goals in a discipline. And there are many accounts of U.S. students who have had composition courses struggling mightily with disciplinary writing requirements, as European students do (Russell, "Where").

The academic literacies orientation—the least common of the three—has developed in the last decade to explain why many students do not meet the expectations for writing after having had study skills instruction and/or time in a discipline. It views writing neither as a set of generalizable skills nor as an unteachable, natural part of entering a discipline, but as an immensely variable, developing accomplishment that is central to the specialized work of the myriad disciplines of higher education and to the professions and institutions students will enter and eventually transform. Each new specialized genre a student or new employee encounters means learning new practices—ways of thinking and acting that have become second nature to old-timers (Russell, "Where"). In this sense, writing development is bound up with issues of identity, authority, and motivation, conditioned by ideological assumptions, institutional structures, and disciplinary epistemologies. Questions of agency, identity, and authority are lurking behind textual choices students make. If writing is not autonomous but instead integral to disciplines, then choosing to write in a particular way is choosing to be one of the people who write that way, to link one's identity, one's future, to these people. Often students resist, or opt out, or fail. The academic literacies orientation asks how writing works differently in various practices and how students move from one to another using writing. A central question of writing development becomes how to simultaneously raise the awareness of students, specialized academic staff, and policymakers to the powerful and varied role of writing in learning, teaching, work, and citizenship, while at the same time integrating efforts to develop writing into the specialized studies and activities that writing mediates—instead of segregating writing development and keeping it on the margin. Each of the essays in this volume addresses these questions from an academic literacies orientation.

The Roles of Writing: Classrooms, Assessments, and Professional Access

Students moving from secondary to higher education are in a liminal state, as Mary Scott reminds us in Chapter 2, situated at the threshold. They are between worlds, and their writing reflects this transition. Generally, students are leaving a more nurturing environment in secondary school and entering an environment of greater responsibility and greater personal challenge. In most systems, students must orient themselves to new institutional expectations, the challenge of disciplinary discourse, and new structures of learning and writing. David Foster describes, for example, how students in Germany must "build new habits and attitudes," often with little feedback from professors (p. 194). German students must learn to work within new institutional and material spaces, develop new rhetorical masteries, and negotiate freedom and autonomy in learning and writing. In Suellen Shay and Rob Moore's account of South African students, the transition to university means negotiating a system in transition, in which deep historical differences in education systems—African, Colored, and White—meet in traditionally White universities that are rapidly expanding to meet postapartheid demands. Scott describes how in England this transition often means shifting from the "pastoral care" of secondary schools to a theory-laden disciplinary environment.

In terms of writing development, students entering higher education are moving out of the relative comfort of writing for teacher, examiners, and classmates, where the conversations are limited to the world of education. They are on the threshold of entering a professional world in which they are preparing to write for other professionals in business, industry, government, and nonprofit sectors. (We use the term *profession* here in the broad sense, as work that ordinarily requires higher education, as well as credentialing from a governmental or professional organization—law, medicine, nursing, and engineering, of course, but also teaching, mortuary, accounting, and literally thousands of others.)

The expectations implied in the genres and activities of secondary school writing are—often without warning—challenged by a different set of expectations from the genres and activities of disciplinary discourse. These expectations are sometimes made explicit for students, but often they remain tacit, folded into the reading and writing required by course work and examinations. In much the same way people learning a foreign language experience what has been called "interference" from their first language, students carry unconscious habits of writing into the university environment—until they experience the shock of difference, and often failure. These misperceptions lead to dissonance and struggle as students reexamine their choice of profession and their identity as learners/writers. They must decide if they want to be one of the people who write in these new and as yet unfamiliar ways. They must appropriate the discourse of a discipline and/or profession, a process made more difficult in highly multilingual countries such as Kenya and South Africa, where they must often use a language not their mother tongue. (Professors also often misperceive student writing, but because of the power differential, they can define what is appropriate writing without listening carefully to students' views expressed in nondisciplinary discourse).

Yet much more than schooling is involved in these textual choices, which are also ultimately life decisions, decisions about identity. Student decisions about what to make of writing in formal schooling grow out of their whole experience, not just their experience of secondary schooling. The IEA study, like this collection, suggests that the students' family, community, gender, ethnicity, and social class are constantly in play. Such "home variables," as the IEA study calls them, are one of the most powerful predictors of successful performance, particularly on the more academic tasks, such as persuasion (Purves et al. 201). Indeed, the IEA study found that "what goes on in [elementary and secondary] school does not account for the differences in ratings of student writing. . . . What seems to make the difference is what goes on in the home" (201).

> What emerges . . . is that for writing, as for many other school subjects, the reinforcement of the home of the values of writing and participation in a "scribal culture" (Purves, *Scribal*) appears in the rated performance of the students. The schools exist within an ethos of particular forms of literacy that is part of the historically literate culture of a country; when children come from families that participate in that ethos, they tend to be seen as "good" writers. (Purves et al. 202)

And when they do not, writing presents particularly complex challenges, which may explain much about which students enter professions and which do not. Shay and Moore's study of the writing readiness of three students from different racial and cultural backgrounds in South Africa, for example, illustrates the importance of family culture in the acquisition of schooled literacy. A central theme that emerges in this collection is that writing involves negotiating identity and authority in the intersection of students' experiences in school and outside of it, which in higher education, at least, also means inside and outside powerful disciplinary and professional networks.

Identity and Authority in the Transition to Disciplinary Conversations

The liminal state in which first-year university students find themselves, on the threshold of disciplines and professions, is most evident in the way they approach argument. The development of new identities and authorities as writers is a major challenge for students in their transition to university. The uncertainty of their new situations as writers manifests itself, for example, in their uncertainty about, and frequent resistance to, the difficulties of entering disciplinary conversations that require them to use the theories of various fields. Students are expected to enter disciplinary and/or professional conversations and eventually to make a contribution to a profession or field after they leave higher education. This is the goal of their university teachers in their own research, and teaching others to do so is an ultimate goal of their teaching.

Students entering university studies must learn to exercise what Foster calls a different kind of authority as writers (Chapter 4). They must make arguments within not only the social system of the classroom, among peers and teachers—as in secondary school—but also within the system of disciplinary debates, entering conversations between and with experts. This involves framing problems in the theoretical terms of the discipline and thus in terms of its fundamental questions, methods, and epistemologies. This is a tall order for students entering higher education, something for which their secondary school has often not prepared them.

U.S. researchers (Russell, "Where") have described students' struggles with academic writing in similar terms, as students try to accommodate their own rhetorical resources to the unfamiliar demands of university writing. They are like "strangers in strange lands" (McCarthy) who must "invent the university" (Bartholomae) as they go, wondering how these new ways of writing will fit with their previous ways of using language and with their futures, personal and professional. Similarly, Foster describes German university students who, aware of their borderline command of disciplinary discourse, decide they must use disciplinary terms and concepts they don't fully understand in order to "maintain authority" in the new environment. In the stress of choosing, there is sometimes resistance, or opting out, or failing.

Shay and Moore's study is especially revealing about students' struggles with the rhetorical demands of university-level writing. They describe three South African students whose history professors *expect* them to practice and display theory-based historical methodological skills by becoming constructors themselves of positions and arguments. Students struggle to move from reproducing "single truth" (textbook) accounts of history as "information retrieval" to a "far more active writer role" that requires them to understand "the disciplinary field of history as a debate made up of multiple and contending narratives" that have to be adjudicated (p. 282). Their instructors, as representatives of a discipline, tacitly expect students to act as agents in the discipline, to construct history—but out of theory-based and therefore authoritative accounts. Yet, say Shay and Moore, university instructors, taking disciplinary authority for granted, are often "silent about how students can develop this agency in relation to the authoritative canon." "On the one hand," they say, "they [students] are asked for their own opinions, but in reality [as one professor put it], 'we want [their] opinions about a historical process, [not] about moral issues,'" as students' secondary school writing had led them to expect (p. 294). Yet the students sometimes resist writing in these "disciplined" ways because those ways of writing seem to disallow their moral and political stances. Students in the transition between school and university cannot yet fully negotiate the various imperatives at play: voices warning against plagiarism, voices of personal experience and resistance, voices of textbook authority, and voices of competing theories in the discipline. Their only resort often seems to be a hollow imitation of the voices of academic texts.

Students find it difficult to develop a personal investment in writing—and motivation beyond getting a good grade—when the discourse requires distance or even detachment from the personal interests and questions that brought them to the course, whether this distance is labeled "objectivity" or the familiar injunction not to use the first person "I." Shay and Moore's study reveals that the South African students are better able to construct an authorial role when they work from primary sources rather than from authoritative secondary sources. They feel and exert greater agency when they are not competing with the theorized voices of professional historians. But the students in Shay and Moore's study don't have the rhetorical and linguistic resources to create the rhetorical authority desired by their professors. Thus they often produce an "'authorless text' about a naturalized world"—writing that does not show them as potential meaning-making agents in the discipline of history (p. 294).

Students' difficulties in making the transition from the controlled rhetorical settings of school writing to the more complex rhetorical demands of disciplinary discourse are also reflected in Scott's study of British students entering university in literary studies. Scott's study finds that students entering university must develop a more distanced and theory-laden subjectivity in order to succeed. They have been taught to write essays in secondary school based on a model of literary criticism that university professors no longer hold (or hold in disrepute): the old Arnoldian, Leavisite model of literary analysis as an argument about "human thought and meaning," which values paradox and ambiguity but does not discuss theory explicitly. Arriving at university, students encounter a new disciplinary epistemology and a set of methods that the newer disciplinary model (tacitly) requires in writing about literature. Their university instructors (often without saying so) expect students to acknowledge and discuss competing literary theories in a "contested space" in the discipline, as they harness evidence to support a particular theory. There is again a profound mismatch between teachers' and students' expectations.

Scott's study, for example, traces the struggle of a student who writes about a short story set in the former colonies not in terms of postcolonial theory—which requires identifying "the other" in nuanced political terms—but in terms that seem to the tutor to sound as though the student views colonization as natural. Unfortunately, the student does not mention her own sense of "otherness" as a member of a minority group from a former colony, even though this revelation might have allowed her to discuss issues of contested postcolonial identity. Another student wants to write about "feminine experience" in a poem but essentializes this in a way unacceptable to her instructor, who operates out of a much richer network of competing theories of feminism. The novice university students hear "the voices of past experience" in the essay questions they are given to write on, but these voices are not the voices the tutors expect or want the students to hear.

Scott proposes ways that secondary school teachers can lead students to appreciate the ambiguities and paradoxes of their *own* writing about literature as well as the ambiguities and paradoxes in the literature they analyze. This reflection on their own writing might move them into a zone of proximal development in which the complexities of theory could become accessible. But such a move will take a much fuller appreciation on the part of the instructors of the complexities of student writing.

In China, expectations for university writing are also radically different from those for secondary school. Instead of writing in a few genres stressing literary effect, imagery, and sensibility, as they did in secondary school, university students must adapt to writing that emphasizes rationality, logic, and "depth of thinking" in discipline-specific argument (p. 76). University papers are much longer, stress theory, and require intertextual reference beyond the standard works taught in secondary school. To write such papers, students need a good command of theory and specialized information, a difficult task that can be accomplished only by much reading and hard thinking. "University writing," one of Xiao-ming Li's sources concludes, "is different from high school in that there is more room for developing one's own ideas, more leeway for one's own inclination, more books to consult, and few restrictions on what to write" (p. 76).

In the United States, high school and college composition teachers often value personal sensibility and expressiveness in writing and see these qualities as freeing. In contrast, many Chinese college students find that the personal sensibility and expressiveness valued in their high school writing is actually restrictive because it closes off the political and social analysis possible with disciplinary discourse. The debates of discipline-specific argument allow students an "openness to diverse ideas" and provide a sense of freedom to address matters of substance, neither of which they had in high school. In the words of one of Li's respondents, "High school writing has fixed structure and fixed thinking," while in college, "the style is looser, content more substantial, and import more profound" (p. 77). Another student described college writing as "more practical, freer to express one's own ideas without being judged 'good' or 'bad'" according to unwritten (and often unconscious) stylistic expectations (p. 76).[2]

France has the only system among the six represented in this book in which the transition in writing from high school to university—and the mismatch in expectations—seems less pronounced. High school *(lycée)* students are relatively well prepared for university writing for several reasons, Christiane Donahue argues in Chapter 3. First, students not only specialize during secondary school (as in many other nations), but they also are expected to do extended, theory-based writing in their secondary school courses. Second, there is a much narrower gap between the training and expectations of secondary and of university teachers. Indeed, both are called "professor." Third, the genres of secondary school writing and examinations are very similar to those of the first university cycle. The major difference is in length.

The most difficult transition for French students in writing comes for students who move from the first university cycle to the second and to the elite *"grandes écoles,"* where they are expected for the first time to make a serious contribution to their fields. Many in France wonder if this early specialization and narrowing of the writing problems to manageable proportions is good, but it certainly has the advantage of providing a smoother transition to higher education.

As the studies in this volume show, students in most educational systems must adapt to major new challenges as writers when they enter university studies. They must inhabit new institutional and material spaces, negotiate the intimidating texts and some-times-incomprehensible lectures couched in new terminologies, and adapt to the dangerous freedoms of unstructured work time. And whether the secondary school has as its aim "single-truth," monologic, textbook-style accounts (South Africa) or complex personal response to primary sources (Germany, England, China), students must also adapt to major new challenges as apprentice writers in their disciplines, immersing themselves in the multivocal—and often theoretical—discussions of various authorities in their disciplines.

Handling Intertextuality: Synthesis and Citation

Another issue that recurs in the studies that follow is the difficulty new university students have in handling intertextuality—paraphrasing, summarizing, synthesizing, and citing sources for writing—while avoiding plagiarism. Though handling intertextuality may seem at first glance to involve a mechanical set of tasks, it actually goes to the core of many students' problems in making the transition to higher education—how to locate their writing and themselves in terms (literally, in the words) of powerful institutions and professions. And it raises a question for their teachers as well—how to represent their specialist knowledge so that students can have progressively deeper access to it and engagement with it.

Because students in higher education are expected to negotiate disciplinary discourse in their reading and writing, they must learn to synthesize the various voices of disciplinary authorities and operate within a much more complex intertextual system of citation and paraphrase. German students in Foster's account, for example, find that the most difficult challenge at university is "learning how to bring together published scholarly voices from the discipline" (p. 219). In navigating the more diverse and complex rhetorical terrain of university discourse, students discover that the personal views often encouraged by high school teachers—however well thought out—become less important. What becomes more important is the ability to integrate views of authoritative others skillfully and coherently into a more complex, multivocal perspective. Some students perceive this as learning the most effective textual strategies, but others see it as a loss of voice to the "impersonal logic of *wissenchaftlich* [scholarly] authority" (p. 221), a silencing of students' personal values and viewpoints.

Similarly, South African history students struggle in selecting from preconstructed authoritative accounts in theory-based secondary sources in order to produce a single account giving their "own" view. As Shay and Moore's study shows, they often fall back on knowledge-telling strategies and are unable, at least initially, to synthesize sources in the knowledge-making way their professors expect.

Chinese secondary students must move from a deeply embedded Confucian tradition of citing canonical texts to the newer and more diverse disciplinary communities of specialized higher education. As Li says, knowing history and "being able to draw instructional or cautionary lessons from history has long been regarded as a salient quality of a good . . . scholar" (p. 67). But the ability to weave together allusions to culturally shared texts only indirectly prepares them to synthesize texts from a disciplinary textual field in order to make an argument that has logical coherence and import in a particular textual field of a discipline in higher education.

French secondary students, as Donahue's study suggests, also learn to write for readers using a relatively narrow range of canonical texts in the disciplines they study. Exam questions often set a passage to comment on, requiring students to use a "reprise modification" structure as a way of building on the passage's main proposition. Intertextuality is common but, as in China, students are trained to give concrete examples from cultural references: "the reflection of rich and varied human experiences, constituting a quasi-infinite reservoir of examples related to every academic domain," as one writing handbook puts it (p. 169). Because the first two years of postsecondary education demand the same kinds of writing as the later secondary years *(lycée)* but with more elaboration, French students have an easier time making the transition as writers—though they may experience shocks similar to those of German students when they enter later stages of higher education (analogous to U.S. graduate school) and are expected to operate within a narrower field. The same classroom genres that students practice in *lycée*—especially the *dissertation* and, to a lesser degree, the *commentaire composé* or other close-reading versions of text explication—will be the two dominant forms in the first years of university. The general expectation for student writing in the university tradition, says Donahue, has been either to "do the same thing [as in the *lycée*] but better," or to "present roughly the same material as in the secondary cycle but in postsecondary form" (p. 176). The French system thus circumscribes for students the problem of handling intertextuality.

Examinations and Writing: Broadening Access, Maintaining Distinctions

Examinations are the most important—and vexed—issue in articulating secondary and higher education. And writing plays an extremely complex and contested role in the educational institutions of each of the nations represented in this collection. Assessments of students' writing often determine who gets into higher education and who completes it—though discussions of access and selection often ignore writing development, focusing instead on what is tested rather than how (and how students are prepared to write).

As knowledge and work become more technical—more specialized and professionalized—nations and professions seek ways to increase the numbers of people entering higher education, where students are selected and prepared to take up specialized positions. Moreover, as democratic ideals spread, governments and institutions of higher education feel greater pressure to increase the numbers in higher education. In one sense, as we noted, these pressures are contradictory. Broadening access runs up against the desire of professions to select only those students who will, the professions believe, make the greatest contribution to their work. And because that work depends—more and more—on specialized writing, the selection process continues in most countries (the United States being the notable exception) to be dependent on extended writing as the main form of assessment.

Thus, written examinations are at the heart of the selection process. But we should note here that the desire to find those people whom the professions believe will make the greatest contribution is a legitimate and ultimately ethical motive. Professions could not serve others effectively if they admitted everyone who wished to enter. Selectivity and qualification are essential to ensure competence. And entrance examinations, particularly written ones, can serve as a motive for individual growth and writing development, for spurring action toward worthwhile goals. For these reasons, examinations are constantly under scrutiny by various stakeholders who represent ethnic groups, business groups, various professions (including teachers), and so on. Indeed, examinations always bring with them a history of language use that was formed along class lines and (in all the nations represented in this collection) those of gender, race, and ethnicity. The effects of examinations on individuals, as well as on identifiable social groups, are never simple.

The United States has the longest history of broadening access (and, not coincidentally, of widespread professionalization; in 1997, 87 percent of twenty-five- to twenty-nine-year-olds had completed high school [Day and Curry]). But in many nations, including those represented here, higher education enrollments are skyrocketing at a rate that will equal that of the United States in the next decade or two. Similarly, increasingly global economic and communications systems are making writing in specialized professional work even more important—and the stakes in written examinations higher. All six of the countries discussed in this study are negotiating these pressures in various ways as they continue to shape the roles that writing plays in the transition from secondary to higher education.

EXAMINATIONS AS GATEKEEPERS

Questions of access surface dramatically in the transition from secondary to higher education. Indeed, writing plays its most important role in the nations represented in this collection in the examinations that qualify students for higher education, in which extended writing is the main—often the only—method of examining students. Clearly, not all who wish to enter a profession—or any work requiring expertise for its safety and effectiveness—are allowed to do so. (We want our surgeons, for example, to have gone through rigorous selection and training.) Specialized reading and writing allows people in specialized practices to learn and to do their work together safely and effectively. But the question of whether and how selection should involve writing assessment is very much contested, in the United States and elsewhere, and rightly so. For written (or any other) assessment can prevent people from entering the roles they desire for reasons that have little or nothing to do with their potential to learn or perform some specialized work well.

Though a few states and districts in the United States have recently instituted high-stakes examinations that incorporate extended writing, admission to higher education is still almost exclusively based on the average of grades in individual courses and nationally standardized multiple-choice, machine-scored tests. Similarly, undergraduate degrees in the United States are granted on the bases of accumulating a certain number of course hours and maintaining a certain grade average. With a few exceptions, written examinations are not required outside of individual courses. Even admission to graduate school (e.g., M.A. and Ph.D. programs) is based primarily on accumulated grades and machine-scored aptitude examinations (e.g., GRE, MCAT, LSAT). In general, students are not required to present an extended piece of writing until graduation from a Ph.D. (and often a master's) program, although both national testing companies, ACT and SAT, as well as a number of professional certification exams, have introduced writing components, usually optional, and are continuing to develop written and other alternative assessments.

In contrast, all of the nations discussed in this study require students to do numerous pieces of extended writing in order to enter higher education—often in a range of disciplines, including mathematics—and to do extended writing in order to obtain a university degree. Though the pervasiveness of writing in the transition from secondary to higher education in other nations may surprise Americans, educators in other nations are often incredulous at the U.S. system, for a variety of reasons. Foster notes, for example, that a German university professor simply could not understand why anyone would study his students' writing in an upper-level seminar. He commented that it really "didn't make sense." After all, he said, all you have to do is look at how the system of seminars and examinations works in order to prepare students to write (p. 192).

Writing ties assessment to teaching and learning in ways that multiple-choice tests cannot, allowing teachers and students (and sometimes other stakeholders) to share expectations. In most nations, examinations are assessed by examining boards made up primarily of teachers and former teachers. In China, France, and Germany, for example, being chosen to grade examinations is an honor for teachers. They are given the freedom and charged with the responsibility to make appropriate evaluative judgments. This means that teachers and other stakeholders must agree on the kinds of writing it is most important to assess. In England, for example, a component of the secondary school leaving (exit) examination is often a portfolio of course work, which is graded by teachers of the subject in the individual school; a sample of portfolios from each school is evaluated by teachers from other schools, in a system called "moderation." The positive effects of moderation on teachers' professional development have been well documented (Gipps). Similarly, in Germany teachers are formed according to discipline into district and regional reading committees that have freedom, within education ministry limits, to interpret assessment criteria as they deem fit. In this way, teachers both use and share their expertise in the grading of examinations. Though human-scored written examinations have less scoring reliability and cost more than machine-scored exams, most nations have judged that the advantages—especially validity—outweigh the disadvantages.

Because in most nations assessment and thus selection have for many decades (and in some cases centuries) been tied to extended writing, cultural values have come to be expressed in examination writing and grading. Thus examinations in many countries are a cherished (critics would say fetishized) part of the culture and therefore resistant to rapid change—just as multiple-choice exams are ingrained in the United States' meritocratic ideology of education and therefore resistant to change. In China, for example, examination writing dates back to the Confucian era, and as Li shows, the genres of secondary leaving essays still have the moral purpose and even at times the generic structure of that ancient tradition. In England there was an uproar in the press and the Ministry of Education when some teachers proposed that not all students be examined on Shakespeare. In France the ideology of democratic *égalité* lies behind the centralized national examination system. For students to have a fair chance at success in the exams, the French generally believe, then it is reasonable to think that all students need an equivalent education. Though to Americans centralization may seem rigid, undemocratic, and antithetical to individual freedom, French teachers often consider the U.S. system undemocratic because, they argue, it masks a system of social sorting under the guise of scientific objectivity and individualism, hiding human decisions and social responsibility for sorting. The French generally view centralized, standardized written examinations as a primary way to offset the inequalities of class and economic privilege as they affect schools and learning. As they see it, only a standard written examination can ensure an immigrant student of color from a working-class district an educational opportunity equal to that of a white student from a privileged middle-class family, though statistics show this is extremely rare, and criticisms of examination bias are increasingly common.

Consequences of Examinations for Pedagogy and Writing Development

Of course, written examinations, like all other examinations, have consequences for pedagogy—"washback," as it is sometimes called. Tests push students to study certain things and not others, and push teachers to teach those things. "Teachers teach to the test," whether their own or one developed by a range of stakeholders over time. There will always be sorting mechanisms, including assessments of various kinds. The trick is to negotiate among stakeholders a test worth teaching to, one that will balance the demands of equity with the demands of disciplinary excellence. If there is collaborative assessment of student writing, then individual teachers must to some extent align their teaching (and the writing they have their students do) with the shared expectations represented by the test.

In one sense, this produces a negative washback called "curricular crowding out," a tendency to exclude from curriculum important genres and content because they are not on the test. And it can also produce alienation in students, who find exam writing and preparation a "dispassionate and perfunctory exercise of finding the information and organizing it acceptably," as Shay and Moore describe one South African student's reaction (p. 302). Chinese writing teachers call such writing *ying4 shi4 wen2*, or exam-coping writing. In writing for university admission, Chinese students must typically display knowledge rather than explore or question it, an approach that attempts to win approval and avoid provoking or offending the reader/judge. Such writing is "rule abiding and conformative" in nature, and explains, Li argues, the persistence of genre expectations over centuries, even millennia (p. 73). But in another sense, shared expectations provide a common core of knowledge and accomplishment that allows students to learn well some genres and develop a sense of accomplishment and cultural solidarity. In this sense, written assessment can balance the demands of equity and excellence. As Foster points out, teachers in German high schools *(Gymnasien)* actively seek continuity between course work and writing through classroom practice.

In every system represented here, there is debate over the choice of genres to be included in written examinations and the relative importance in the university selection process of examinations as opposed to the judgments of teachers. In Germany, for example, secondary teachers are held in high regard, and a primary element of selection for higher education is based on the collective judgment of teachers in individual schools about students' course work. In other nations, by contrast, selection is based almost solely on students' written performance as judged by outside examiners—as in Kenya, for example, as Muchiri's essay suggests. In England the conflict between the role of the local teachers' collective judgment versus that of outside examiners has been a matter of fierce contention between teachers and the government. But in all cases except that of the United States, writing is central in the selection process leading to university matriculation.

Examinations using extended writing become the focus of

debates over the content and direction of education in ways that don't often occur in the United States, where multiple-choice exams produced by national testing companies and grade point averages calculated from students' final grades in individual courses form the primary basis for selection, reducing the need for extended writing and debate about it. In China, moves to modernize the economy have elicited pressure to extend the examination genres to more communicative, "practical" writing. In Germany the recent unification provoked debates about the role of individual versus official interpretation in student exam writing. Similarly, in France a controversy over the relevance of exam genres led to a revision of the genres available to students on the baccalaureate, the secondary exit and higher education entrance exam, though recent studies show that exam readers in France still favor students who answer literary questions over those who answer the new nonliterary questions.

Debates continue over whether preparation for secondary leaving exams is good preparation for university writing. Foster, for example, suggests that German students' interactive participation in a responsive rhetorical setting in secondary classrooms, which provides them with a familiar, "well-defined rhetorical situation," does not necessarily prepare them for the more formal and agonistic environment of the university seminar-style classroom (p. 208). Li finds that in China university students, "in an almost unanimous voice . . . dismiss high school writing as 'writing for exams,'" and describe it as "utilitarian," "programmed," "formularized," "dry and rigid" (p. 79). More individualistic than the older generation, they may view that kind of education as limiting personal freedom.

As the essays in this volume attest, these debates over writing focus attention on the character of both secondary and higher education, and thus can be healthy for reexamining education at both levels. When writing is a major element of assessment and selection within a nation's educational system, it can illuminate issues important to crucial national discussions about a country's educational directions, though this comes at the price of virulent disagreement among stakeholders.

Language Policies and Traditions: The Debate over Writing in School and Society

Questions of writing development are conditioned by tacit traditions of language use as well as explicit language policy. All the nations represented in this volume are increasingly multicultural and multilingual. Just as the United States has experienced controversies over the teaching of writing to speakers of other languages and dialects, particularly in the form of disputes over bilingual education and English-only movements, other nations have seen similar conflicts over language policies. In Kenya and South Africa, where many languages are spoken (nine official languages in South Africa alone) and where most people speak at least two languages, language policy poses major challenges to writing development in secondary schools and at university. In Kenya, says Muchiri, "code switching . . . is a way of life" (p. 258), which can create serious difficulties for students matriculating at university who are unaccustomed to functioning in English, the dominant language of education in Kenya. Students often attempt to render phrasings from their native tongue (Kiswahili, for example) into written English, only to discover that such renderings do not work. "Code switching," she concludes, "may affect writing at both the lexical and grammatical levels," making it difficult at times for students and teachers to understand each others' meanings (p. 259).

The challenges to educational access are particularly sharp in countries where native speakers of languages other than the dominant language—immigrants, guest workers, migrant laborers, formerly enslaved peoples, and marginalized native peoples—begin entering secondary and higher education in significant numbers. When this occurs, writing for educational access and academic success becomes a particularly contested issue. In countries such as Kenya, the need to negotiate multilingual environments creates difficulties for students and teachers at all levels when well-intentioned efforts to standardize writing and speaking punish those not sufficiently fluent in target languages. Resistance to allowing access for users of nonstandard languages also emerges in areas where a once-dominant language cherished by the majority becomes a potent symbol of political and cultural identity. In France, for example, writing French correctly and elegantly is held in such esteem that applicants for jobs are often required to provide handwriting samples to be analyzed for indications of the applicant's personality and character. Indeed, efforts to broaden notions of what is "standard" French may run counter to deeply held assumptions about social and educational equity. As Donahue points out, French national policy is that every child "must have equal access to the same tools and experiences, and one standard must be used to judge his or her work." Moreover, "the national exams at the core of every stage of French education are the accepted basis for that one minimum standard. . . . Because [most of these] exams are heavily essay based, writing ability is one of the keys to advancement" (p. 138). The emphasis on correctness can signify to non-native speakers that educational and professional access may still be grounded in long-standing educational customs.

In many nations, as in the United States, written correctness— a general marker of social class—becomes a specific signifier of fitness for high-status work. In the United States, language correctness as a component of general "aptitude" examinations plays a distinct role in the selection process for colleges and universities and for postbaccalaureate professional and graduate programs. In this sense, language correctness determines which candidates can "write like ladies and gentlemen," who is "college material," and who has the "quality of mind" to pursue higher education according to the linguistic constructs underlying the examinations. Clearly, any national emphasis on social equity or economic opportunity will incur debate over whether such policy-grounded correctness should remain an important marker of educational advantage and how students from excluded groups can be drawn into the mainstream.

Writing Development and Processes of Writing, Learning, and Teaching

Students develop their writing in a host of ways, tacit and explicit. Tacit traditions of writing instruction that emerge in course work affect this learning, as do explicit instructional guidelines in educational policy documents and other venues such as examinations. All vary widely across nations. As this collection reveals again and again, what is common sense in one education system may be simply unthinkable in another. And it is in this taken-for-granted dimension—what Stephen North in the United States has called "lore"—that formal writing instruction operates most powerfully and enduringly. As Li's study of China's educational system dramatically shows, for example, millennia-old Confucian genres, pedagogies, and attitudes persist in the most humble of student compositions—whether or not they are officially sanctioned or even acknowledged. In the United States, general composition courses are so pervasive that teachers in other disciplines sometimes assume that they themselves don't "teach" writing or even that their students don't "write" when they compose genres such as laboratory reports instead of compositions or essays. Through cross-national comparisons, the familiar can indeed come to look strange, as Geertz puts it.

Writing and Learning to Write: Implicit and Explicit Values

Because writing is so deeply embedded in modern education in the form of lecture notes, exams, reports, journals, research papers, and countless others, it tends to be transparent, an element that in many systems cannot be separated from the larger work of learning. It often disappears, becomes unavailable as an object of discussion, as do discussions of its teaching. But writing is being taught nevertheless, often in tacit and unexamined ways. Elementary school teachers around the world are held responsible for teaching their students to write their native language at the most basic levels. But in the United States (and in many other nations), teachers at higher levels—except secondary English teachers and English professors specializing in composition—often do not view themselves as having direct responsibility for helping students improve their writing about the subject matter of the courses they take. In the United States, because access to higher levels or tracks ("ability groups") of education depends largely on machine-scored aptitude and achievement tests, writ-

ing does not play a dominant role in the ongoing work of learning assessment. And U.S. English teaching in secondary and higher
education has as its major focus the reading and criticism of literature, with relatively little time devoted to instruction in writing (see Applebee).

Although writing in U.S. schools and universities is a visible
element of students' learning development, its teaching and administration are also politically charged and divisive. In the link
between universities and the world of work in the United States,
writing is a contested issue. Among secondary and postsecondary
instructors, there is a widespread perception that writing is a
"basic" skill that students should have learned earlier, in elementary school, and that the improvement of writing is a task for
English teachers. General writing instruction in the form of first-
year composition has borne the burden of academic development
for U.S. students making the transition to colleges and universities. English departments have generally been at the center of this
tradition of complaint and cascading blame. Employers blame
higher education teachers, who blame secondary teachers, who
blame elementary teachers, who blame parents, who blame all of
the above.

But while the United States has for over a century pursued
this course of teaching writing directly in high schools and universities, other nations have viewed the development of academic
writing skills very differently. In most other nations (as, actually,
in most disciplines outside English in the United States), writing
is structured into the environments of teaching and learning, for
better or worse, rather than being taught in separate courses and
programs. To see writing development from this integrative
perspective, one must look at the ways in which writing is embedded in the work of learning itself and examine writing development across the curriculum.

Teaching Methods

Teaching methods also vary greatly among the nations discussed
in this study. In the United States, the traditional (and still dominant) methods of instruction in secondary and higher education

are lecture and a form of recitation designed to elicit the responses the teacher has in mind (sometimes erroneously called whole-class discussion, even though there is little open dialogue) (Nystrand 6). U.S. teachers—including English teachers—have inherited a tradition of textbook recitation from the nineteenth century, when teachers with little training relied on textbook questions to structure the discourse of overcrowded classrooms. Studies go back to the 1860s, when one observer remarked, "Young teachers are very apt to confound rapid questioning and answers with sure and effective teaching." A 1909 comparison with European teachers concluded that European teachers "build up new knowledge in class," whereas U.S. teachers act as though they were chairing a "meeting, the object of which is to ascertain whether [students] have studied for themselves in a textbook." And a long series of studies suggests that things have not changed much (Nystrand 6). Similarly, in most South African and Kenyan secondary schools, large classes, underprepared teachers, and lack of adequate materials have produced a tradition of textbook-based lecture and recitation with little extended writing, and that writing is mainly "single-truth" accounts of textbook knowledge. In China, Li argues, a secondary school tradition of teaching writing based on the close study and memorization of models, combined with ethical teaching, seems to crowd out the relatively freer examination of ideas and expression of views that Chinese students value in university writing.

England, Germany, and France, by contrast, have long traditions of valuing students' opinions, at least in secondary school literature and mother-tongue language courses, though the notion of "opinion" differs among the educational cultures of each country. Students are expected to share their views of texts and engage in a great deal of open dialogue and critical analysis before writing. In England, for example, "talk" is central to much secondary school teaching in English courses. Students are expected to share their views in large and small groups before and during writing. In France there is much "pre-text" (prewriting) discussion. In Germany students are "pushed to articulate" opinions orally and in writing in the classroom, and articulating their own ideas is a crucial goal (p. 207). In China students read about

twenty model essays each semester, mostly excerpts from literature, and there is much memorization of poetry and line-by-line
explication.

The genres of student writing also vary greatly, though in all
these nations students typically write in only a few genres in each
subject. In the United States, school themes (sometimes called
essays) dominate English courses, with summaries of facts (called
research papers) most prevalent in other courses. Some fields have
specialized genres, such as book reports in history and laboratory reports in the sciences (Applebee). In France there are only
two or three genres in each subject, and these are codified by the
examinations. In England, however, there is some movement toward allowing a wider range of genres in student portfolios,
though a few traditional classroom genres dominate the timed
examinations—and often the teaching.

Writing processes are also taught in various ways, mainly
implicit. In U.S. writing pedagogy, at least in high school and
first-year university composition courses, an explicit emphasis
on "process," conceived as stages of composing (prewriting, drafting, revising, editing, publication) is increasingly prevalent (see
Applebee and Applebee et al. for evidence of the growing focus
on process). But in other nations, various processes of writing
are for the most part tacitly embedded in the pedagogy. In England, at least in English classes, there is a thirty-year-old tradition of writing fewer pieces (perhaps only four or five a year) but
polishing these for a course work portfolio over a long period of
time, with much revision along the way.

In Germany, France, and China, the emphasis is on extensive
preparation for the one-draft writing that is useful on examinations—and in much workplace writing. In these countries, students repeatedly practice the examination genres in timed writing
over a period of months or years, until students get good at them.
The writing process embedded in this pedagogical practice emphasizes writing in a few genres well, for timed examinations,
but it restricts the genres available. In education systems emphasizing timed written examinations, one-draft writing is king.

Several educational systems represented in this collection have
evolved structures as part of the general work of teaching and

learning in many disciplines that help students develop as writers. In the United States, there has been some movement toward small-group work in some disciplines and schools. The U.S. writing-across-the-curriculum (WAC) movement (profoundly influenced by British theory and pedagogy) has begun to encourage greater awareness of the wider range of roles that writing can play in learning in all disciplines. In Germany the seminar format of discussion generally begins in the first year of university. Students discuss work together and write papers over a long period of time—often longer than the seminar itself. They have the time (for some students, too much time) to do extensive reading as preparation for writing and to reflect on it individually and in discussions. Similarly, English universities often provide a system of tutoring for each course, either individually (in the most elite institutions) or in small groups. Tutorials focus on the writing students do, whereas lectures focus on the reading. Informal structures also help to develop students' writing. In Kenya, for example, the community ethos of the society leads students to create informal study groups, which support students' writing and learning outside the purview of formal instruction.

In each of these traditions, students generally develop their writing (or fail to) without benefit of much explicit writing instruction. Writing development is usually folded into the activity of a discipline without becoming a conscious and formal component of the curriculum—for better or worse (or a bit of both). Recently, however, writing has become a more explicit focus of education.

Conclusion: Toward New Articulations

We began where the IEA study concluded:

> We suspect that writing is not as unitary a construct as many national assessments and writing researchers would have it. . . . We cannot say that someone is a better writer than someone else. All we can say is that at this particular time we think a person wrote a good composition on this topic. (Purves et al. 200)

This collection suggests that even this formulation is not strong enough. The "we" making the judgment of a student text is a variable and dynamic construction, dependent on a dynamically shifting articulation of institutional organization, selection structures, and traditions of teaching, learning, and language policy. Indeed, the essays here point to the need for a broader and deeper understanding of what has often been called the "articulation" between secondary and higher education. In their writing, students "articulate" their differences, and in doing so negotiate the difference between secondary and higher education. Writing is central even where (as in the United States) writing is not usually a direct part of the official sorting and teaching mechanisms.

Increasing access to higher education has sparked a worldwide interest in writing development, and many nations have begun organized efforts to address the perceived problem. In England student support units that formerly served only international students are being rapidly expanded to serve "home" students from nontraditional backgrounds. Many support units offer courses and programs for writing development, and there is now a professional organization for writing support staff—Writing Development in Higher Education (WDHE)—that represents some eighty institutions, supports its own publications, and holds an annual conference. The Ministry of Education has begun a major WAC initiative, influenced by the U.S. WAC movement, to raise the awareness of secondary teachers across the curriculum about the role of writing in learning (SCAA). Additionally, an Academic Literacies organization for higher education supports an ambitious program of research. In Scandinavia there is a wide range of curricular and research efforts. In Germany approximately one-third of educational institutions have some course or program to support student writing development. South Africa is seeing a young but burgeoning effort, with writing-across-the-curriculum programs often attached to student support units. Kenya has for two decades systematically addressed the problem of writing development through national curriculum reform initiatives designed to develop courses and programs that support student writing development. Even in France, there is a budding effort to address student writing development with courses and programs.

Writing development is now an international effort. In Europe the International Association for the Improvement of Mother Tongue Education sponsors a biyearly conference and supports a large research effort (see http://www.ilo.uva.nl/development/iaimte). The recently formed European Association for the Teaching of Academic Writing specifically addresses writing in higher education, and brought together program developers and researchers for its first annual conference in 2001, in conjunction with another new organization, the European Writing Center Association (http://www.hum.ku.dk/formidling/eataw). Though these efforts sometimes look to the older efforts of the United States, they are bringing original perspectives to the problems of articulating writing in secondary and higher education that grow out of their own national and local experiences. And as higher education expands enrollments to traditionally excluded groups, and as specialization of work—and writing—for graduates of higher education expands with the globalizing economy, these efforts will surely expand. Indeed, the increase in students demanding help with their writing has been a major factor in the increased administrative and faculty interest in academic writing.

We end this introduction by proposing questions we believe are central to new secondary-higher education articulations, questions raised repeatedly in the chapters that follow and answered in many different ways. We offer them both as heuristics for teachers and policymakers considering rearticulations and as questions for cross-national research—theoretical, historical, qualitative, and quantitative.

What contradictions are created in writing development through early versus late specialization? Early specialization allows teachers to focus on particular genres, engaging students more deeply in the conversations of a discipline by the time they begin higher education. But such focused disciplinary socialization may mask subtle differences in disciplinary discourse between secondary education and higher education unless there are conscious attempts to articulate writing development between secondary and university courses. Moreover, the disciplinary socialization model tends to make the role of writing invisible and thus provides little conscious support for writing. Late specialization provides more opportunities for general education—and for writing in a wider range of genres, perhaps in courses and programs specifically devoted to writing. But it is costly, and the relation between general writing instruction and writing in specific disciplines is also difficult to articulate—as U.S. WAC programs have found (Russell, *Writing*).

What contradictions in national traditions and ideologies of education affect writing development? Each national system and each institution embodies traditions and ideologies in tension, such as those we've noted: for instance, general/liberal education versus professional training, social equity versus disciplinary excellence and status, individualism versus communitarian solidarity. We might productively analyze these in cross-national perspective to see what possibilities exist for rearticulations in debating fundamental stakes, forming alliances, mobilizing stakeholders, and forging compromises. Comparative historical studies may prove useful here.

What are the trade-offs in centralization versus decentralization? More centralized systems can make writing development a priority, mobilizing resources quickly and massively, as with England's language-for-learning initiative (SCAA), but centralization can also inhibit innovation. More decentralized systems can breed many local innovations but may have difficulty disseminating and sharing best practices, as in U.S. composition. It will be interesting to see what distance education can do for (or against) writing development, as it may be used both to centralize educational control and to decentralize control, to spread innovation either from the top or from the bottom.

How do tracking and selection affect writing development? The IEA study highlights the fact that "the institution of the school serves not only to educate a portion of the population, but to sort the student population as well," and concludes that we need further exploration of "how best to teach these students who are not in the academic tracks. [The IEA study] calls into question the system of tracking itself. It also suggests that teachers probe more deeply into their beliefs and practices as teachers of writing to all kinds of students to see whether they are in fact helping them succeed" (Purves et al. 202). This collection suggests that we must also take into account the writing development that happens (or fails to happen) in higher education, in order to ensure greater equity in both education and selection for education. Do assessments in secondary education take into account the needs of students in higher education, and vice versa? What is the "washback" of assessments, written or not, on students' writing development at both levels and between levels?

What contradictions exist in institutional attitudes toward writing development, and how do these influence the structure of programs and allocation of resources for them? The educational systems discussed in this collection are undergoing rapid and far-reaching changes as they expand their higher education systems in response to social and economic changes. There are widespread efforts to improve students' writing in order to make university access and success more likely for previously excluded groups. In educational systems that do not support composition courses (the great majority), for example, study or communication skills centers are being established to deal with the problems of writing and access to higher education (and have led to much nation-specific research, as this collection reflects). These efforts uncover deep-seated attitudes toward writing development. Will such efforts move toward (and fund) general skills instruction (perhaps ignoring the social, disciplinary, and personal dimensions of writing development), toward academic socialization (perhaps ignoring the institutional, cross-disciplinary, and civic dimensions of writing development), or toward academic literacies (and undertake the very complex and potentially costly effort to balance tacit disciplinary and explicit formal instruction)? Cross-national research can illuminate potential problems and propose solutions—particularly through comparisons with the United States, which has a longer history of explicit teaching of writing (and virulent debates over attitudes toward and resources for writing) than other nations.

What kinds of support do students need to gain authority and identity as academic writers when making the transition to disciplinary conversations? In what ways is writing used to help students enter disciplinary conversations and, conversely, to restrict students' access to professions? New articulations of writing development must take into account the profound mismatch in expectations of teachers in secondary and in higher education. The goals of the two are often different, and this may well be necessary and right, given the responsibility of higher education to select and prepare people for specialized work and greater responsibilities as citizens. But if teachers, examiners, and policymakers on either side of the secondary/higher education divide do not talk to each other, directly and/or indirectly, about student writing and writing development, then the mismatch will continue—and may grow as specialization in higher education increases. Trade-offs between general/liberal education and professional training will have to be continually renegotiated for students' writing development, particularly as access to higher education widens.

What kinds of support do students need in handling intertextuality—citation, synthesis, and plagiarism—and when? Instruction in the mechanics of citation, documentation, and paraphrase is only the first step in handling the complex intertextual conversations that make up academic discourse. Yet this is often the only explicit instruction students get. We know very little about how students develop the ability (and motivation and authority) to successfully carry on written conversations in a discipline over time. How might we, in Mary Scott's phrase, "move students on" from the more general and personal written responses, to the reading typical in many secondary schools, to the complex conversations mediated through intertextuality in the disciplinary specialties of higher education? And because the epistemologies of various disciplines are often radically different, students must develop a chameleon rhetorical capacity to move from one to another, to converse differently in different networks of people through their written response to specialist reading and talk. A great deal of work needs to be done across disciplines and nations to understand these problems and formulate pedagogies that go beyond the typical writing textbook formulations of intertexuality as a set of discrete mechanical skills.

How, where, and when are students assessed through writing? There will always be assessments, which will always enable and constrain the work of teachers and students. The goal is to create assessments worth teaching to, assessments that have the greatest positive and fewest negative consequences for teaching, learning, and writing development. Each teacher, institution, profession, and national education system must continually negotiate those assessments among the many stakeholders—at each level of education. Should writing play a role in assessments in various fields, or in general writing instruction only? Should extended writing be a high-stakes part of assessment early (as in most nations) or only late (as in the United States)? Who has a say (and how much) in the kinds of writing assessed and the evaluation of it? For all these questions, cross-national research can illuminate local and national practices, but only if such comparisons take into account the particular cultural-historical factors that make assessment of and with writing so difficult and so contested.

What are the effects of language policy and traditions on writing development? Economic and business structures, non-governmental organizations, professional associations, and academic research are increasingly global (with English the dominant language). This means that students will increasingly write across cultures and languages when they leave formal education. But at the level of teaching, national and local language policies and traditions condition writing development in powerful and increasingly contested ways. As students move from secondary to higher education, language policy and tradition intersect with the demands of selection. How do language policies and traditions enable and constrain writing development, opening and closing opportunities for students—particularly those from previously excluded groups—to enter and succeed in the new networks of global communication?

What mixture of explicit and implicit support for writing exists—and might exist? As we noted, writing is often "taught" implicitly, as an apprenticeship or disciplinary socialization, with little conscious attention to writing per se. General composition courses and writing support (tutoring) units often teach writing as a set of general skills. The essays that follow suggest that some mixture of the two approaches might provide more effective articulation between writing development in secondary and in higher education. As with the U.S. WAC movement, efforts in several nations represented here (Kenya, South Africa, the United Kingdom) to improve writing across the curriculum involve faculty in the disciplines working in partnership to make writing development a more conscious part of teaching and learning, while at the same time recognizing and valuing the varied and specialized nature of writing in both secondary and higher education. But we know very little about how these programs work and how they might work better. By sharing insights across nations, we might learn, for example, how faculty and students in various disciplines come to see writing as integral to teaching and learning: what is best made conscious, explicit, and open to critique and what can be left unsaid, or unconscious, about writing.

Just as it is common for writing researchers in various nations to talk past each other, so also it is easy for us as teachers in secondary and higher education to talk past each other and miss the crucial role that writing plays in students' work and in the transition from secondary to higher education. We hope these essays will spur broader and deeper discussions among teachers, researchers, and policymakers that will help bridge the divides and rearticulate the differences. The international studies offered here come at a time of increasing international interest in writing development, assessment, and pedagogy. We hope they will stimulate readers to examine their own assumptions about the roles that writing plays in the transition from secondary to higher education and thereby generate more reflective practice. It is essential for educators to explore the often tacit traditions of writing and learning that shape each new effort at reform. We believe it is vital to continue the dialogue begun by the IEA study and the few cross-national studies since then and to encourage the global circulation of writing research, innovations in pedagogy, and a reexamination of educational policies that shape and are shaped by writing pedagogy.

Notes

1. Also, two collections on mother-tongue education have been published, one for western European countries (Herrlitz et al.) and one for English-speaking countries (Britton). Though these studies provide useful context for this collection of research, they do not specifically address the transition from secondary to higher education.

2. See Cope and Kalantzis for a similar critique of Australian and U.S. expressivist writing pedagogy.

Works Cited

Applebee, Arthur N. *Contexts for Learning to Write: Studies of Secondary School Instruction.* Norwood, NJ: Ablex, 1984.

Applebee, Arthur N., et al. *NAEP 1992 Writing Report Card.* Washington, DC: U.S. Dept. of Ed., 1994.

Bartholomae, David. "Inventing the University." *When a Writer Can't Write: Studies in Writer's Block and Other Composing-Process Problems.* Ed. Mike Rose. New York: Guilford, 1985. 134–65.

Britton, James, ed. *English Teaching: An International Exchange.* London: Heinemann Educational, 1984.

Cope, Bill, and Mary Kalantzis, eds. *The Powers of Literacy: A Genre Approach to Teaching Writing.* London: Falmer, 1993.

Day, Jennifer, and Andrea Curry. *Educational Attainment in the United States: March 1998.* Washington, DC: U.S. Census Bureau, 1998.

Geertz, Clifford. *Local Knowledge: Further Essays in Interpretive Anthropology.* 3rd ed. New York: Basic Books, 2000.

Gipps, Caroline V. *Beyond Testing: Towards a Theory of Educational Assessment.* London: Falmer, 1994.

Herrlitz, W., et al., eds. *Mother Tongue Education in Europe: A Survey of Standard Language Teaching in Nine European Countries.* Enschede, Neth.: SLO, 1984.

Lea, Mary, and Brian Street. "Writing as Academic Literacies: Understanding Textual Practices in Higher Education." *Writing: Texts, Processes, and Practices.* Ed. Christopher N. Candlin and Ken Hyland. New York: Longman, 1999. 62–81.

McCarthy, Lucille P. "A Stranger in Strange Lands: A College Student Writing Across the Curriculum." *Research in the Teaching of English* 21 (1987): 233–65.

Muchiri, Mary N., Nshindi G. Mulamba, Greg Myers, and Deoscorous B. Ndoloi. "Importing Composition: Teaching and Researching Academic Writing beyond North America." *College Composition and Communication* 46 (1995): 175–97.

Nystrand, Martin, with Adam Gamoran, Robert Kachur, and Catherine Prendergast. *Opening Dialogue: Understanding the Dynamics of Language and Learning in the English Classroom.* New York: Teachers College P, 1997.

Ohmann, Richard. *English in America: A Radical View of the Profession.* New York: Oxford UP, 1976.

Purves, Alan C. *The Scribal Society: An Essay on Literacy and Schooling in the Information Age.* New York: Longman, 1990.

Purves, Alan C., et al., eds. *The IEA Study of Written Composition II: Education and Performance in Fourteen Countries.* Vol. 6 of *International Studies in Educational Achievement.* Oxford, UK: Pergamon, 1992.

Russell, David R. "Where Do the Naturalistic Studies of WAC/WID Point? A Research Review." *WAC for the New Millennium: Strategies for Continuing Writing-Across-the-Curriculum Programs.* Ed.

Susan H. McLeod, Eric Miraglia, Margot Soven, and Christopher Thaiss. Urbana, IL: NCTE, 2001. 259–98.

———. *Writing in the Academic Disciplines, 1870–1990: A Curricular History*. Carbondale: Southern Illinois UP, 1991.

SCAA (School Curriculum and Assessment Authority). *The Use of Language Across the Curriculum*. London: SCAA Publications, 1997.

Street, Brian V. *Literacy in Theory and Practice*. Cambridge: Cambridge UP, 1984.

CHAPTER ONE

"Track (Dis)Connecting": Chinese High School and University Writing in a Time of Change

XIAO-MING LI

Long Island University, Brooklyn Campus

In September 1976, the "Great Helmsman" Chairman Mao passed away and the so-called Cultural Revolution, which had started in 1966 and ravaged the country for ten long years, finally ended. Yet for most young people, the first sign of a return to normalcy was the restoration of the university entrance exam in the summer of 1977 under the direction of the new Party Chairman Deng Xiaoping. The university entrance exam had been abolished in 1966 at the start of the Cultural Revolution as the first revolutionary act to end the "feudalist and revisionist" education system. But Deng told the country that to catch up with developed countries, China needed talents, and the exam was necessary to give everyone who had talent a fair chance to be recognized. Young people (and many not-so-young thirty-year-olds) who had been denied an education during the Cultural Revolution rejoiced at the decision. Almost overnight, intellectuals were no longer the "stinking ninth," and reading books was again a respectable, if not the most desirable, pursuit, for the restoration of the exam signaled that one's command of knowledge rather than political loyalty—or at least not that alone— would be the basis of academic selection.[1] A student's mastery of knowledge was to be displayed at the exam mainly through the medium of writing, as it had been for thousands of years (the Cultural Revolution constituting only a brief interruption).

At that first exam after the Cultural Revolution, candidates were tested in four areas: Chinese, math, politics, and science (physics and chemistry). For the exam on Chinese, every candidate had two hours to compose an essay of five hundred characters on a designated topic; for the exam on politics, they had to answer a number of essay questions on the history of the Chinese Communist Party and political issues of the day. Given the intense competition, no one who failed any one of the exams—still less two of them in which writing played a crucial role—could possibly be admitted to any university. After all, for the longest time in Chinese history, learning was synonymous with reading and writing. Although that tradition had been altered considerably over time for reasons I discuss later, in post–Cultural Revolution China it was still a commonly held view that a learned person should be a decent writer.

The restoration of the university exam, part of Deng's ambitious plan carried out in the next two decades, is still shaping China in many ways. The early 1980s saw Deng launch the Open Door policy and the movement of Four Modernizations—the modernization of agriculture, industry, science, and the military. Education was the cornerstone of that grand enterprise. As a result of this process, many things have changed in China in the past two decades, some more slowly than others. Although most Chinese happily drive on multiple-lane highways, move into more spacious buildings with little hesitation, and even crowd into the McDonald's and Kentucky Fried Chicken restaurants, educators are ambivalent about the changes in the classroom.

Some see the influx of foreign ideas and language from the West as a threat to the purity and integrity of a literary heritage held dear by many even during the most tumultuous years of the Cultural Revolution. Mr. Gong, senior lecturer of Chinese at a high school in Nanjing, whom I met when working on my doctoral dissertation in China in 1992, lamented the "new problems" in student writing:

> Problems arise because some students have rapidly adopted new concepts and ideas, but their language is lagging, thus creating a gap between the content and language. Some simply transplant new terminology and new concepts into their writing without fully understanding the meanings of those words; some use Europeanized sentence structures and esoteric references, produc-

ing writings that are "neither fish or fowl," very awkward, often unreadable. (22)

On the other hand, some educators see the coming of the information age as the rounding of a full circle that started in China. As one of them comments,

> Our great country known for its brilliant literary tradition has traveled a long and tortuous "Z" path in the past two thousand years. From the traditional Confucian view that "[writing] is the primary means of managing a country" and that "a gentleman is judged by his writing," we gradually evolved to the view that "science outweighs writing."

But the pendulum is swinging back, the author enthuses:

> Now we are facing another important radical change because of the arrival of the "information age" via high volumes of digitized writing symbols. . . . In this information age writing, the "fountain of information," has attained an extremely important status. (Liu 1)

How language fares in the new environment is for many educators a crucial issue, and their impulse is to preserve rather than tamper with China's "brilliant literary tradition."

One common slang term among Shanghai residents, who are known for their quick absorption of things Western, is *jiegui* (connect tracks). A relative who knows how to use a beeper but not an answering machine, for example, explains why he failed to leave a message on my machine when he visited New York City: "We have *jiegui*ed with beepers but not with answering machines yet." During my last visit in 1996, the second since I left China in 1985, I became interested in the impact of modernization on the teaching of writing, the most ancient and venerable profession in China. The term *jiegui* crystallized the issue I was confronting: how does the teaching of writing jibe with the Four Modernizations? The theme of this collection, the secondary to higher education transition in students' writing development, provides a serendipitous segue into that larger and more elusive topic. In this essay, I focus on how the teaching of writing in Chinese high schools *jiegui* with university education, the former rooted in the Chinese traditional "private education" and the latter imported from the West and run mainly by the government since its inception. More specifically, I review China's education history, look at the current official guidelines for teaching Chinese in high schools, and examine how writing is evaluated in the university entrance exam, the storied "baton of high school education." Finally, I discuss the results of surveys completed by students in three Chinese universities, offering opinions on how well high school writing instruction prepared them for university writing, and suggesting ways to improve the *jiegui* of the two tiers of education. I cite the insights and expertise of Mr. Gong and Mr. Xu, two prominent teachers of Chinese in Nanjing, to provide context and background for my discussion.

First, to provide structural context for readers, I want to offer a brief overview of important similarities and differences between the Chinese and U.S. educational systems. At first glance, the current Chinese educational system is a near replica of its U.S. counterpart. It is a three-tier system consisting of elementary school (six years), middle school (three years of middle school and three years of high school), and university (four years except for five-year medical colleges) (see Figure 2). Elementary and middle school education is mandatory and tuition-free. Students still have to pay for books and other fees, which, though minimal according to Western standards, are prohibitively expensive for families in poverty-stricken areas. Students start to take math and physics (second year) and chemistry and biology (third year) in middle school, along with other traditional liberal arts courses such as Chinese, foreign language, history, geography, and political education. Similarities stop there, however. Education in China is, first of all, a highly centralized system, in which the Ministry of Education controls the curriculum and textbooks, and all teachers are government employees. Private education had been nonexistent in mainland China since the founding of the Communist government. In the last two decades, some changes in government policies have allowed the opening of private schools at all levels, but such schools still constitute an insignificant component of the entire educational system.

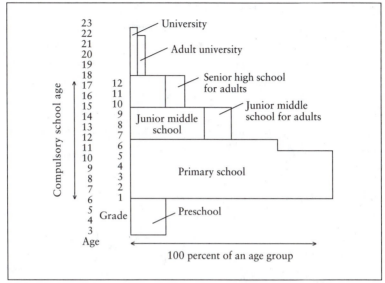

Figure 2. *People's Republic of China: Structure of the formal education system.*

Chinese education also includes a rigorous tracking system, and students specialize much earlier than in the U.S. system. Tracking—separating the more academically successful students from the less successful—starts from an early stage: the better scorers after the middle school entrance exam go to "key" middle schools; thereafter, these students have a better chance of entering "key" high schools, and finally, after surviving two rounds of rigorous screening, they are almost guaranteed admission to universities. In recent years, some local governments have taken steps to eliminate entrance exams at the elementary and middle school levels to avoid early tracking, but those key schools, still the preferred schools for most parents and students, continue to be more selective than others. Selection in China is best described as "academic orientation," since it sorts students into two large categories—those planning to major in liberal arts and those planning to major in science—in order to prepare the students for different college entrance exams. Students identify their own orientations, always in consultation with their parents and teachers, and follow the curriculum that gravitates toward one or the other orientation. A more subtle but equally important difference is the forceful presence in China's educational system of an indigenous humanist tradition that for centuries has centered on character formation through the teaching of reading and writing. In the next section, I explore this tradition, with its powerful grip on Chinese educators' imagination and practices. I trace its beginnings in Confucius's time and identify radical changes that have occurred since the beginning of the twentieth century, changes that have transformed the tradition without forcing it to lose its identity.

The Shadow of History

Private education made its debut in China during the Spring and Fall War period (770–476 B.C.) when the old court-run education fell apart. Confucius (551–479 B.C.) and educators of his time laid down the cornerstones of the Chinese educational edifice (Zheng, *History* 5–7). They pronounced the goal of education to be the training of high-minded scholars who were "saints inside and kings outside" *(nei4 xian2 wai4 wang2)*, "gentleman scholars" whose sole purpose in life was to realize "Tao."[2] To restore Tao, these scholars were expected to know history well, for despite changes in time and dynasty, a study of the past allowed one, it was said, to "cope with the myriad through the unvarying principle." Therefore, wise rulers were the ones who "used history as guidance for the present" *(yi2 gu3 chi2 jin1)*.

These saintly scholars were entrusted with running the government and, more important, with providing living examples of moral leadership for the larger society. A recurring theme of *The Great Learning*, one of the seminal Confucian texts compiled by later Confucius scholars, is the crucial role of education in society: "The goal of education is first and foremost to bring forth the nobility inside each and every scholar, and these scholars, in turn, will influence the populace to reach its best, and hence the peace of the universe" (qtd. in Zheng, *History* 6).[3] The book draws heavily on the educational theory and practices of the Western Zhou Dynasty (1100–771 B.C.), the model of Confucius's education. In education, as in government, the past is viewed as offering the best guidance for current practice. The assumption underlying this belief is that human nature can be perfected through institutional education (Confucius himself cautiously circumvented the thorny issue of whether human nature was inherently good or evil). Schools are envisioned as the incubating grounds for all levels of the ruling elite, with the emphasis on moral uprightness and knowledge of the past. From this perspective, students ought to be dedicated to the good of society and nourished with the knowledge of history.

How, then, do the select few connect with the uneducated majority? *The Great Learning* further suggests that the populace will be receptive to the influence of the superior if the scholars are "sincere" *(cheng2)*. Sincerity is indicated not just by the consistency between what one preaches and what one actually does, but also, since the ruling and the ruled never took residence in the same quarters, by the persona a writer projects through writing. Noble messages, in other words, have to be carried by honest brokers to touch the hearts of otherwise apathetic commoners. The teaching method employed, as seen in *The Analects*, a collection of Confucius's exchanges with his disciples, reflects the same human touch: it is dialogical, interactive, and personal.

Confucius and his contemporaries started the humanist tradition in education, which had character formation at its core and state welfare as its goal, but not until the Han Dynasty (206 B.C.–A.D. 220) was Confucianism elevated to the status of state religion. Confucianism was formalized and solidified by the Imperial Civil Service Exam held regularly to select government officials at all levels. "A good scholar will make an official" *(xue2 er3 you1 zhe2 shi4)*—an old Confucian adage—took on a new meaning after the institution of this exam. Historian Ray Huang describes the momentous impact of this highly competitive system in its declining years (Ming Dynasty: A.D.1368–1644):

> With very few exceptions, members of the Civil Service had qualified for it through the competitive examinations held once every three years. . . . Counting the screening tests and qualifying examinations at the county level which the candidates had to pass before they were even admitted to the [national] contest, the system, when in operation, must have involved close to one million aspirants to official positions, and included virtually all of the empire's literary talent.

An important aspect of the examination system was that, aside from the Civil Service, avenues for individuals to gain prominence and demonstrate their creative energies were extremely limited, in many cases nonexistent. It was not unusual for the success of a candidate to depend upon the concerted effort of his whole family. Although when success came he could go from rags to riches in his lifetime, his way to good fortune had as a rule been paved by his parents or even his grandparents. (54)

Given its unparalleled scope and impact, China's Imperial Civil Service Examination is probably the most successful government-run social engineering program in human history. With the reward for hard work and family support so instant and life altering, the exam not only dictated what and how students learned in school, but also left an indelible print on China's cultural and social fabric. Much of the Chinese's high regard for education and family values can be directly attributed to the two-thousand-year tradition of this exam.

The content of the examination was exclusively on the Five Classics and Four Books, and the sole medium of evaluation was writing. Applicants were expected to compose an impromptu essay on a designated topic, invariably on a *thema* selected from the classics, within a given time period at places in the capital under close supervision. A good scholar, it was commonly agreed, was one so steeped in Confucius classics that he could expound on cue any Confucius precept in writing. Gradually lost in this massive screening process, however, was the human touch that characterized early education. Perhaps because of the difficulties for exam administrators in reading and assessing the many examinations submitted on each occasion, writing over the years became set and mechanical. During the Ming Dynasty, exam writing was eventually formalized into the so-called "eight-legged" essay, a format that allowed little room for individuality or creativity. The Imperial Civil Service Examination ended with the last dynasty, Qing (A.D. 1644–1911), but its influence, according to many educators and students, continues to be felt in today's school writing classes. Because passing the Imperial Civil Service Examination had been the ultimate goal of education until the exam was discontinued, other subjects disappeared from the curriculum.[4] During those years, going to school was synonymous with reading and writing about the classics. Once learning was no longer a means of inquiry but instead a stepping-stone to officialdom, the method of instruction also changed from inter-active dialogue to rote memory, and teaching was transformed from offering personal guidance to earning a living for those who, despite all their years of burning the midnight oil, failed to achieve officialdom. Teaching, though in a way a profession for the los-ers, had always received respect from people of both high and low status. Though education had come to represent personal advancement more than moral leadership, the educational enter-prise was carried out with rigor and dedication by generations of teachers. Undergirding their efforts was the hope that knowl-edge of saints' books might still produce saints, and the recogni-tion that if the lure of the good life provided an incentive, all the better.

The reading-and-writing-centered educational system de-signed for character molding started to tip toward science and technology in the nineteenth century after the infamous Opium War ended in 1842. Having been soundly defeated by "solid ships and powerful cannons" *(chuan2 jian1 pao4 li4)* of Western pow-ers, many believed that the way to contain "foreign devils" was to learn from them *(yi3 yi2 zhi4 yi2)*. A new type of school, col-lectively called "foreign affair schools" *(yang2 wu4 xue2 tang2)* and specializing in foreign languages or ship-building technol-ogy, appeared in some parts of the country (Zheng, *Modern* 22–38). The goal of education shifted from the classical training of moral leaders to the technical training of practical experts. The first Western-style school, the Capital Teachers' Learning Insti-tute, later part of the Capital Teachers' University, was founded in 1867. It was funded entirely by government revenue, and the school's top administrators were appointed by the royal court. It started with an eight-year program, combining middle and high school and college educations. Since traditional students trained in reading and writing, the classic Confucius texts were not ap-propriate for the new science-heavy curriculum of the institute. Graduates from the Capital Teachers' Learning Institute would enter civil service directly without taking the Imperial Civil Ser-vice Examination. Consequently, the Four Books and Five Clas-sics were no longer part of the curriculum; instead, classes were taught on specialized subjects: reading and writing in the first and second years, world geography and history in the third year, math and chemistry in the fourth to seventh years, and astronomy in the eighth year. The study of a foreign language started in the second year and continued throughout the seven years (Zheng, *Modern* 38–44). In retrospect, it is clear that these changes—the replacement of Confucian classics with scientific study and specialization in disciplinary knowledge—signaled the beginning of the end of centuries of China's humanist educational tradition.

The Imperial Civil Service Exam was finally jettisoned in September 1901 when the foreign powers, in retaliation for the violence of the Boxer Rebellion against foreign missionaries, destroyed the city by ground-burning arson and systematic looting. When the exam ended, traditional private schools, whose goal had been preparation for the exam, were gradually replaced by schools with curricula compatible with that of schools such as the Capital Teachers' University. The teaching of Four Books and Five Classics was completely discontinued in mainland China when the Communists took over in 1949. The teaching of reading and writing has remained the focus of Chinese studies, but this is only one of the ten subjects that high school students are required to take.[5] Yet despite profound political and structural changes, the humanist tradition has never surrendered completely.

Official Guidelines

High school students in China nowadays spend considerably less time on reading and writing compared with their counterparts of a century ago, yet the study of Chinese is supported by a significant number of class hours. According to the current "General Guideline for High School Chinese Language Education" issued by China's Ministry of Education, students majoring in humanities should take a total of 384 hours of Chinese in high school, averaging four hours a week, while science majors take 332 hours (two hours a week in the final high school year). The only other subject that receives comparable class hours is mathematics.

In regard to the goal of Chinese education, the same government document assigns importance to the development of students' linguistic and intellectual capacities, as well as their moral and ideological correctness:

> During the teaching process, [teachers] should guide students to further broaden their horizon, enrich their knowledge, foster fine sentiments, and develop intellect, personality, and specialty. [Teachers] should cultivate in students love for their native language and fine national cultural heritage, cultivate in them healthy and noble temperament and interest and certain aesthetic abilities, and cultivate in them socialist ideology, moral values and patriotism. (Ministry of Education 2)

It further states that the goal of teaching Chinese is to help students "possess the ability to read, write, listen to and speak modern Chinese, and the rudimental ability to appreciate literature and to read simple texts in classical Chinese." Classic Chinese, by the way, no longer denotes the Four Books and Five Classics; instead, it is literature produced in the classical Chinese, a language for the literati. The language in the guidelines obviously responds to both the Confucian tradition and the changes in education since the beginning of the twentieth century. It affirms the traditional view that teaching Chinese should develop character and transmit historical and cultural heritage, and at the same time it emphasizes the communicative and intellectual functions of language.

Writing constitutes one of the most important activities in Chinese classes. The Ministry of Education guidelines stipulate that during a student's three-year high school education (grades 10–12), he or she should receive no fewer than twenty-five in-class writing assignments (averaging once a month, in most cases), producing a minimum total of 20,000 words, and that other kinds of writing should amount to an additional 30,000 words. At the end of such training, students should be able to compose about 600 words of practical writing (hiyongwen) in forty-five minutes.[6] Narrative writing is the main genre of student writing till the first year of high school, during which some class time is devoted to the teaching of practical writing. From the second year on, the focus is on opinion writing (yilunwen), a genre that comes close to Western argument but with marked differences, as discussed later.

Writing is taught mostly through reading and analyzing model texts. Each semester a student reads around twenty model texts by distinguished Chinese authors, primarily modern, while assigned classical texts increase proportionately as students advance. Model texts can be short essays, poems, or excerpts from longer literary works. These model texts are taught to students in ways I can describe from my own schooling. I studied in a key middle school in Shanghai from 1963 to 1966, the year the Cultural Revolution started and all schools were closed to "do" revolution. In class the teacher would first have us, collectively or individually, read part or all of the text. Shorter texts, particularly poems, we were required to memorize, and we were called on in class to recite them from memory. Then the teacher would read some selected sentences and paragraphs from the text—an illuminating detail, an apt metaphor, a well-chosen word, or a historical allusion—to illustrate the merits of the text. With classic poems and prose, however, the teacher would usually explicate the text line by line to ensure our understanding. Another popular activity in Chinese class is the analysis of macro- and microstructures of the text, focusing on central themes and stylistic strategies. Such close analysis generally starts late in elementary school, and by high school graduation an average Chinese student has examined hundreds of essays and internalized features of "good" writing in a piecemeal, cumulative fashion. In my experience, writing was practiced at least once a month but always in class (no take-home writing assignments), so that students learned to improvise on designated topics under time pressure, with the attendant habits of rapid composing and the use of clichés and ready-made ideas (Li, "Writing").

These classroom strategies are largely a response to the demands of the university entrance exam. Despite the goals for the study of Chinese stated in the official guidelines, teachers and students understand that it is performance on the university entrance exam that really matters. Since a university degree guarantees a secure job in the government or a government-owned enterprise, or even, in the last decade, a lucrative position in a foreign company, passing the university entrance exam is an opportunity to reap the reward of twelve years of schoolwork. Seats at the universities, however, are severely limited for a population as vast as China's. In Nanjing, the main site of my research, only around 50 percent of applicants from high schools were admitted to university in 1998, a percentage lower than in such megacities as Shanghai and Beijing, but much higher than in average cities and towns with low, single-digit admission rates. Mr. Gong describes the situation as "all armies marching towards a single-plank bridge." Mr. Xu, a senior lecturer at the high school affiliated with Nanjing Teachers' University, the "key" of "key" high schools in Nanjing, calls the exam "the baton of high school education."

What kind of writing, then, is valued in the university entrance exam? To answer that question, I examined the writing section of the 1998 university entrance exam, looking closely at two highly praised student exam essays, with Mr. Gong's and Mr. Xu's comments.

The university entrance exam is conducted by the central government, as was the ancient Imperial Civil Service Exam, but there are important differences.[7] A century ago the Imperial Civil Service Exam was an endgame for candidates: winners at the exam immediately became new members of the bureaucracy, while winners at today's college entrance exam will continue their more specialized education in preparation for eventual professional and technical careers. This difference plays an important part in the *jiegui* between the two tiers of the educational system in China today. The contents of the exam are markedly different. Now the exam tests five subjects, commonly referred to as "three plus two." All candidates take exams in Chinese, math, and a foreign language. Liberal arts majors must take political studies and history (both combine multiple-choice questions with essay questions) in addition to the first three, and those who intend to pursue science take chemistry and physics in addition. Writing is perceived as much more important for prospective liberal arts majors than for science majors. The role of writing, as a result, is much diminished in the modern version of the Imperial Civil Service Exam. Chinese accounts for 150 points, one-fifth of the total score of 750, and of those 150 points, only 60 are for writing (the rest are for reading, grammar, and vocabulary, tested by multiple-choice questions).

Although writing makes up less than 10 percent of the total score, the competition to get into university is so intense that no one can slight the subject, especially prospective liberal arts majors, whose writing ability can directly affect their performance in Chinese, history, and political studies. For that reason, writing is still vigorously taught and learned in high school, particularly among students who are oriented toward liberal arts. Just as important, Mr. Gong maintains, is the traditional view that "writing, as always, is still regarded by most teachers in high school and university [as] the most important measurement of a student's comprehensive capability" (3–4). But though this view may be widely shared among educators, it is not necessarily shared by students. A doggerel popular among students since my school days goes, "Master math, physics and chemistry; walk all over the world with no fear"; writing was commonly seen as "growing flowers with the pen" *(bi3 xia4 sheng1 hua1)*—a mere decorative work.

The composition section of the university entrance exam in 1998 consisted of two parts: a short narrative of two hundred characters (about a page), also called "minor writing," and the major essay, or *yilunwen* (opinion writing or commentary writing). The perfect score for the former is 20 points, and for the latter, 40 points. The entire exam on Chinese takes two hours, of which usually fifty minutes are devoted to the writing of the two essays. Most students spend ten minutes on the minor essay and forty minutes on the major one. To limit the scope of this discussion, I examine only the major essay. Following are the requirements for the major essay in the 1998 college entrance exam:

> Compose an essay according to the following information (40 points).
>
> Nowadays high school students demonstrate radically different levels of mental strength: some have a mental strength as fragile as an eggshell, some tough as nails. How about yours? Select from the two topics one that suits your situation, use real life examples, and write an essay on your mental strength.
> (1) "Endurance, the Character that I pursue" (2) "Overcoming Frailty." Requirements:

1. Cross out the topic that you choose not to write about. You may also replace both topics with one that expresses the state of your mental strength.
2. You are free to choose one genre or a combination of a few from the narrative, descriptive, lyrical, expository, and commentary.
3. Poetry, novels, drama, and other kinds of fictional writing are not acceptable.
4. The total number of characters of the writing should be no fewer than 600.

A team of university professors and selected high school teachers of Chinese grades the exam. Mr.Gong and Mr. Xu, both senior lecturers teaching at key high schools in Nanjing, were invited to read the exam in 1998. The grading took place in June when Nanjing, known as "one of the three stoves," was boiling hot and the compensation for the work was nominal. Mr. Gong told me that he participated in the grading every year to get a sense of grading criteria and practices in order to better prepare his students for next year's exams. But other teachers as well as next year's examinees and their parents also want that information. The demand to know how the writing is actually evaluated is so high that after the results of the exam are delivered, local newspapers publish student essays that scored high grades, accompanied by participating teachers' comments. Mr. Gong and Mr. Xu, both well respected in the profession, are in high demand, and they have written comments on dozens of student essays for local newspapers. "Everyone Should Have Some Spirit," commented on by Mr. Gong, was published in *Chinese News (High School Edition)* in September 1998, and "Thank You, Hardship," selected and commented on by Mr. Xu, was published in the *Yangtze Evening News* in June 1998.

From these two essays and the two teachers' comments, perceptive readers would be able to recognize the influence of both Confucianism, with its stress on morality and historical knowledge, and the eight-legged essay, with its distinctive form (discussed later). Both reflect the influence of China's literary past.

The first essay, which scored the perfect 40 points, was selected and commented on by Mr. Gong:

Everyone Should Have Some Spirit

Everyone should have some spirit. Can one have it sometimes and not at other times? No. One should have some
spirit in times of crisis. What spirit? The spirit of "surmount-
ing every difficulty to win victory."[8] Why should one have
that spirit? Because in face of crisis, when the pressure from
outside weighs heavily, if the pillar of spirit falls, one would
surely collapse. Has anyone seen *tofu* withstand pressure?
No, because it has no spine. If a person does not have spine,
what kind of humiliating and soulless behavior would one
commit? History has already provided us with answers.

Then, can we discard spirit in times of peace and comfort? No. The phrase "riding a hobby weakens one's will"
means that indulgence in leisure saps one's spirit.[9] What spirit
can get lost in leisure? The spirit of worry and concern. Ancient Rome, having expanded across Europe and Asia and
boasting high civilization and prosperity, perished for its indulgence in wanton extravagance. In another ancient state
also known for civilization, however, Mencius cautioned,
"Live with worry and concern, die in comfort and compla-
cence."[10] Why is it that for eons those kings and emperors
who abided by his advice prospered and those who ignored
it ended in self-destruction? Again Mencius put it well: "A
state will inevitably perish without wise and loyal counselors
inside, or foes and threats from outside." We should keep in
mind the lessons of history. Despite that, however, we see
spoiled "little emperors" everywhere nowadays. Isn't that a
dangerous sign? The spirit of worry and concern is a fundamental quality for finding a foothold in modern society; therefore, it is more urgent, more pertinent to talk about spirit in
times of comfort than in crisis. If not, why do we say that it is
easier to conquer the land than to safeguard it?

In regard to respect, one has to uphold dignity. Some
believe that insults are not humiliating as long as I don't care.
Then why is it that the more triumphant his psychological
victories, the more Ah Q-ish that Ah Q becomes?[11] Looking
back at history, Boyi and Shuqi would rather die than feed
on the enemy's handout.[12] Why did Li Tang, known for paint-

ing beautiful ladies, paint the "picture of picking roses" for the two emaciated old loyalists of the Shang dynasty? Because he admired their moral integrity and their persistence in upholding their dignity. In modern times, Professor Zhu Ziqing refused American charity.[13] Why did all men of standing applaud him? Because they salute that similar spirit of unyielding defiance. Is it acceptable to discard the spirit of "not taking handouts" and for people of ideals and integrity to surrender to power? No, because without the spirit of "laying down one's life for a just cause," we as a nation will lose respect and dignity, and nothing is more precious than national dignity.

Likewise, does one also need to have spirit in times of triumph? Of course, one has to have the spirit of modesty. If one's head is turned by small victories, one is likely to consequently "keel over in a gutter." It will be too late to regret when that happens. I remember that after the debate team from Fudan University won the national debate contest in 1993, the coach told the team to "hang your tail between your legs when you go back." Some team members, perplexed, asked why they should shrivel like defeated dogs. One should know that it is only human to be feel superior when one prevails, yet people with high aspirations would remind themselves to be modest in order to avoid pitfalls. For ordinary people like you and me, what reason do we have to swagger around, swollen-headed?

In final analysis, no matter what the circumstances are, one has to live like a man and have some spirit. (Score: 40)

Mr. Gong's comments:

The essay[14] revolves closely around the topic. Structurally it poses questions and answers them, advancing the thesis layer upon layer, one proposition built solidly upon another. The examples cited cover both the ancient and the present; the reasoning is both correct and down to earth, the content rich and interesting. This is an essay of first class, which deserves a perfect score.

The second essay was selected and commented on by Mr. Xu.

Thank You, Hardship

As I trembled with fear when I talked to my stepmother, I was unaware that humiliation was breeding inside; when I was mocked by peers and felt lonely and helpless, I was unaware that fire was burning under my chest. But then, I was little.

Dozens of scars on the back of my hands are from cutting grass; layers of calluses are witnesses of hoeing in the field. I have never intentionally sought out trial and tribulations, yet they have always been my company. I don't see myself a strong person, yet strength is what has sustained me in darkness.

Graduating from middle school, I was qualified to go directly to high school without taking the exam. While my classmates went home to consult their parents, I, without hesitation, had already signed up. With the admissions letter in my pocket, I informed my father, and he acquiesced, but other people, either surprised or angry, called me a "heretic." Faced with the question, "What if you can't get into university?" I held up my head and answered, "I will work in the local factory." With support only from my father's silence, I became a high school student.

When I was awarded the title of "Model for Youth Volunteers," the young girl sweating under the merciless sun appeared again in front of my mind's eye; when I was commended as "Student of the Three Good Qualities," I could feel again the sensation of my feet in wet shoes on summer nights. . . . I experienced all this with peaceful acceptance. I never desired the same life as those who have an air conditioner in the bedroom and go to school in a private car. But I have long stopped pitying myself. Maybe they are luckier than I am, but they did not work for those privileges.

I am not quite sure what "endurance" pertains to specifically, but I know that I am definitely not a person easily defeated by hardship. Sick in the cold rain, I went to the hospital alone; deep at night, I stayed in the dorm alone to write for the radio station; failing exams once in a while, I kept my eyes wide open to force back tears on the brink of falling, clinging to conviction.

I have come to this examination site on my own, while others entered the classroom with the loving company and expectation of their parents. I brought with me the determination I made three years ago. As I write this essay, I am filled with only gratitude: thank you, hardship! Thank you for endowing me with strength. (Score: 38)

Mr. Xu's comments:

> The essay is highly focused on the theme. The author relates repeatedly her real life experiences and uses plain and sincere language to look back at the hardship she went through, demonstrating how she overcame mental weakness in the process.
>
> Hardship can crush a person, but also toughen a person, all depending on how one handles it. The growth of this examinee is a good lesson for most high school students who have grown up with privilege and comfort. Viewed from this particular perspective, the spiritual import of the essay is probably more significant than the grade it achieves.

"Everyone Should Have Some Spirit," as highlighted by Mr. Gong's comments, won high points for the author's demonstrated knowledge of history. The author's familiarity with history and his ability to instantaneously cite from memory examples such as the decline of the Roman Empire; the quotations from Mencius, a saint-philosopher of the same standing as Confucius; and a host of historical incidents and personages, put his writing in the highest order. Being able to draw instructional or cautionary lessons from history has long been regarded as a salient quality of a good Confucian scholar. What is not mentioned directly in Mr. Gong's comments but surely impressed him just as much is the writer's command of the classic language when alluding to those historical lessons. The writer wrote fluently and fast, producing a cogent essay in forty minutes, and appeared to be at great ease with "four-character proverbs," idioms that started as shorthand references to some widely known historical anecdotes and incidents. The use of these four-character proverbs adds "literary grace" (*wen2 cai3*) and an air of learnedness to a piece of writing in the same way that the use of words with Greek and Latin roots does in English. I have provided the historical references of these proverbs in the endnotes for readers unfamiliar with Chinese history. Unfortunately, the succinctness of these proverbs, as well as the special cadence produced by four characters, composed of two symmetrical pairs, does not survive translation.

In comparison, the essay "Thank You, Hardship," which scored lower than "Everyone," does not demonstrate the same degree of command of history and linguistic prowess, but it succeeded by pulling the reader's heartstrings. The outpouring of emotions and personal trials and tribulations, which are often viewed by U.S. readers as "sentimental," "peevish," or "a gush," is judged by Chinese readers as an indication of the writer's "sincerity" (Li, *Good Writing* 108). Good writing, according to Confucius, "flourishes with emotion and literary craft" (*qing2 wen2 bing4 mao4),* the two wings that carry Tao far and wide. Literary critic Liu Xie of the Liang Dynasty (907–923) elaborated on this view of good writing:

> Feelings are the warp of writing, and literary grace the weft. . . . It is said that a man who grew an orchid but did not love it could not smell its fragrance. Even a small plant has to be nurtured by genuine feelings, let alone writing, which has the expression of feelings at its core. If the feelings expressed run contrary to what the writer claims to believe, how can such writing be convincing? (Zou 318–319)

"Everyone," which received the highest score, is any teacher's preference, yet "Thank You" represents the genre of writing most popular among high school students: *sanwen* (loose writing). Writing *sanwen,* as we can see from "Thank You," serves the purpose of disseminating Tao and provides the kind of therapeutic effect that U.S. students find important in writing the personal narrative.

Professor Bei, vice president of the Chinese Writing Association, defines *sanwen* as "a familiar genre that traditionally has a broad and a narrow denotation. Broadly speaking, all non-verse is *sanwen.* . . . Narrowly defined, it is a writing genre in the same ranking as poetry, novel, [and] drama" (474). What separates *sanwen* from other prose is its attention to artistry and the expression of "subjective feelings": "Most artistic *sanwen*, unlike other prose such as reportage, biography, and *zawen*, is for the purpose of emoting," adds Professor Bei. "Whether it is employed to describe, narrate, or explicate, it ultimately expresses the author's subjective feelings" (475).[15] *Sanwen* became the most popular genre among young people after the May Fourth movement in 1919, the Chinese literary renaissance that followed the demise of the eight-legged essay and the Imperial Exam. Like the Renaissance in the West that marked the transition from medieval to modern Europe, the May Fourth movement marks a turning point in Chinese literary history, when the dominance of the archaic classical style of writing ended and a vernacular style close to everyday speech became dominant. The popularity of *sanwen* harks back to the early Confucian period when poetry, for its attention to form and literary grace, was revered as the highest form of literature. Poetry, however, was not accepted in the Imperial Civil Service Exam. Cherished more for its aesthetic value than any utilitarian function, *sanwen* remained a pastime of the literati for the expression of their personal experiences and feelings. *Sanwen*, to some extent, is prose written in the tenor of poetry, a public discourse opened to the personal. "The uniqueness of *sanwen*," says Professor Bei, "is that it is both 'loose' and not 'loose'"; it provided a new form for the linguistic and political freedoms of the May Fourth movement:

> It is based on real life, but not confined to one's own life experience; it expresses genuine emotions, yet it also gives room to poetic imagination; its style is free-flowing yet at the same time its language has to be concise and distilled, and images vivid. All in all, *sanwen* allows freedom in a limited space, unrestrained expression of subjectivity within restraining rules. (481)

That *sanwen* is favored by writing instructors and students alike is evident if one browses current anthologies of student writing. Publishing prize-winning or recommended student compositions is one of the most brisk and thriving businesses in China. Solicited by education publishers, supplied by teachers such as Mr. Gong and Mr. Xu (each of whom has published at least one anthology of model student writing), and eagerly bought by parents for their university-bound children, such publications fill the shelves of bookstores and libraries. As more students and teachers put aesthetics above message, *sanwen* becomes a more attractive genre than *yilunwen* (opinion writing), the traditional genre for exams. *Sanwen* is favored by teachers for its teachability—it is usually two or three pages long, short enough to be read and discussed in a class period—and because *sanwen* writings are often crafted to reflect its poetic lineage (called "beauty writing" disparagingly by its critics). Students prefer *sanwen* to the more traditional *yilunwen* because it allows them to express their subjective feelings and opinions without constantly seeking the sanction of history and other sources of authority. In such a context, it is little wonder that the essay "Thank You, Hardship," wrung out of the author's personal life and written with powerful emotions, was deemed exemplary by the exam readers.

The styles of the two student essays cited reflect their different traditions. Consistent with its informal style and emotionally charged content, "Thank You, Hardship" goes directly to the writer's personal experiences in the introduction, an approach commonly referred to as "open-the-door-and-see-the-mountain." From the introduction of the essay "Everyone Should Have Some Spirit," on the other hand, one hears an echo of the formulaic eight-legged essay, the official genre of the Imperial Civil Service Exam, which is sometimes translated as the "octopartite composition."[16] In its traditional form, an eight-legged essay invariably begins with an elaborate four-part opening consisting of "breaking the topic" *(po4, ti2)*, "continuing the topic" *(cheng2 ti2)*, "starting the explication" *(qi3 jiang3)*, and "entrance" *(ru4 shou3)*. It then proceeds to the four-part body: "the initial leg" *(qi3 gu3)*, "center leg" *(zhong1 gu3)*, "hind leg" *(hou4 gu3)*, and "tie-up leg" *(shu4 gu3)*. Since each leg includes two statements matching both in rhyme and sense, the essay has a total of eight legs. The rigid format and complex wordplay of the eight-legged essay had a stifling effect on the writer's creativity and free expression, and it was rightly removed from school curricula after the demise of the Imperial Civil Servant Exam. Yet the essay "Everyone Should Have Some Spirit" shows clear signs of that legacy. The first paragraph conforms to the four-part opening, although reduced and simplified. The first sentence "breaks" the topic with the statement, "Everyone should have some spirit." The first round of question-and-answer reinforces the topic by asserting that its applicability transcends time. The next few questions and answers further explicate the topic, and finally, the statement that "[h]istory has already provided us with answers" establishes the historical approach that is followed in the body of the essay.

How do students learn to write such essays if they have not been formally introduced to the eight-legged form? The answer can be found in the textbooks they read. The first essay in the textbook for the second grade of senior high (grade 11) in Nanjing provides a handy example. The essay, "On Diligence," opens with the following two paragraphs:

> There is an old Chinese saying, "With diligence, nothing under the sun is too hard to crack." ["Breaking" the topic, so to speak.] Han Yu, a great man-of-letters in the Tang Dynasty, once said, "Excellence is born out of diligence," which means, extensive knowledge and profound scholarship come from assiduous work. ["Continuing" or reinforcing the topic by quoting from a renowned scholar.]
>
> Diligence is a virtue for those who are eager to learn and eager to make progress. By diligence, we mean that people should cherish time, study diligently, think diligently, explore diligently, practice diligently, and sum up the experience diligently. [Brief explication.] On every page of the chronicles of all men with great accomplishment, in the past or present, in China or the world, is the giant character glistening with sweat: diligence. [Entering the topic from an all-encompassing perspective. The essay then proceeds to enumerate examples of Chinese and international personages and their accomplishments, some historical and others contemporary.]

The essay is certainly not used to illustrate the eight-legged essay, a term never evoked in class in a positive sense in mainland China since the founding of the People's Republic of China. Most postrevolution generations learned about the eight-legged essay in Mao Tse-tung's famous polemic, "Combating 'Eight-Legged' Party Writing," in which the eight-legged essay is condemned as full of bureaucratic jargon and empty of substance. The propensity for an elaborate opening found in the student essays cited here reflects a traditional practice cultivated through repeated exposure to textbook models and teachers' influence.

The two essays "Thank You, Hardship" and "Everyone Should Have Some Spirit" reveal a similar structure in the body, known as the "associative structure." Professor Bei suggests that

> the associative structure *(zu3 he2 shi4)* holds on to an idea, a poetic sentiment, or a thought as a thread that stitches together people, incidents, scenes, and objects that are otherwise unrelated. It is an organic realignment of reality. As such the writer ruminates over the one idea, one sentiment, or one thought over and over again from different angles and experiences. (488)

"Thank You, Hardship" moves from one episode to another in the writer's life—as many as nine of them—in an essay of about six hundred words. "Everyone Should Have Some Spirit" criss-crosses a larger terrain from the past to the present, from China to the world. The author quotes from Mao and Mencius, and alludes to fictional characters in Lu Xun and no fewer than seven other historical and literary incidents. The accumulation of facts and the free association of ideas and incidents from different times and places, all threaded together with a single idea, effectively drive the message home. The narrative is not as specific as Western teachers would like, and the ideas are not as fully developed, but obviously none of the teacher-commentators perceive these qualities as flaws.

Finally, following the Confucian tradition, both essays convey a strong moral message. The student writers, however, did not choose the moral message; it was decided by the designated topic of the essay, a moral proposition in itself. Yet a clear structure, emotional power, and historical awareness would not alone earn a high score; a strong moral message is essential. This is where traditional Confucianism and Chinese-style Marxism agree. Confucius asserted that writing is "the vehicle of *Tao*," and Mao, whose thinking still guides China's ideology today, admonished, "Proletarian literature and art are part of the whole proletarian revolutionary cause; they are, as Lenin said, cogs and wheels in the whole revolutionary machine" ("Talks" 86). Thus the goal of the eight-legged essay has traditionally been to advance the dominant morality of the time—Tao in Confucius's time and the proletarian cause in Mao's era. The student writers of both essays speak, in Bartholomae and Petrosky's words, with "moral authority rather than intellectual authority" (34)—an authority borrowed from the expectations implied by the question itself. The writers did not assume the authorship of their thesis, which was assigned to them, nor did the source of their authority come from the validity of their arguments or the strength of the evidence, but from their reading of the readers' expectations. (Did anyone, the examiner or the examinee, seriously believe that he or she needed to defend the value of endurance?)

Writing the essay portion of the university entrance examination is thus a test of rhetorical skill and the mastery of knowledge and language, but decidedly not an intellectual venture into the unknown or the controversial. As Freedman and Medway point out, such writing is "a way of responding to a specific reader (or readers) within a specific context on a specific occasion" (5). Chinese writing teachers call such writing *ying4 shi4 wen2,* "exam-coping writing." The candidate, writing for the sole purpose of gaining admission, must display knowledge rather than question received wisdom and produce texts that are inherently rule abiding and conformative. That is why writings produced in the university entrance exam bear so much resemblance to the long-abandoned eight-legged essay even though the latter is never explicitly taught in school. Those who take the exams write within the same rhetorical situation as those who took the Imperial Civil Service Exam. Moreover, as with the exam a century ago, the current university entrance exam wags the dog of education. The exam is an invisible but all-powerful hand that controls the teaching of writing in high schools across China, and its influence is as pervasive as ever. Given the force of this tradition, however, it must now be asked how well students are prepared for the writing they must do at university.

Voices of Dissent

What do today's Chinese university students think of their writing experiences in high school? How is an education that remains faithful to a disappearing tradition "track connecting" with an imported, specialized, career-oriented university education? The last part of this essay examines the transition between high school

writing and university writing in China from the student's perspective.

The basis for the discussion that follows is a survey distributed to students in three universities, two in Nanjing and one in
Shanghai. The survey posed three related questions:

1. What kinds of writing have you done in university? How are
   they different from what you did in high school?

2. Do you think high school Chinese education prepared you well
   for university writing? Why?

3. Is there anything about the teaching of high school writing that
   you want to see changed? [See the appendix.]

A total of 241 students in thirteen different majors returned
the survey, many with extensive responses. About half of the respondents are liberal arts majors. The distribution includes humanities students majoring in history (66), philosophy (29), and
Chinese (16); other majors include economics (26), computer
science (25), law (23), education (15), finance (11), information
technology (5), and physics, chemistry, and other sciences (11).

Two hundred and eight respondents, 86 percent of the total,
observed that the writing they face in university is quite different
from their high school writing. It is important to note, however,
that there is no universal genre—general university or academic
writing—in Chinese universities and that writing varies considerably across disciplines. The responses range from science majors' assertions that they "have not written anything" (which
probably accounts for their low participation in the survey) to
Chinese majors' reports that they do a wide variety of writing,
including poetry, vignette, *sanwen*, informal essay, political commentary, reading notes, literary criticism, and so on. In between
are humanities and social science majors, which make up the
majority of the survey respondents (76 percent). These students,
regardless of their concentration, are required to take "public
courses" (similar to general education courses in U.S. universities
but more limited), which include credit-earning, nonmajor electives offered to all disciplines, and supplementary courses (courses
taken in evenings and on weekends, which result in certificates

and some credits). Students in humanities and social sciences report that they engage in three main types of writing: *xiaolunwen* (a short research paper, an in-depth investigation of a topic, or a social phenomenon); *duhougan* (formal book reviews); and short exam-based essays. Several respondents report that they do not engage in narrative writing, "practical writing," or "opinion writing"—the writing they were trained to do in high school. One student says that "high school writing is not real writing"; others propose that university writing is too unimaginative and bland to be viewed as real writing.

Several points in respondents' comments mark their perceptions of differences between university and high school writing:

1. Many observe that university writing is much longer, more complex, and covers more ground in terms of content. One history major describes university writing as "huge and complicated." Another offers some statistical comparison: "In high school the average length of an essay is 600–800 words while in university it is 2,000–5,000 words."

2. Many note the importance of the library in university writing tasks. "The difference from writing in high school is that in high school writing is like cooking something out of the thin air, all coming out of one's own mind," comments an education major, "while in university, one goes to the library for information." An economics major has the same observation: "Writing in university is assisted by reference books. . . . In university there is no writing teacher; the best teacher in university is books." Most students find the collection, selection, synthesis, and organization of information from various sources a challenging task— one not taught in high school—that must be learned through trial and error.

3. More important, respondents note the stress on logic and theory in university writing, in contrast to the expression of feelings and opinions in high school writing. A law major lists the topics he has written on since entering university: "Reading *White and Black*," "Refuting the Chinese Threat Fallacy," "A Quick Analysis of the 'Conflict between Civilizations' Theory," and "On a

New Round of Government Restructuring." He points out that to write these papers, one has to have a good command of theory and information.

This perception is shared by several philosophy and economics majors who point out the difference between *li3 xing4* (rationality) and *gan3 xing4* (sensibility) in their tasks—thinking in logic as opposed to thinking in images. One of them observes that "university writing enforces rational thinking, so that one can understand issues at a deeper level; whereas high school writing emphasizes feelings and intuition, so we wrote mostly narratives and opinions." Another respondent, a philosophy major, characterizes university writing this way: " More emphasis on thinking, logic proof, as well as strong theory and factual evidence." A student of economics gives a similar characterization: "In university, writing has to have sound logic, indisputable evidence, and, on top of that, one has to have his own views." A law student says that "the writing [in university] is acceptable as long as you can round your words." This openness to diverse ideas gives many students a sense of freedom they did not have in high school. "In high school, once the topic was given, the point of view was already decided. To support that given view, [students] can only put in some examples copied from books mechanically. There is little thinking involved. There is more freedom with university writing," remarks a respondent from the Department of Information Technology.

This view is echoed by a great number of respondents, and one of them sums up the differences between writing in high school and university this way: "University writing is different from high school in that there is more room for developing one's own ideas, more leeway for one's own inclination, more books to consult, and few restrictions on what to write." Another writes about university writing as "more practical, [one is] freer to express one's own ideas without being judged 'good' or 'bad.'"

4. Students also report that the emphasis on language and structure in high school writing gives way to a stress on depth of analysis and interpretation in university. A history major describes it as the difference between "depth of thinking" and "literary grace" *(wen2 cai3)*. A history major comments, "high school writing . . .

was particular about the correct style, elegant language, etc.; i.e., more attention was paid to surface features."

While some respondents describe their writing in terms of Western rhetoric, others refer to a Chinese notion, *zi4 yuan2 qi2 shuo1* (round up one's words; i.e., no loopholes in the argument), to explain the criteria for university writing. A law student believes that the difference between high school writing and university writing is that "in university the writing is specialty related. The professor has higher demands in terms of logic, yet as far as language is concerned, he only expects it to be simple and clear." Others see university as less demanding about following a prescriptive structure. One student remarks that with university writing, "all you need is some order," yet in high school one had to "follow so many rules." Respondents repeatedly mention that the attention paid to structure in high school writing was restrictive, attributing it to "excessive" analysis of texts. A law student writes, "high school Chinese classes did too much analysis of each sentence and paragraph; a text is mutilated into scattered pieces to dig at its deeper meaning. This does more harm than good." An alternative, suggested by an economics major, is that "teachers do not have to analyze a text paragraph by paragraph; all they have to do is give some general guidance." Some assert that the preoccupation with structure weakens the content. One respondent, for instance, writes that "high school writing has fixed structure and fixed thinking," while in university "the style is looser, content more substantial, and import more profound."

Despite perceived differences between university and high school writing, most respondents said that high school writing prepared them well for university work. Sixty-four (26.5 percent) give an unqualified "yes" to this question, and ninety-five respondents (39.4 percent) think that high school Chinese classes prepared them to write well in university "to some extent" or "in some areas." A significant portion of the respondents (31.9 percent), however, believe that high school education was of little or no help at all. Most who answer yes claim that high school Chinese classes provided a sound foundation in writing. Others point to the training in basic language skills, particularly in building vocabulary, constructing sentences, and structuring an essay.

One student believes that he benefited from the emphasis on putting ideas in an orderly fashion: "I learned organization, the arrangement of the structure and paragraphs." An economics major wrote, "high school Chinese taught me the basic skills in writing, cultivated in me interest in literature and my capability to read. All these are of great help to writing in university." The same student, while valuing the language skills he learned in high school, says that high school writing developed his "ability to polish language . . . but not the ability to polish ideas." Most respondents see high school writing instruction as helpful for teaching them vocabulary, syntax, and organization (which many found restrictive but still useful), but they consider its moral and ideological content ineffective. They generally see themselves as having gained a set of skills from high school writing that was useful but stripped of content or purpose.

A skill-oriented education in writing does not prepare Chinese students to assume the authority that university writing requires, so it is not surprising that a decisive majority (89 percent) of survey respondents suggest that changes in high school curricula are urgent and necessary. They express a desire for more control over the topic and structure of their writing in order to freely express their own minds. They hope to have "more freedom" and "less restriction on thinking," and one respondent suggests that the practice of assigning "one fixed topic for one writing assignment should be abandoned." The following comment typifies suggestions for change:

> To be honest the course I liked least in high school is writing. In class the teacher always assigned a topic, discussed the topic for a while and then we proceeded to writing. Nothing new happened. Haven't many writers said that good writing comes from observation, understanding of life, and expressing them when you feel compelled to? Therefore, to reform writing classes, I suggest that for junior middle school students, the teacher can take them out to observe life and then write about their observation and comments. Often with the same object, when looked at from different angles one would have different points of view. . . . Teachers should not force them to write about the same topic; they should allow students to write what they feel like. . . . Besides, teachers should not impose form or their views on students. Rather, they should try to work with students to reach

some common understanding. . . . Any style is as good as the other. It is not necessary to follow the same model. Am I right?

Such sentiment is echoed by many other students. An economics major says that "high school writing is too restricted in topic and form; we are bound feet and hands. Besides, all writing has to be high-minded, which makes it hard to express one's real mind." Still another respondent simply requests, "Let me write my genuine feelings and thinking. Let me write what I want to write."

Survey respondents reserve the strongest negatives for the university entrance exam. Many respondents suggest that changes will be slow to come if high school education cannot free itself from the grip of the university entrance exam. In an almost unanimous voice, they dismiss high school writing as "writing for exams," a "modern version of [the] 'Eight-Legged' essay," "utilitarian," "programmed," "formularized," and "dry and rigid." They believe that as long as the goal of writing in high school is to pass exams, both teachers and students will have to conform to prescribed forms and ideas, making writing a "burdensome but inescapable chore." As one of them comments:

> High school writing is too much controlled by the university entrance exam, which creates the serious tendency to write the "Eight-Legged" essays: the opening, arrangement, and conclusion as the unalterable mould. Teachers recommend and students try to memorize essays that received high scores and praises; consequently, we all write the same kind of essay, repeat the same ideas, and create nothing new. . . . As we enter the university we found that universities generally do not teach how to write [the] research paper, so students do not know where to start and many simply plagiarize. If we were better prepared in high school, such problems could have been preempted.

A history major was more forceful: "to solve the problems in high school writing, we have to fundamentally change an education that revolves around the exam. That is the crux of all cruxes. Barring that, all is empty talk."

Students in this survey most often characterize university writing as "thinking" and high school writing as developing linguistic and organizational "skills." They rarely mention ideological and moral goals, which are emphasized in government guidelines and implemented strenuously through the design of the university entrance exam. Respondents to this survey recognize that university writing requires more than the ability to simply apply the skills learned in high school to a different set of writing tasks. At university, no longer is it acceptable, for example, to string together anecdotes with a thematic thread; it is not enough to be fluent with four-character proverbs or to command an encyclopedic knowledge of history. University writing entails a different epistemology, a different worldview.

Bizzell characterizes the academic worldview as one in which there are no absolutes, in which one must constantly (re)examine one's assumptions, reflect on one's own thoughts, and compare these thoughts with those of others. One's views, choices, and conclusions, therefore, are based on careful analysis, deliberation, and examination of evidence. Basically, one has to make sound critical judgments of one's own views and those of others. This way of thinking and writing could hardly be further from the world these students come from, where the truth is immutable and proven by history, and the writer's role is to shore up the existing truth. It is encouraging to discover that most respondents are glad to have the opportunity to exercise their critical faculties and relish the freedom to form their own views at university. They welcome change despite its daunting challenges.

The survey clearly indicates a gap between what high schools intend to teach and what students want to learn. On the one hand, schools take it as their mission to transmit the moral and literary traditions that have distinguished China from the rest of the world, and the university entrance exam is an effective enforcer of that tradition, just as the Imperial Civil Service Examination was a century ago. On the other hand, students living in the time of modernization have little interest in the past. Seeing the exam as a set of shackles, they want to be liberated from it and the tradition it embodies. Because the larger society is moving toward a "socialist market economy," in Deng Xiaoping's words—a culture in which people are rewarded for initiative and creativity—students see little value in following conventional principles. More individualistic and independent minded than the older generation, they want to use writing to develop their own thinking. In this way, students are ahead of the modernization curve. The contrast between the new and the traditional is acutely visible at the level of the university because, as a Western import, the university is responsive to the demands of the job market. Most universities in the last ten years have added majors that are in high demand on the market, while high schools are insulated from the hot breath of time—though students, with their eyes on the endgame, are not. Entering university, Chinese students travel a long distance, one that spans two worldviews reflecting two historical times in China.

Looking toward Change

Lao-tzu, reputedly a philosopher and Confucius's older contemporary who advocated a peaceful mind rather than a social hierarchy, famously advised, "If you realize that all things change, there is nothing you will try to hold on to" (74). In China today, changes are happening more rapidly and meet with greater acceptance than ever before. As I am finishing this project, Mr. Xu informs me that a new high school Chinese textbook with a very different approach and possibly more contemporary texts will be published next year. The current high school Chinese textbooks were last revised in 1995.

Of more significance is the government's decision to transform what is called "exam education" into "quality education." In Shanghai, for example, as part of this national movement the entrance exam for junior middle school was eliminated last year; all children now go to the nearest junior middle school regardless of their test scores. An even more dramatic step was taken last month, when it was announced that the national enrollment of university students would increase from last year's 1,080,000 to 1,530,000, an increase of over 40 percent ("1999: Higher Education" 1).

In Shanghai that means two out of every three applicants will be admitted to university. The impact was felt instantly, according to the report in *China Youth Daily*. This is particularly good news for students in nonkey high schools; as one high school graduate told the reporter, "Key high schools usually send 95%

of their graduates to university, the increase in enrollment does not mean much to them, but in my school only 20% of the graduates were able to go to university in the past. Now with the increase in enrollment, admission grades will become lower, which gives us more hope of being admitted" ("1999: Higher Education" 2). Educators also predict a positive impact on future education. A high school principal remarked, "By opening the door of high education wider, the single-planked bridge is widened, the pressure of exam is much alleviated, so we can focus more on the quality of education rather than passing the exams" (2).

Yet the real engine behind expansion is the market economy, as the president of Shanghai Education Research Institute suggested in describing the three benefits of increased university enrollments:

> First of all, by adding 300,000 freshmen, more students have the opportunity to receive university education, which will prepare them for the challenge of the next century. . . . With a well-educated labor force, our country will be better positioned to compete in the international market.
>
> Second, by expanding the internal demand, it will accelerate our economic development. Most parents are willing to invest in their children's education; their investment will in turn stimulate other related industries, such as the construction of new school buildings and the manufacturing of educational accouterments. Since an expanded higher education will need more logistic services, that will also create more jobs.
>
> Third, this creates a better environment for quality education. As the opportunity to enter university expands . . . and all qualified graduates can go to university, exams will gradually lose the power to control education. ("1999: Higher Education" 6)

China has come a long way from the view that education is a sacred ground for breeding moral and intellectual leaders. Will this change improve the quality of education, or instead reduce it to a mere commodity on domestic and international supermarkets? The jury is still out. Tradition continues to exert a strong hold on the reformer's imagination. My nephew, a computer science major in a Nanjing engineering university, recently e-mailed me:

> Our department started to offer Chinese as a required course for everyone from this semester [spring 1999]. The course mainly teaches the history of Chinese literature, yet we had to take an exam at the end, during which we were asked to write 600 words on the topic, "On Joy." I looked around during the exam and saw many sour faces in the classroom. It took me an hour to finally find "joy."

The exam also included translating and annotating excerpts from classical literature. Instead of creating Chinese courses that help students succeed in university, my nephew's school seems to have transported high school Chinese to the university campus. The pendulum continues to swing between broadening education for the future and paying homage to China's homespun tradition.

Appendix

Survey Form [translated from Chinese]

Whether the teaching of writing in high school meets the need of writing in university is an issue both high school and university educators are concerned with. Therefore we conduct the following investigation. Your support and participation in the survey are greatly appreciated. Please complete the form based on your high school and university writing experience.

Name: (optional)   Major:
Year: School Name:

Question 1: What kinds of writing have you done in university? How are they different from what you wrote in high school?

Question 2: Do you think that high school Chinese classes prepared you well for university writing? Why?

Question 3: Is there anything about the teaching of writing in high school that you want to see changed? Please give your suggestions.

Again, thank you for your cooperation and support.

Notes

1. During the Cultural Revolution, class enemies were classified into eight categories, and intellectuals, who were not denounced as class enemies but were regarded as politically unreliable, were denigrated as the "stinking ninth."

2. *Tao* has been translated in different ways, one of the most frequent being truth. Yet what is truth shifts with the user and time. Most Confucian scholars believed that the core of Tao was summed up by the Three Guiding Principles *(san1 gang1):* the minister submits to the emperor, son to father, and wife to husband; Five Constants *(wu3 chang2):* benevolence, righteousness, propriety, knowledge, and sincerity; and the Four Social Bonds *(si4 wei2):* propriety, morality, modesty, and sense of shame. These precepts were not articulated by Confucius but inferred from his works by later Confucian scholars.

3. This text was one of the traditional series called Four Books and Five Classics. The Four Books are *The Analects of Confucius, Mencius, The Great Learning,* and *The Doctrine of the Mean.* The Five Classics, commonly believed to be compiled under the personal guidance of Confucius and his disciples, are *The Odes (Shi1), The Book of History (Shu1), The Book of Rites (Li3), The Book of Changes (Yi4),* and *The Spring and Autumn Annals (Chun1 Chou1).*

4. Before neo-Confucianism took hold, a curriculum typically included rites, music, archery, charioteering, reading and writing, and counting.

5. In most high schools, students take ten subjects: Chinese, math, foreign language, physics, chemistry, biology, history, geography, political education, and physical education. In political education, students typically study the history of the Chinese Communist Party and current government and Party policies.

6. Practical writing usually includes business letters, notices, receipts, reports, documents, and so forth. Although it is theoretically the most useful genre in real life, it traditionally receives little instructional attention. The current high school Chinese textbook (1990), which consists of six volumes, one for each semester, does not contain a single piece of practical writing. The low status of practical writing is also indicated by the fact that it is not used as an exam genre. It is certainly not used in university entrance exams, and according to research by Mr. Xu, of the genres tested in high school entrance exams in 1996, practical writing was not required for the major essay on any of the exams offered in eighteen provinces and municipalities. (The narrative is the predominant

genre, and in three areas, opinion writing was offered as an alternative to the narrative.) Although more than half of the eighteen surveyed locales (10) claimed to require the examinees to do practical writing for the minor essay, in fact only one did. The others instead had examinees "correct the wrong sentences" in a given piece rather than produce practical writing. Obviously, teachers and administrators see little educational or literary value in putting practical writing on the testing block. Students' academic careers do not seem to be hampered by the neglect; however, none of the university respondents in my survey indicated that they composed any kind of practical writing in their university studies.

7. In recent years, as an experiment the exam has been waived for students with outstanding academic records from key high schools, with the recommendation of the teachers and administrators, but such privilege is strictly limited to the truly exceptional.

8. A quotation from Mao Tse-tung.

9. A proverb.

10. Confucius's successor, often mentioned in parallel with Confucius, as in "the doctrine of Confucius and Mencius."

11. Ah Q is the self-delusional protagonist in a short story by Lu Xun, widely regarded as the forefather of China's modern literature.

12. The first and second sons of the last king of the Shang Dynasty (16th to 11th century B.C.). They went to King Zhou to stop his invasion of Shang. After King Zhou conquered Shang, they hid in a mountain and, refusing to eat the handouts sent by King Zhou, starved to death.

13. Professor Zhu Ziqing (1898–1948), essayist and poet, died in poverty in August 1948 in Beijing.

14. The original Chinese is *wenzhang*, meaning "a piece of writing." For the purpose of this study, and following the practice of Lynn Bloom, *essay* in this study is meant as a "protean genre"—i.e., "whatever is not poetry or fiction" (405). The difference between Chinese and Western essays, however, is a complex subject that warrants a separate study.

15. *Sanwen* (miscellaneous writing) is short commentary on topical issues of politics and society. Mao Tse-tung describes it as a "short and sharp dagger."

16. Father Angelo Zottoli in his *Cursus Litteraturae Sinicae* translated the terminology of octopartite rhetoric into Latin, which led some scholars to believe that there was actually a parallel between schoolboy Latin prose composition and the octopartite composition.

Works Cited

Bartholomae, David, and Anthony Petrosky. *Facts, Artifacts and Counterfacts: Theory and Method for a Reading and Writing Course.* Upper Montclair, NJ: Boynton/Cook, 1986.

Bei, Xiansheng, ed. *New Manuscript on Writing.* Huaiyin: Jiangsu Education, 1987.

Bizzell, Patricia. "What Happens When Basic Writers Join the Academic Discourse Community?" Panel on Discourse Communities: Social-Rhetorical Perspectives. CCCC Annual Convention. Sheraton Centre, New York. 19 Mar. 1984.

Bloom, Lynn Z. "The Essay Canon." *College English* 61 (1999): 401–30.

Confucius. *The Analects (Lun yü).* Trans. D. C. Lau. Harmondsworth: Penguin, 1979.

"Everyone Should Have Some Spirit." *Chinese News (High School Edition).* 1 Sept. 1998: 1.

Freedman, A., and P. Medway, eds. *Learning and Teaching Genre.* Portsmouth, NH: Boynton/Cook, 1994.

Gong [pseudonym]. "An Overview of Teaching Writing in Chinese High Schools." Letter to the author. May-June 1991. 29 pp.

High School Textbook: Chinese Vol. X (required). Beijing: People's Education Press, 1995.

Huang, Ray. *1587, a Year of No Significance: The Ming Dynasty in Decline.* New Haven: Yale UP, 1981.

Lao-tzu. *Tao Te Ching: A New English Version.* Ed. Stephen Mitchell. New York: HarperCollins, 1988.

Li, Xiao-ming. *"Good Writing" in Cross-Cultural Context.* Albany: SUNY P, 1996.

———. "Writing from the Vantage Point of an Outsider/Insider." *Non-Native Educators in English Language Teaching*. Ed. George Braine. Mahwah, NJ: Erlbaum, 1999.

Liu, Xiqing, ed. *Collected Commentary on Chinese Writing Theories*. Liaotong: Inner Mongolia Education Press, 1992.

Mao, Ze-dong [Tse-tung]. "Combating 'Eight-Legged' Party Writing." *Selected Works of Mao Ze-dong*. Vol.III. 2nd ed. Beijing: People's Publisher, 1991. 830–46.

———. "Talks at the Yenan Forum on Literature and Art." *Selected Works of Mao Ze-Dong*. Vol. IV. London: Lawrence & Wishart, 1956. 63–93.

Ministry of Education, People's Republic of China. "General Guideline for High School Chinese Language Education." Brochure.

"1999: Higher Education Expanding Enrollment." *China Youth Daily*. 28 June 1999. 1–8 <http://www.chinayouthdaily.com.cn/gkzt/9543^Q107.html>.

"Thank You, Hardship." *Yangtze Evening News*. 15 June 1998: 7.

Yu, Xuechu. "Chinese, Teachers of Chinese, Individuals." *Newsletter for Educators of Chinese*. April 1989: 47–49.

Xu, Shaowu. *Gallery of Best Writing by Middle School Students: Essays from High School Entrance Exam*. Nanjing, Jiangsu: Jiangsu Education Press, 1997.

Zheng, Dengyun. *The History of China's Higher Education*. Shanghai: East China Teachers' UP, 1994.

———. *The Modern History of China's Education*. Shanghai: East China Teachers' UP, 1994.

Zou, Wei, ed. *The Selection and Translation of Traditional Theories on Writing*. Henan, China: Wenxin, 1990.

CHAPTER TWO

Cracking the Codes Anew: Writing about Literature in England

MARY SCOTT
University of London

Current Contexts

As in some other countries referred to in this book (such as South Africa and Kenya), higher education in the United Kingdom has been the site of huge changes in recent years. The changes can be broadly characterized as representing a move away from a highly exclusive system, in which the participation rate of eighteen- to twenty-year-olds was still only 15 percent in the mid-1980s, to a more open system in which over 30 percent of that age cohort had gained access by the mid-1990s (Scott 2). It can thus be said that, broadly speaking, higher education in Britain has undergone a transformation. If we borrow Trow's yardsticks, this transformation can be described as a move from an elite system (i.e., one that enrolls up to 15 percent of the age group) to a mass system (one that enrolls between 15 and 40 percent). The process of transformation is not yet complete, however. The current government would have the participation rate of eighteen- to twenty-year-olds leap to 50 percent in the near future, a rate that would conform to Trow's criteria for a universal system of higher education (i.e., a system that enrolls more than 40 percent of that age group). (For a diagrammatic overview of the educational system in the United Kingdom, see Figure 3.)

While this concern to increase access might seem to bring the United Kingdom closer in ideology to the United States or France,

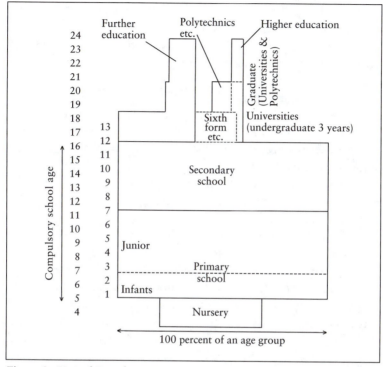

Figure 3. *United Kingdom: Structure of the formal education system.*

where social equity is a primary aim, the situation in the United Kingdom is more complex. Because they are so recent, the moves toward a universal system are the subject of competing discourses. While many teachers in both schools and universities welcome the opening up of the universities to "nonstandard" entrants as a democratic initiative, others view it as a "dumbing down" of higher education. The former polytechnics, which concentrated on professional fields such as business studies and journalism, have been renamed universities, but popular discourse refers to them as "new" universities and maintains that "old" universities are superior. To quote Scott again, "elite instincts and mass forms presently co-exist" (9).

These changes in higher education provide the frame for my discussion of student writing in the transition from school to university. It is a frame I enlarge in the concluding section of this chapter when, looking to the future, I concentrate again on government goals and initiatives. Taking the photographic or filmic analogy further as a means of articulating the structure and purpose of this chapter, the opening and concluding parts of the chapter offer a long shot of the higher education scene in the United Kingdom, while in the intervening sections I seek to provide a close-up view of the difficulties of three first-year undergraduate writers in English literature courses. This close-up will not, however, reflect "elitist instincts" since I do not regard the students' academic difficulties as the inevitable outcome of the expansion of higher education. I aim instead to show that the primary problem lies in the gap between what is expected at school and what is required in the university.

While I have selected undergraduate essays that clearly were considered problematic by the markers, who gave them low grades, I would argue that the gap between school and university approaches presents problems for almost all first-year undergraduates when they write essays about literature. A marked parallel can in fact be drawn between many novice undergraduates' experience of writing such essays and Turner's anthropological conceptualization of the *rite de passage,* in which a separation from an "established set of cultural conditions" is followed by a "liminal period." Turner describes the state of the "passenger" or "liminar" during the *rite de passage* as "ambiguous, neither here nor there, betwixt and between all fixed points of classification" (232). As the following comment indicates, it is a transition that can confront student "passengers" with the unsettling realization that what they learned in the past has become mysteriously inappropriate:

> I got good marks for my essays about literature at school. I can't understand why I am not doing well now [at university]. I always think I understand the essay questions but clearly I don't. I am not the only one who is confused about what's expected. In fact I would say that most of us are. (First-year undergraduate)

Giving novice undergraduates access to new understandings that they can then make visible in their essays is, however, no easy task. A number of researchers have shown that students do not often attach the required meanings to the terms we teachers use in the essay questions we set and in our attempts to offer helpful guidance and feedback (see Hounsell; Mitchell, "A Level"; Lea and Street). My own experience as a tutor[1] matches these research findings. Terms such as "analyze," "discuss," "argue," and "give your personal response," which I use in framing essay questions or in feedback, make sense to me in that they reflect my *habitus* (Bourdieu), my internalized ways of knowing and doing, but to many new university students in the humanities and social sciences, these conventional instructions are codes they cannot crack.

This failure on the part of the students represents a paradox, however. It is a failure deriving not from the unfamiliarity of the encodings but from their apparent familiarity—at school the students were also required to "argue" and to give their "personal response." Consequently, and unsurprisingly, they tend as undergraduates to assume a continuity between school and university essay-writing requirements, but it is a continuity that does not in fact exist.

This discontinuity within apparent continuity provides the central focus of this paper. Using sample essays placed in the "highest category" (i.e., were awarded the highest marks) in the final school examination (General Certificate of Education: Advanced Level) in English literature, as well as the examiners' comments on the essays, I first identify the meanings attached in practice to the principal criteria stated in the document. What I find is that these criteria—viz., "argument" and "personal response"—derive their meaning from a particular conception of literature and literary criticism that applies across all essay questions. I then turn to essays by first-year undergraduates following a course on (or in U.S. English, majoring in) literature in English—essays the tutors considered problematic. I suggest that the essays can be read as evidence of how the students have tried intuitively to make the essay questions correlate with approaches that brought success in the Advanced Level (A-level) examinations. But the unified conception of literature and literary criticism giving meaning to essay questions at A-level is no longer what is required. The undergraduate needs to be able to assess just which of many competing theoretical orientations a particular essay question may encode.

While discontinuity within apparent continuity is the central paradox that I aim to make visible in this essay, it is not the only incongruity I detect. There is also an irony that my own approach can be said to have constructed. In the concluding part of this chapter, I trace that irony to my initial failure to perceive how my readings of the student essays do not do justice to the theoretical focus within which they are explicitly framed. Anticipating this later discussion, I briefly characterize that failure here in the following way: my readings of the students' essays rest on a narrow conception of a "student essay" as a text to be assessed, rather than an indicator of individual understandings and ways forward. In looking again at features of the undergraduates' essays in the final part of this chapter, I introduce problems that keep the meanings of "argument" and "personal response" under review.

Theoretical Orientation

These comments imply a particular view of writing and of the writer, a view that derives largely from Kress (*Making*, "Representational"). Kress presents the writer as the producer of motivated signs (words, texts, or images). *Motivated* in this context does not, however, denote a Romantic view of the individual as spinning meanings from his or her own self-substance, nor that writers consciously control all aspects of what they write. It also excludes a view of the sign as fully motivated by the social environment. In short, Kress steers a pathway between the extremes of Romantic individualism on the one hand and social determinism on the other. For him, the individual is social, and writing remakes the forms and meanings that have been socially made. In adding detail to this broad perspective, Kress describes the writer as engaged in the remaking of available resources (which are of many different kinds—linguistic, social, cultural) out of her "interest," a term that denotes the focusing (both intuitively and consciously) of many factors, including social and cultural histories and present social contexts.

When I apply the concept of motivation as interest to student writing, an essay (i.e., an essay assignment, in U.S. context) takes on the character of a writer's hypothesis that this is what is required by this essay question assigned in this course. This leads me, the reader, to form my own hypotheses as to why the essay is as it is and not otherwise, or to consider why the student writer has made the meanings he or she has. I do not, however, assume that I can identify all the reasons why the student has remade his or her knowledge, understandings, and experience in a particular way. In fact, the completeness or accuracy of my reading is not actually the issue. What is important is the style of pedagogy suggested by the idea of a text as motivated. It emphasizes self-reflexivity on the part of student and tutor that is promoted by tutor-student dialogue grounded in the tutor's careful attempt to identify the assumptions and meanings in the student's essay and to consider their possible origin.

The view of writing thus sketched can clearly accommodate poststructuralist intertextuality as Barthes maintains it, especially the reminder that "creativity" and "originality" are not absolutes since textual meaning is tethered to the social by references to other texts. The concept of the "motivated sign" also resonates with Bakhtin's perception of the "life of the word" as "contained in its transfer . . . from one context to another context," a process in which "the word does not forget its own path and completely free itself from the power of those concrete contexts into which it has entered" (*Problems* 202). Consequently, Bakhtin argues that "there are no voiceless words," and any word cannot but speak to, hear, and understand meanings deriving from its past contexts. To these abstract formulations Kress adds a concern with text as testimony to writers' active engagement with their past learnings and experience, and with their perceptions of their role and writing task.

The theoretical framework thus outlined contains a brief comment on pedagogy. As that comment suggests, my view of writing and the writer finds its pedagogic corollary in Vygotskian perspectives on learning and, in particular, in the "zone of proximal development" (ZPD). In writings about education, typified in Daniels's work, ZPD is usually interpreted as indicating the distance between the problem-solving abilities exhibited by a learner working alone, and that learner's problem-solving abilities when assisted by, or collaborating with, more experienced people. There are, however, other interpretations of ZPD, one of which Lave and Wenger refer to as the "cultural" definition. In this interpretation, ZPD is the "distance between the cultural knowledge provided by the sociohistorical context—usually made accessible by instruction—and the everyday experience of individuals" (144).

This interpretation of ZPD can be used to refocus the betwixt and betweenness of the novice undergraduate's situation. To demonstrate the enlargement of meaning that then emerges, I return to the student comment quoted earlier: "I always think I understand the essay questions but clearly I don't. I am not the only one who is confused." Considered in light of a cultural interpretation of ZPD, this comment suggests that new undergraduates bring with them approaches to writing about literature that have become so much a part of their everyday experience as essay writers that they cannot conceive of other possibilities. In other words, the students have been inducted into a particular way of writing essays about literature and are unaware of the theoretical underpinnings of their approach or of how it relates to other approaches. The task for me as teacher, then, is to move the students on from their largely intuitive view of what is required to what is actually required.

Setting this task within the theoretical framework just outlined, I suggest the following implications for my approach to student essays: While reading the individual essay as a "motivated sign" is essential, it need not be the final stage in my thinking. It is just as important to consider an essay as indicating where a new approach might have its beginnings—i.e., indications of the student writer's ZPD. To borrow Doris Lessing's metaphor, I need to look for the cracks through which the new may flood. I attempt to do just that in my analyses of undergraduate essays.

Research into Argument

"Argument" is a key term in the codes that confront the student writer both at school and in university. In the United Kingdom, this has been recognized in recent years in the granting of funding by the Leverhulme Trust for research into the teaching and learning of argument in school and university. This research is, however, based on a theoretical focus different from that outlined here. In fact, my theoretical orientation was developed out of my criticisms of the Leverhulme projects and takes on a sharper outline when considered in relation to the view of argument developed in those projects.

The research to which I refer has been largely carried out by Mitchell (*Teaching, Improving,* "Quality"), Andrews ("Learning," *Teaching*), and Riddle ("Introducing"). To provide a theoretical description that teachers in schools and higher education can translate into practice, these researchers draw on several different sources, particulary Toulmin's elements (Toulmin, Rieke, and Janik)—claim, warrants and grounds—from which they derive the underpinnings of all performances of argument. Their reliance on Toulmin coexists, however, with references to the Bakhtinian "dialogic" (Mitchell, *Teaching, Improving*; Andrews, "Learning"). Here I find an unacknowledged contradiction at the core of the research's theoretical framework. It derives from the fact that Toulmin and Bakhtin are incompatible. Bakhtin was primarily concerned with the historicity and specificity of performance. While he certainly did not reject the notion of systematicity, he treated systems as "existing only with respect to the subjective consciousness of members of some particular community" (Clark and Holquist 224). His focus was thus not on a given utterance's significance within an underlying system, but rather on its "actual meaning," which can only be "understood against the background of other concrete utterances on the same theme" (Bakhtin, *Dialogic* 281). This focus invites a consideration of the historicity and specificity of the meanings in students' essays. But while the research into argument did not initially ignore learners' meanings, in recent years more and more emphasis has been placed on framing an answer to the question, "What is this thing called argument?" (Mitchell, *Improving*). Since such a question implicitly attributes essential qualities to argument, its effect has been to move the research away from Bakhtin's emphasis on the specificity and historicity of performance and toward Toulmin's abstract categories. In the process, the learner has tended to disappear from view.

In obscuring the learner, the question, "What is this thing called argument?" implies a focus on pedagogy that is very different from the Vygotskian perspective I have suggested. In short, it invites a model of teaching and learning in which teachers transmit their knowledge and students receive what has been transmitted. The transmission model of pedagogy is currently in fashion in higher education in the United Kingdom, where the Quality Assurance Agency[2] (QAA) links it to a call for explicitness in the statement of course aims and criteria and in tutor feedback and guidance. While I recognize the need to aim at explicitness, however, I question the particular exemplar of explicitness in pedagogy that the Leverhulme research projects offer. It is an explicitness that invites the naming of parts by teacher and taught—this is a claim; that is the warrant, these are grounds. I seek here to propose instead a focus on explicitness as constituted by the lending of consciousness by teacher to undergraduate on the basis of a reading of the student's essay as a sign that is "motivated" by subjectivities formed at A-level, and in particular by the meanings attached to the primary criterion, argument.

What argument means in the context of A-level examiners' practice is the main subject of the next part of this chapter. First, however, some background needs to be provided concerning the role and place of A-level examinations in relation to university entrance.

University Admissions: The Role and Place of A-Level Examinations

When a student proceeds to an A-level course (typically at age seventeen), he or she exchanges a broad curriculum with seven compulsory subjects for in-depth, narrowly specialized study in two or three subjects, studied over two years. Criticism of the narrowness of the A-level curriculum abounds, and some head teachers argue for the French-style *baccalauréat* (see Chapter 3). Yet most universities still regard A-levels as the "gold standard," claiming that they provide an essential foundation for further academic study, and that the degree of specialization required in any one subject matches the level of academic achievement students in many other countries do not attain until at least the end of their first year at university. A-level students take high-stakes essay examinations at the end of their studies, assessed by an examining board, which largely determine their admission to university.

In the United Kingdom, all applications for full-time undergraduate programs of study are managed by the Universities and Colleges Admissions Service (UCAS), a government agency.[3] Prospective students have to apply through UCAS in the early part of the second year of their two-year A-level course. In filling out the UCAS application form (at about age eighteen, typically), they can list up to six universities and/or courses. Although the applications are then sent to each of the universities the applicant has listed, students are admitted to a specific degree program (curriculum or major in the United States) and are expected to remain in that program. In this sense, a successful applicant is admitted to a degree program and not to a university. Consequently, it is the course admissions tutors within each discipline who decide the outcomes of all applications. In short, the A-level examinations loom large in the lives of students in their last two years at school, and their teachers give considerable time to preparing the students for the kinds of questions they are likely to encounter in the examinations.

How then does it come about that students who have been successful at A-level can be "confused about what's expected" in essays about literature at university? I would suggest that the problem derives both from the nature of literature as a field of academic study and from the empirical realities imposed by the perceived need for a large-scale end-of-schooling public assessment system. The academic study of literature is characterized by many different approaches whose diversity is greater by far than that which typifies the study of science, where knowledge is more codified at the A-level. An A-level science course can thus serve as a strong foundation for university courses in science. A-level and first-year university courses in English literature, on the other hand, differ considerably in that familiarity with a diversity of critical perspectives is not required at A-level but is necessary for success even in first-year undergraduate courses. The reasons for this relate to the fact that at A-level, literature is a public examination subject taken by thousands of students who do not have access to well-stocked libraries where they might research different critical approaches to literature. In other words, to make English literature teachable and examinable across the country (and in some overseas centers too), the examination boards, which supervise the A-level examinations, have imposed a particular approach centering on the study of set literary texts in certain ways. But there may well be an even stronger reason for the approach adopted, since, as I indicate later, it can be said to suit larger educational aims within the British context.

Several different examining boards offer A-level examinations. Schools decide which board's examinations their students should take. In this chapter, I refer to the University of London Examinations and Assessment Council's (ULEAC's) examinations. In order to identify the view of literature and how to write about it (i.e., the kind of subjectivity) that is required for success in ULEAC's A-level examinations in English literature, I draw on the *Teachers' Guide* that ULEAC publishes. The stated general aim of the guide is to "give straightforward advice with direct reference to the ULEAC English literature syllabus[4] at Advanced Level" (1). The guide contains samples of students' examination answers to particular questions together with the examiner's comments. It also includes samples of course work, since students can choose to submit a portfolio of essay assignments they have done on their own time in place of an examination. In such cases, the course work portfolio makes up 20 percent of the total assessment.

The Examiners' Criteria

The *Teachers' Guide* emphasizes two criteria—viz., "argument" and "personal response" or "personal involvement." At one level, the emphasis on the personal is, of course, examiner code for candidates' need to avoid the stock, prepackaged answer. But care is also taken to distinguish personal response from uninformed personal opinion. Personal response or involvement is in fact an elaboration of argument and its cognates, namely, "critical analysis" and "judgment." The guide thus offers a Janus-faced view of literature: literature resonates with the reader's experience of life even while its formal devices and structures distance it from the world of everyday events and experience. Consequently, the guide advises teachers to help students appreciate that although empathizing with a character is desirable, it should be contained within an awareness of the character's particular function or role in articulating the themes of the text under discussion.

This focus on a literary text reflects a critical tradition of seeing a text as a self-contained object that represents a moral perspective. I outline that tradition shortly. For the moment, however, my aim is to describe the kind of subjectivity an A-level essay is expected to reflect. With that end in view, I consider two A-level essays in relation to the examiners' comments on each.

Writing about Literature at A-Level: Two Essays

I have selected two examination essays that were each placed in the "highest category" by the examining board and were therefore included in the *Teachers' Guide* as exemplars of the kind of approach the examiners expect. The first essay is on *Madame Bovary* (in translation) and *The Great Gatsby*. The second essay is on Sylvia Plath's poetry. I do not know the name or the gender of either writer and so I use androgynous pseudonyms, referring to the writer of the open-text examination essay on Sylvia Plath's poetry as Jo and to the writer of the course work essay on *Madame Bovary* and *The Great Gatsby* as Sam. Following feminist practice, however, I use the pronoun *she* and the possessive adjective *her* for both writers.

In Jo's and Sam's essays, as in the guide's other exemplary essays, "argument" and "personal response" are realized in the description and assessment of a character's, or a poem's, moral and emotional qualities, and in particular in the perception of ambiguity and paradox. In fact, the examination question on Plath's poetry invites attention to ambiguity. It reads:

> It has been suggested that even at its most destructive Plath's poetry is always counterbalanced with tenderness. Have you found this to be so?

Jo responds to the question in the way intended: she is quick to see that agreement with the given statement is what is actually required. Thus, after initially giving an obvious and brief example of tenderness, she addresses the paradox of tenderness in destructiveness:

> However, Plath's underlying tenderness is most evident in one of her most vicious poems, "Daddy," perhaps reflecting her ambivalent love/hate attitude towards her father:
>> Daddy I have had to kill you
>> You died before I had time.
> In these two lines the poet's wish to murder her father is combined with her regret and her grief over his death in a startling, contradictory couple of lines.

This paradox of love within hate is the dominant theme of Jo's essay and is the note on which she concludes her discussion of "Daddy," the poem to which she gives most attention. She writes:

> However much Plath would like to hate her father, . . . she is unable to do so and despite the increasingly vicious triumph of the last stanza . . . the final line of the poem reads more like an acknowledgement of her own defeat than a victory.

In Sam's essay, too, argument is realized in the elucidation of a paradox. Her opening sentence states that her essay is about the "tragedy" of two characters—Gatsby and Emma Bovary—who could "hardly be more different at first glance," but who "beneath the surface have much in common in their inner worlds of romantic fantasy: both are simultaneously sustained and destroyed by their dreams." In short, as in Jo's essay, argument is a matter of looking below the surface of events and actions, and implicitly excluding simple moral categorizations. This is clearly demonstrated in the final paragraph of Sam's essay in which she emphasizes the ironic similarities and contrasts she finds in the characters of Emma Bovary and Gatsby:

> They are both tremendously romantic figures because of their powers of imagination and dreaming. Emma's tragedy is that she is a fantastically sensual woman who is capable of inspiring great

love, but she has not grasped the true nature of love and of compromise. Gatsby's tragedy is that this most hopeful and most loving of men has surrendered himself to a woman unworthy of his trust and devotion.

In their assessment of character or feelings, Jo and Sam both adopt a judgmental mode of discourse that reflects a particular set of values. Their statements gather authority from assertive third-person linguistic structures. Emphasizing a paradox once again, for example, Jo informs the reader that Plath's destructiveness is actually a virtue in that it is a mark of her courageousness:

> Although undoubtedly some of Plath's more rational poetry contains undercurrents of tenderness, there are some poems which hit the reader with their lack of it. In some ways, however, this is one of Plath's strengths—she never shirks a completely bitter sentiment. (p. 61)

Sam likewise confidently categorizes Emma and Gatsby. This is graphically illustrated in statements in which, writing in the third person, as throughout the essay, she passes judgment with an air of authority:

> Emma's fantasy is self centred whereas Gatsby needs to give love as much as to receive it. Emma's love is selfish, Gatsby's, however, is entirely unselfish. But despite the elusive qualities of their fantasy worlds neither Gatsby nor Emma is an idle dreamer. (p. 68)

As these examples show, Jo and Sam implicitly ascribe an unquestionable validity to their judgments and to the moral norms on which those judgments are based. This in turn sheds further light on what the examiners mean when they ask for a personal response, the criterion the examiner picks out as particularly important when commenting on Jo's essay:

> The question makes a number of quite specific demands, . . . but more significantly it signals ("Have **you** found . . .") that what is being sought here are personal involvement and personal response." (p. 62)

Jo interprets the question in a way that meets the examiner's expectations. She perceives, no doubt intuitively rather than consciously, that "personal involvement" and "personal response" signal that the examiners require an interpretation based finally on values that can be assumed to be shared by the reader. In short, both Jo and Sam treat the literary text as a comment on life's complexity that they explicate for a reader inhabiting the same moral world.

This assumption that the reader occupies the same universe of values is reinforced by the absence of detailed analysis of how the texts under discussion create their effects. Although Jo quotes extensively from Plath's poems, for example, she tends to gloss the lines, embedding the quotations in her interpretations, as in:

> Although the poet seems to attach blame to both her father—
>   No less a devil for that, no not
>   Any less the black man who
>   Bit my pretty red heart in two—
> and her husband, she also acknowledges her own capability—
>   If I killed one man I've killed two

Sam similarly tends to use quotation as an elaboration of her interpretation:

> Emma's first attempt at securing herself a reality of eternal romantic love ironically contributes still further to her need for dreams, for the happiness derived from her marriage to Charles falls horribly short of expectations. He is incapable of fulfilling her fantasies. "Before the wedding she had believed herself in love. But not having attained the happiness that should have resulted from that love she now fancied she must have been mistaken. And Emma wondered what exactly was meant in life by the words 'bliss,' 'passion,' 'ecstasy' which had looked so beautiful in books."

Writing about Literature at A-Level: Some General Conclusions

What general conclusions might be drawn from this discussion? Significantly, Jo and Sam each reveal a no doubt largely intuitive awareness of paradoxical assumptions clustering around the conception of literature and literary criticism set out in the *Teachers' Guide*. They implicitly subscribe to the view that literature both is and is not about life, and that a personal response both is and is not personal in that it has to be transformed into a general comment within a shared community of values while not ceasing to be an individual interpretation. They demonstrate this process in an assumption of authority reflected in two habits: their use of the third person and their use of general themes that sweep up the text into comments about thought and feeling—comments that eschew simple either/ors, replacing them with the identification of ambiguity and paradox.

But while the generalizations universalize attitudes and feelings articulated in the text, they also throw into relief the particularities of the text. This is a critical process Connor describes as the use of examples for their "exemplarity." He contrasts "exemplarity" with "exemplification," which denotes the subordination of the example to the delineation of certain concepts or principles. This is a distinction that, as I shortly show, illuminates the nature of the difference between the essay questions set at A-level and those that students are required to address in an undergraduate course.

Connor links exemplarity to practical criticism, a method of analysis associated mainly with I. A. Richards. Practical criticism (which is also the title of the book Richards published in 1929) is the British counterpart of American New Criticism. In their emphasis on the study of texts largely in isolation from their sociopolitical, biographical, and literary-historical background, the A-level students' essays, and the examiners' comments, do in fact echo the primary principles of practical criticism. Richards shared with F. R. Leavis an insistence that the purpose of literature is to teach about life and to transmit humane values that transcend time and place. This too is a shaping and strongly visible influence on the study of literary texts at A-level. Leavis and Richards both began teaching at Cambridge University in the 1920s and came to represent what has been termed the "moral intrinsic" approach to literary texts. Birch summarizes this approach:

> For this method of reading the reader does not need to know
> about the situations in which the text was produced, the histori-
> cal/economic contexts, or the biographical contexts of the writer.
> It is basically a criticism that produces an interpretation free of
> any contextual influences. . . . The object of analysis is not the
> specific text, but rather the phenomenon of subjectivity—that
> which makes us human. (16)

In short, the reader needs to be a "sound judge of value" (Richards
87). Birch makes some harsh criticisms of the moral intrinsic
approach, using excerpts from a paper by Cleanth Brooks, an
American New Critic, as an example of the shortcomings he perceives in the approach. The following lines are part of a longer
passage, which Birch quotes to exemplify Brooks's mode of criticism. Brooks is referring to Faulkner's poem "The Marble Faun":

> How much more brilliant is Faulkner's account of how the idiot
> found a "brown creep of moisture in a clump of alder and beech"
> and scooped out a basin for it "which now at each return of light
> stood full and clear and leaf by leaf repeating until (cow and
> idiot) lean and interrupt the green reflections." (qtd. in Birch 75)

Birch's purpose in quoting these lines is to accuse Brooks of
"expecting a series of quotations to function as critical comment."
When I now look back at Jo's and Sam's essays, I see that they
can be said to use quotations in the same way. The stance they
adopt does in fact resemble that of the professional practitioners
of moral intrinsic criticism, who assume a reader crediting them
with privileged access to the meanings in the text. It is a stance
that assumes that "ultimately we can talk of . . . texts only in so
far as we can talk with them" (Carter 384).

Earlier I suggested that certain real-world constraints cause
the A-level study of English literature to focus on the study of set
texts from a particular critical perspective. Now that I have traced
that perspective to its source, however, I perceive another, even
stronger reason. Leavis, Richards, and the American New Critics all argue that literature has a morally educative role that distinguishes it from other uses of language. As Barry points out,
this view of the educative powers of literature has deep roots in

the past. A brief account of its history, however, will reveal the political nuances that have been attached to literature's educative role.

The Political History of the Moral Intrinsic Approach

In 1840, F. D. Maurice was appointed professor of English at King's College, University of London. He was convinced that literature connects the reader to what is "fixed and enduring." But Maurice also regarded English literature as the expression of Englishness. Though he recognized that it was a middle-class Englishness, he believed that a potential "political agitator" who studied English literature would feel "his nationality to be a reality" (qtd. in Barry 13). He thus considered the study of English literature to be a way of giving people a "stake in maintaining the status quo without any redistribution of wealth."

This view of literature's potential role as a socially cohesive, antirevolutionary force continued to be prominent in education in the United Kingdom into the 1980s and 1990s. It has been at the center of debates about which texts should be studied in schools. In his 1986 Arnold Palmer lecture, for example, Kenneth Baker, then secretary of state for education in England and Wales, echoed Maurice's perspective when he referred to the English language and English literature as "our greatest asset as a nation . . . the essential ingredient of the Englishness of England" (qtd. in Donald 14). Baker's narrow conception of "Englishness" not only ignores Wales, but it also reflects a blindness to the multicultural composition of the population of England. Opposition comes from academics and educationists such as Green and Medway who have sought to raise awareness of the cultural politics of English teaching. In discussions of classroom actualities, however, much of the debate concentrates only on the selection of set texts. "Englishness" and the canon of "great literature" are at the center of this debate, with opponents arguing for a broader view of literature and the replacement of "English literature" with "literature in English." To a certain but definitely limited extent there has been a broadening of this kind. The ULEAC

A-level syllabus now includes works by U.S. and commonwealth writers, and translations are also permissible, as we have seen.

This concern with the choice of set texts, however, tends to hide from view the continuing presence in the A-level examination of the liberal humanist conception of literature. As the essays in the "highest category" show, students need to adopt the role of a moral intrinsic critic and to write about human actions and feelings whether the genre is poetry or fiction. In short, they are expected to conform to the very view of literature that the academic study of literature in higher education, with its emphasis on theory, has come to problematize. The transition from school to university thus requires students to perceive and unsettle their assumptions if they are to succeed.

Writing about Literature at University

Having outlined the characteristics of the best essays about literature at A-level, I now move to the university. Here we university teachers' statements of criteria are likely to sound familiar to novice undergraduates in that we tend to say we expect critical analysis, argument, and a personal response, as do A-level teachers. But something different is actually required: viz., the ability to handle the theoretical diversity of literary criticism. It was his perception of how unprepared most students are that led Barry to produce a book titled *Beginning Theory*. This introduction offers a summary of the situation in which novice undergraduates tend to find themselves on courses in English studies:

> If you are coming to literary theory soon after taking courses in such subjects as media studies, communications studies, or sociolinguistics, then the general "feel" of the new theoretical approaches to literature may well seem familiar. You will already be "tuned in" to the emphasis on ideas, which is one of their characteristics; you will be undaunted by the use of technical terminology, and unsurprised by their strong social and political interests. If on the other hand, you took a "straight" A Level literature . . . course with the major emphasis on set books, then . . . initially you will have the problem of getting on the wave length of these different ways of looking at literature. (6)

To illustrate the problems that students writing about literature can encounter on moving from school to university, I discuss three undergraduate essays, since the essay continues to be seen as an essential component in the assessment process. In English, as in most arts and humanities subjects, *essay* tends to mean an extended piece of writing drafted and redrafted over months, intended to give students the opportunity for in-depth reflection and critical thinking leading to the construction of an argument. All three essays were considered inadequate by the tutors. But while I consider that judgment just in terms of what was required, my reading of the students' essays is an attempt to identify what each student is doing and to suggest the source of the approach that each student adopts. My analysis reveals that the students assume a continuity with A-level ways of writing about literary texts, whereas something very different is actually required. To show that discontinuity between A-level and undergraduate essays, I preface the discussion of each essay with a brief account of the approach reflected in the essay title (essay prompt or topic assigned), each of which represents a different critical perspective on literature. In keeping with the Vygotskian perspective outlined earlier, I conclude my discussion of each essay by suggesting ways in which each student might be helped to move on as a writer of essays about literature.

I had not taught these students, who were in fact studying at another university; nor did I interview their teachers. These omissions were, in fact, the product of a deliberate decision to concentrate exclusively on the students' texts. I was thus in the same position as most internal or external examiners.

Jack's Essay: The Essay Question and Its Meaning

Jack's essay addresses the following essay question:

> Write an essay on the accumulation of evidence—the significance given to "clues"—in an example of early crime fiction.

This essay question is clearly different from the questions of the A-level essays discussed earlier. Here there is no explicit demand for personal response, nor is there an emphasis on character or feeling. What is required is encoded in "essay" and in the abstractions "accumulation," "evidence," and "significance," while the quotation marks around "clues" turns this word into an abstraction too. In this context, "crime fiction" denotes a distinctive genre in which the relation between fiction and reality is of central theoretical importance. The difference between this essay question and those of the A-level essays is contained in Connor's distinction between "exemplarity" and "exemplification." Although the student is asked to concentrate on only one literary text, he is required to focus on how the text exemplifies concepts rather than on the exemplarity of the text or parts of it.

Jack chose to write about Poe's Dupin tales. Poe uses many of the motifs that are still to be found in crime fiction: a murder in a locked room, the innocent suspect, a detective with superior reasoning powers. What the essay question suggests, however, is that such details are not important in themselves. A student who read the essay question in the manner expected might concentrate rather on the tales as presenting a theory of how detection works in a fictional world. In other words, he would focus not on the details of the evidence itself but on the manner of its discovery and interpretation. Such a discussion could lead finally into a consideration of conceptions of "truth" in crime fiction. This is the kind of analysis pointed to by, for example, van Leer in his paper on Poe. Jack, however, seems not to have consulted any critical works, which is in keeping with the A-level emphasis on personal response to set literary texts. He thus concentrates on narrative detail and in particular on character and theme—the focus of attention in A-level questions on literature.

Jack's Approach

Jack begins his essay by stating that he has chosen to discuss Edgar Allan Poe's *Tales of Mystery and Imagination,* "concentrating on 'The Murders in the Rue Morgue.'" He then states that the police are baffled by the available clues. In the next paragraph, he introduces the argument on which his essay is based—the significance of the clues lies in the light they shed on Dupin's abilities. Referring to Dupin as the "hero" of the tale, Jack recounts how he uses his superior analytic ability to solve the crime that had been baffling the prefect of police:

> The hero, C. Auguste Dupin, defeats the Prefect of Police "in his own castle" by solving a seemingly insolvable crime. Dupin and his companion read about the extraordinary murders of Madame L'Espanaye and her daughter, Mademoiselle Camille L'Espanaye. The newspaper report gives all the clues that have been found and are dumbfounding the police. The police's inability to solve the murder enables Dupin's "peculiar analytic ability" to come into play. The report provides us with evidence from the scene of the crime, including the confusing, conflicting evidence of different foreigners each claiming to have heard a European voice, different from their own, shouting out at the time of the crime. Nearly everything in the room is presented as a clue to the murderer.

Jack then turns to the obvious clue the police overlooked but that Dupin identifies:

> Dupin visits the apartment and begins to unravel the mystery. He refuses to believe that there is no means of escape. All doors and windows seem securely locked and the chimney is too small for escape. It is astonishing that the police did not pursue the investigation of all means of escape further and it is their failure to do so which makes Dupin's success seem astonishing. Unsurprisingly Dupin finds a concealed spring and a broken nail which made the window look locked from the inside even when it had been closed from the outside.

Jack concludes this discussion of *The Murders in the Rue Morgue* by commenting on the construction of the tale. He focuses on how the presentation of the clues emphasizes Dupin's brilliance:

> Dupin presents the reader with each of the clues separately and how he formed a suspicion of who the murderer is but he will not reveal this. Instead the narrator (and the reader) must guess at how the clues link together to form a solution, again creating an impression of Dupin's brilliance in the reader's mind.

Jack then rounds off the essay by emphasizing the contrast between Dupin's brilliance and the police's ineptness:

> The clues should have provided enough evidence to give the po-
> lice a lead and this allows Dupin to carry out ordinary police
> procedure successfully and so to heighten our admiration for his
> "peculiar analytic ability."

As these excerpts show, Jack concentrates on the fact of
Dupin's "peculiar analytic ability" far surpassing that of the police. He treats the tale as an account of battle and victory in which
there is an ironic twist—Dupin is judged "stupid" by the police,
who are supposed to be adept at solving crimes, but he finally
emerges as the real "hero" in a contest of minds. This reading of
the tale leads Jack into significant omissions from the point of
view of the university tutor. He fails to mention the philosophical discussion that frames *The Murder in the Rue Morgue*. Nor
does he critically explore the precise nature of the difference between the police's concentration on what can be observed and
Poe's primary concern with concepts that organize what is observed—concepts such as predictability, unpredictability, and
probability, which have a direct bearing on the significance of
"clues."

Continuities with the A-Level Approach

Jack's tutor did not regard this essay as deserving of a pass mark.
The essay's shortcomings take on a different appearance, however, if we consider Jack's essay in light of A-level requirements
for success. Jack has in fact translated the essay question into a
familiar A-level approach, in which the emphasis is on the kind
of coherence given to narrative detail by a character in his relation to a unifying theme, which in this case is presented as the
victory of analytical brilliance over ignorance. Like the two A-
level candidates whose essays I have briefly discussed, Jack makes
confident pronouncements in the third person. While the essay
would probably not have been placed in the "highest category" at
A-level since the details of the action in places submerge the theme
being traced, the conception of literature and literary criticism is

basically the same as that reflected in Jo's and Sam's essays. In fact, so influenced is Jack by a view of literature as a comment on life that he overlooks the implausibility of Dupin's actions and of the events, an implausibility that the assigned question implicitly suggested he analyze.

Jack has, however, almost certainly not drawn only on assumptions developed at A-level. While crime fiction is not a genre in A-level examination syllabi, the theme of clever detective outwitting authority figures is one with which Jack is surely familiar from other detective stories in print or on film. Poe is, in fact, often referred to as the inventor of the detective story (Stern), and, as I mentioned earlier, many of the motifs in his tales are to be found in the stories of those who came after him. Jack had encountered the Sherlock Holmes stories during his course and was probably also familiar with the film versions in which Holmes demonstrates his superior analytic ability. In reading Poe's tales, Jack may also have heard echoes of popular TV crime fiction such as *Inspector Morse* or *Frost* in which the protagonist emerges as more insightful than doubting superiors or colleagues. These kinds of echoes are, however, precisely those to which Jack now needs to turn a deaf ear. The essay question that confronts him demands a different template for argument and a different subjectivity. In other words, whereas in the A-level context an argument or personal response signaled the interpretation of the particularities of meaning and effect in a text, now the given essay question requires the reader to place himself at a greater distance from the text; to stand back, as it were, so that the text can be seen to exemplify a particular position or positions in a theoretical debate about the nature of literature and of criticism.

Helping Jack Move On

How might Jack be helped to move on? The brief written feedback at the end of the essay reads: "You give a lot of detail but you do not do much analysis of its significance in relation to the essay [question]." This comment seems fair though uninformative from a student's perspective. Oddly enough, what Jack needs to do to be successful is to adopt the focus on evidence that Poe favors—i.e., he needs to see "evidence" as not residing mainly in the particulars observed but in the categories that organize those particulars. Jack's interpretation of the significance of the clues is not implausible from the critical perspective that he adopts. In fact, it is a reading suggested by Stern's argument that *The Murders in the Rue Morgue* marked the birth of the detective story. The attempt to move Jack on could thus include encouraging him to perceive the theory within his approach to the tale. This could then lead into a discussion of the different critical approach implied by the question and how it focuses on more than theme and character.

A starting point might be found within the "lot of detail" that Jack provides. There are places in Jack's essay that imply an awareness of the implausibilities of the tale. Jack's use of the term "hero," for example, and his choice of "unsurprisingly" in the sentence beginning "Unsurprisingly Dupin finds a concealed spring" suggest a perception that this is fiction and not a slice of life. A discussion of these word choices could open out into talk about concepts such as probability and predictability and so to the difference between fiction and life. This would throw into relief the significance of those parts of the tale that Jack overlooked.

The next two essays I discuss address essay questions that reflect a dominant focus in contemporary literary theory—the relation between a literary text and extra-text cultural and political issues. This focus challenges the liberal humanism that went unquestioned at A-level. As I show next, however, neither of the essay writers indicates an awareness of that challenge.

Jessica's Essay: The Essay Question and the Politics of English

The course tutor provided the following essay question:

> How useful is the term "post-colonial" as a critical concept? In your answer refer to at least two texts.

The inclusion in university English courses of questions relating to postcolonialism seems pertinent in postimperial Britain. In that historical context, attention to postcolonialism marks the redrawing of the boundaries of English as an academic field of study—a redrawing that denotes an awareness of the injustice and ethnocentrism of past omissions. The link between those omissions and issues of power is summed up by Ashcroft, Griffiths, and Tiffin, who state that the "formation of English Studies involved the denial of the value of the 'peripheral,' the 'marginal' and the 'uncanonised'" since the "study of English and the growth of Empire proceeded from a single ideological climate," which established a "privileging norm" (3).

While the term "postcolonial" originally denoted a challenge to the powerful impact of that "privileging norm," it has acquired different significances over time and has itself become the subject of debate. In an attempt to offer students a map of the territory, Barry suggests three phases in postcolonial literature, which he summarizes, rather too neatly, as "adopt," "adapt," and "adept." The "adopt" phase was marked by the assumption that colonialist models of writing were universal and thus to be unquestioningly accepted. The "adapt" phase involved adapting European forms to the subject matter of the formerly colonized, while the "adept" phase represents a "declaration of cultural independence in which writers remake the form[s] to their own specification" (195).

But the essay question Jessica addresses looks beyond these neat categorizations to the complexities and problems relating to "postcolonial" as a "critical concept," a phrase clearly indicating that—to borrow Hall's distinction—it is the epistemological and not the chronological meanings that are the intended issue. These meanings offer a rich field of possibilities since "postcolonial" is now a "contested space" (Hall). Moreover, when considered in relation to literary criticism, "postcolonial" raises questions concerning the very nature of a literary text.

Jessica's Approach

Jessica is, however, unfamiliar with the theoretical and political debates surrounding the concept of "postcolonial." In place of a detailed discussion of the usefulness of the term as a critical concept, she begins with a definition in which "postcolonial" is what comes after "colonialism." She writes first of colonialism:

"Colonialism" means the domination by the British Empire over smaller colonies and continents. Britain had an empire, which was controlled by the ruling classes. Millions of people had a new religion forced upon them, their literary works were destroyed, their way of life eradicated.

She then states that postcolonialism, by contrast, "represents the coming to an end of colonisation imposed by the West."

In turning to literature, Jessica treats "postcolonial" as marking the kinds of content that became the primary concern of writers in the newly independent former colonies. She draws a line between colonial and postcolonial periods of history, stating that in postcolonial times, the oppressed were able for the first time to give an account of their historical experience and suffering. Using George Lamming's *In the Castle of my Skin* and Joan Riley's *The Unbelonging* as her two texts, she writes:

> *In the Castle of my Skin* and *The Unbelonging* could not have been written during the colonial era. Firstly the colonisers' information was known to be "correct," and to critically challenge it would have caused a confrontation with the dominant institutions. . . . To highlight racial issues, breakdown in social services, to acknowledge the existence of slavery, black history and the repressive environment—such information would have caused an uproar in the colonial era.

This quotation lists the themes that Jessica finds particularized in the experience of communities and individuals in both *In the Castle of my Skin* and *The Unbelonging*. Discussing *In the Castle of my Skin* first, she singles out Lamming's concern with the slave trade in its effect on the colonized:

> Slaves were taken to Jamaica, Antigua, Grenada and Barbados. Lamming describes a calamitous situation. Individuals "trying to live, some die . . . families fall to pieces and many a brother never again sees his sister nor father his son." Here Lamming is giving an accurate historical account of the slave trade.

Turning next to *The Unbelonging*, Jessica focuses on Riley's treatment of racial issues as represented by the experience of the novel's main character, Hyacinth:

> The Unbelonging by Joan Riley discusses racial issues from the 1950s to the 1960s. . . . Riley raises issues relating to the non-exposure of black students to black history. Hyacinth who was placed in care due to the abuse she suffered at home at the hands of her father had a stereotypical view of blacks. She lived in a white environment and she received no education that addressed blackness or black issues while she was in care.

Jessica then draws the two writers' concerns together, stating that both focus on the effects of displacement:

> Both authors highlight the trauma of displacement. In the Castle of My Skin displacement is caused by slavery. In The Unbelonging displacement for Hyacinth was caused by economic hardship. Hyacinth had to leave Jamaica at the age of eleven at an age when she most needed care but was then exposed to the harsh reality of emigration.

Jessica's essay bears several traces of the approaches that are required at A-level. Like the A-level candidates, Jo and Sam, she focuses on a central unifying theme, in this instance the suffering caused by colonialism. Like them, too, she writes in the third person, confidently making her points. She thus implies a view of argument as the articulation of a focus that is supported by but at the same time illuminates the particularity of the text under discussion. In this instance, however, the essay question requires a different conception of argument. Jessica is not required to choose one meaning of "postcolonial" and then to apply it to at least two texts, but rather to discuss the issues embedded in the concept and debate its range of possible meanings. In fact, Jessica inadvertently demonstrates what Dirlik claims to be a danger attached to the chronological meaning of postcolonial. She seeks to universalize the postcolonial experience, editing out difference, complexity, and the transnational, relying on the binarism of "colonial" versus "postcolonial." This is unsurprising since she seems to have assumed that, as at A-level, she need concentrate only on set literary texts. The essay contains no evidence that Jessica has read any of the critical discussions of the meaning of "postcolonial."

In one respect, however, Jessica's essay represents a marked departure from the criteria reflected in A-level essays. As I pointed out earlier, the A-level student is expected to appreciate that literature both is and is not about life. Jessica, however, obliterates that doubleness of perspective. In choosing a chronological definition of "postcolonial" and texts that are strongly and avowedly autobiographical, she is drawn into focusing on *In the Castle of My Skin* and *The Unbelonging* as simply offering a view of how things were. In treating the texts as historical documents, she tends to present narrative details as if they are simply factual evidence to be flatly stated. Furthermore, the details she selects all emphasize the one view of colonization that fits her chosen theme—viz., colonization as the cause of "trauma" in the colonized. Thus she fails to comment on the nostalgia for the colonial past that coexists with Lamming's condemnation of colonialism and gives his novel its complexity and subtle emotional character. Neither does she move beyond content into a discussion of the novels' use of nonstandard English and the political significance of that choice.

Helping Jessica Move On

How then might Jessica be helped to make progress? Like Jack, Jessica has provided an answer to the given question. As in Jack's case, the problem is that the answer relies on an inappropriate paradigm. There are, however, points in Jessica's essay that touch on critical perspectives that her tutor could take up and explore with her; in particular the relation between literature and its historical and sociopolitical contexts. Jessica explicitly attaches a political purpose to her use of "postcolonial." For her it represents a critical focus on the past, a reevaluation. But she confines the reevaluation to a discussion of the content of the novels, treating them as historical documents and failing to comment on the theory of literature and criticism they reevaluate by example. As in the case of Jack's essay, a way into relevant literary theory could begin with Jessica's own text—that is, with a discussion of how a postcolonial perspective on a text would reevaluate the A-level assumptions on which her essay is based. Such a discussion could start from Jessica's construction of a unifying theme across two texts from different countries and would seek to indicate how she implicitly relies on the very emphasis on the universal and on the exclusion of difference that "postcolonial" seeks to subvert.

A more immediate starting point, however, might be found in an incompatibility within the essay of which Jessica seems unaware, but which could become the source of new insights. I refer to Jessica's manner of contextualizing quotations from Lamming's novel. The following lines are a good example of the clashing perspectives that result:

> "Families fall to pieces and many a brother never sees his sister nor father his son." Here Lamming is giving an accurate historical account of the slave trade.

"Historical account" fails to capture the feelings that the evocatively rhythmical quotation communicates. Yet behind that failure may lie an important issue that Jessica may be intuitively groping toward. The clash of styles may point to an as yet unformulated awareness that while in an A-level approach to the text Lamming's poetic style might well be taken to suggest the universality of the feelings presented, the "postcolonial," by contrast, seeks to highlight the historicity and specificity of the suffering described.

There is, of course, a glaring omission in Jessica's essay. She has not referred to "postcolonial" as a critical concept leading to a reinterpretation and reevaluation of novels long part of school and first-year university syllabi. *Mansfield Park* is such a text, with Mr. Bertram's ownership of estates in the West Indies now being treated as significant in ideological readings of the novel. Had Jessica extended her focus beyond the marginalized and silenced people depicted in the novels to silences in the literary criticism of those novels, she would have got closer to the issues around the usefulness of "postcolonial" as a critical concept. And yet, in asking myself what might have motivated her selection of, and particular approach to, two novels from the "edge," I came eventually to significant omissions in my own approach. But that is a subject for the final part of this chapter.

I turn next to the third essay selected for discussion. It is by a female student whom I call Diana. I focus on an aspect of Diana's essay that distinguishes it from all those discussed so far. Jo's and

Sam's essays show that A-level students can be highly successful without explicit recourse to published literary criticism of the set texts. Jack and Jessica both seem to have assumed that undergraduate essays also need refer only to the works of fiction under discussion. Diana has, however, drawn explicitly and obviously on a particular critical text. Her use of that text does not, however, raise issues concerning plagiarism. On the contrary, what is significant about Diana's essay is how little she has "got" of what she so clearly saw as relevant in the critical text. Her essay thus suggests that we should not assume that referring novice undergraduates to "the critics" will necessarily help them do what an essay question requires.

Diana's Essay Question

The essay question set by the tutor was:

> Discuss the social or psychological meaning of an early crime fiction text including in your analysis a close analysis of form and meaning.

There are echoes here of A-level essay questions in that this question clearly calls for detailed attention to one text. Diana chose to write about the social meaning of Wilkie Collins's *The Woman in White*. Students selecting that novel were referred to Tamar Heller's *Dead Secrets: Wilkie Collins and the Female Gothic*. This critical text contains a chapter on *The Woman in White*, which in fact fleshes out a possible "social meaning." Diana explicitly refers to that chapter in her essay, but she transforms it in ways that echo what was expected at A-level. In order to highlight the nature of Diana's transformations, I preface my discussion of her essay with a brief account of Heller's approach.

Heller's Approach: A Demonstration of Feminist Criticism

Heller gives the reader a clear statement of her focus:

> I am concerned . . . with Collins' gender politics. But I place my analysis of Collins' representations of gender in a more fully

historicized context. In examining Collins' representations of gender through the female Gothic plot I link the relation of Collins' generic choices to his position as a male writer in the Victorian literary market. (4)

As "gender politics" and "representations" suggest, Heller approaches Collins's novel as a signifying practice with a political purpose and not as the kind of exploration of moral complexities found in "intrinsic criticism" (Birch) and featured prominently in A-level essays. "Gender" links the text to its ideological context—that is, to the attitudes and beliefs reflected in the unequal social positioning of men and women in Victorian society. Heller's critique views literary texts in Foucault's perspective, as dealing in discourses that reflect socially constructed differences in power. From this perspective, generic forms such as the female Gothic[5] become a political issue; they carry contestable meanings relating to differences in social identities and so in power.

A corollary of the political focus is that a literary text might be said either to naturalize a socially constructed difference in power, or to challenge received views to make a difference in the world. Heller chooses the latter of these possibilities. She emphasizes the ideological challenge that Collins mounts, giving detailed attention to his "liberal views" and showing how he uses the female Gothic to draw his readers' attention to the unjust position and plight of women in Victorian society. She concludes, however, that Collins presents a flawed critique in that he finally breaks with the Gothic novel's support for female subversiveness. Like most of Collins's novels, *The Woman in White* ends, she states, with the "containment of female power and subversion" (8).

Heller is, of course, also engaged in gender politics as she analyzes Collins's views on the plight of women. She writes from a particular ideological position that she does not, however, hold up to reader scrutiny. That position is evident not only in her criticism of Collins's containment of women's subversiveness, but also in her choices within the genre of literary criticism. Through her citations, for example, she locates herself in a body of feminist writing—that is, in a particular committed discourse community—that seeks to encourage resistance to the representation of gender and its social meanings as they pertain to women. The citations refer to writing from different periods in history (e.g., Wollstonecraft; Showalter). In this way, Collins's representation of women's inequality in Victorian England is given a historical continuity and drawn into an alliance with late-twentieth-century gender politics and a commitment to female subversiveness.

This alliance between then and now is also indicated by the significance Heller attaches to the role of writing in *The Woman in White*. The control of the signifier and the silencing of women's voices are central feminist issues, as Olsen and Miller have demonstrated. Heller also takes up those issues. She points to the fact that, while the story is written by several of the characters, it is a man, Walter Hartright, who edits the text and who finally has the last word in which he describes the active and potentially subversive Marian Halcombe as "our good angel." Feminist criticism is also woven into the lexis of Heller's text, most notably in the reference to women as blank pages to be "inscribed" by men, and in nouns that—to borrow Bakhtin's metaphor *(Dialogic)*—carry the "voices" of their use in other contexts, such as *resistance, subversiveness, identity.*

Diana's Approach: A Demonstration of Transformations

Diana refers explicitly to *Dead Secrets*. But while she focuses on gender inequalities in *The Woman in White*, she does so from a theoretical perspective that is very different from Heller's. Echoing the approach required at A-level, Diana begins with the statement that "the primary theme [of *The Woman in White*] is the gender theme." She then breaks that theme down into other versions of the same theme: she refers to women's "lack of power" in Victorian England; to "the helplessness of women"; and to "the greater social power of the male." She particularizes these abstractions by linking them to details of the plot. She says, for example,

> Throughout the novel the lack of power women have over their own destiny is constantly conveyed to the reader. Laura has no legal power over her marriage to Sir Perceval. She must submit herself to him in order to obey another male, her father, who the

reader discovers has committed his daughter on his deathbed to the marriage with Sir Perceval. Thus Laura must dismiss her true love for another man, Walter Hartright.

The details of the plot, however, tend to become the primary focus of Diana's attention, the themes both illuminating and being supported by the particularities of the text. As this excerpt indicates, Diana is actually engaged in dramatically retelling events, thus creating a narrative of her own that is analogous to *The Woman in White*. She does this effectively and with insight. Although the sentence structures she uses are simple, they indicate a not unsophisticated, even if largely intuitive, appreciation of the women characters' situation and of the melodrama in *The Woman in White*. Laura's only possession, for example, is seen to consist ironically in nonpossession: "she has no legal power." This statement is followed by a further irony: the only action open to Laura represents the absence of spontaneous or willed action, and thus scarcely qualifies as action—"she must submit"; "she must dismiss." This theatrical dramatization of powerlessness is intensified by the contrast between the grammatical agent, Laura, and the "real" agent, the man whose authority in forcing her to submission and obedience is reinforced by the law. By this point, however, story has ousted plot.

Such writing represents an empathic response of a kind that is acceptable at A-level, but in this instance it received only a low mark. By replacing Diana's "themes" with "issues" in his marginal comments, the tutor indicated that he wanted a discussion that would perceive ambiguity of a different kind from that which was central to Jo's and Sam's A-level essays. In this case, the ambiguity to be identified is not confined to characters or feelings within the text, but extends to the relation between author and text. In other words, an essay question once again looks to critical theories other than those that typify A-level writing about literature.

Helping Diana Move On

As in the case of Jack's and Jessica's essays, aspects of Diana's could lead her to perceive the theoretical issues at stake. While her essay imposes a particular, school-learned coherence on *The Woman in White*—the coherence of theme with illustrations—there are ruptures and ambiguities in her text through which tutor intervention might enable Diana to gain access to Heller's text, understand the theory on which it is based, and so, perhaps, critique it. These places are marked by a change of modality—i.e., by a movement from an assertion of what is the case to the suggestion of what might be the case. For example, "Collins does show through Anne the social invisibility of women and their rights" contrasts with the sentence that immediately follows it: "Marian Halcombe's outburst after her sister's marriage may embody Collins' beliefs upon the subject of female inequality within his society." Behind both sentences lies a concern with evidence. The first sentence implies that there is reliable evidence in the text that Anna is an effective means of developing one of the novel's central themes: the social invisibility of women. At this point, "Collins" is primarily an authorial function, an intention that the text realizes. The second sentence, on the other hand, presents Collins as a person inhabiting the world beyond the text. The tentativeness of "may" is echoed by "Collins' beliefs." This tentativeness can be read in several ways. First, it can imply that the novel cannot be read as evidence of its author's views. The change of modality may thus denote the hold on Diana's thinking of an A-level focus on texts, a focus in which "close analysis of form and meaning" means treating the text as a decontextualized linguistic object. Since, however, in this particular instance the sentence concerns Marian Halcombe, whom Heller presents as the embodiment of the female subversiveness that Collins finally seeks to contain, "may" and "beliefs" could mean that Jessica is suggesting an ambivalence on Collins's part toward the qualities and attitudes that Marian represents.

There is a third possible reading, too. As in other parts of the essay where Diana refers to what Heller "believes," the tentativeness here suggests a resistance to the authority of Heller's text that could develop into an understanding of Heller's argument and the feminist ideology it reflects. In other words, tutor intervention at this point could help Diana both understand Heller and separate from her. This separation should enable her to arrive at a clearer understanding of her own theory and its sources.

It should also help her to appreciate that literary criticism is characterized by different approaches and that essay questions rest on trends in literary criticism.

I conclude this discussion of the three undergraduate essays with a brief summary of the differences that have emerged concerning writing at A-level and writing in the university. At A-level, "argument" (like its synonymous partner in practice, "personal response") derives its meaning largely from the critical approach associated with I. A. Richards's practical criticism and F. R. Leavis's emphasis on literature as a repository of humane values. From this perspective, the details of a literary text are to be subsumed by themes that illuminate the particularities of the text. The novice undergraduate is indeed required to "argue" (and to give a "personal response"). But the meaning of the term has now changed. In fact, a number of meanings now cluster around the practice of argument, depending on the theory or theories an essay question encodes. Looking back at the essay questions the three undergraduates had to address, I note how each points to a different theoretical issue. The question on the accumulation of evidence in an example of crime fiction draws attention to the subordination of narrative detail to philosophical concerns, centering on the relation between fictional events and reality. The question on postcolonialism as a concept is based on different theoretical issues. It raises questions about the relation between a text, an author, and the sociopolitical context, and problematizes the effect of dominant ideologies of empire on the reading of literary texts. The question on the social meaning of an early crime fiction text also raises issues concerning powerful ideologies in historical contexts. In this instance, in view of Diana's particular choice of literary text, the theory and practice of feminist criticism are relevant.

I do not intend to suggest that a program of lectures on literary theory would solve student essay writers' problems in the transition from school to university. Such lectures could tempt students to assume that a theory is a template into which numerous texts can be forcibly slotted in spite of the texts' differences. This would be taking exemplification to a point where theory was considered more important than the literary text. Furthermore, while I would not suggest that students should never be

"told" anything, the Vygotskian focus on pedagogy that I outlined earlier leads me to avoid simple transmission models of
teaching and learning as far as possible. In the next and final part
of this chapter, I pull together what I have learned from my reading of the students' essays. Those lessons include a strong conviction that I and in fact all university teachers need to look beyond
our role as assessors of students' writing to give more attention
to how we can best help students develop as writers on the particular programs of study we teach. I am also convinced that the
"motivated sign" and "interest," as Kress uses the terms (*Making;* "Representational"), are concepts of central relevance to our
attempts to ease student writers' transitions from school to university. But, and most important, these concepts apply not only
to students' essays but also to tutors' readings of those essays.

Self-Reflexivity for Students and Teacher

It could be argued at this point that my attention to individual
essays evades the realities of the current situation in higher education in the United Kingdom where there is little time in many
undergraduate courses for one-to-one tutorials. My counter-
argument would take the following form: Time is not in itself the
major issue. More important is our disposition as tutors toward
teaching and learning. Thus, though I personally regard the individual tutorial as indispensable, I recognize that there are, fortu-
nately, other ways in which the lot of the novice undergraduate
writer could be improved. I would give priority to a change in
our self-perceptions as tutors—a change in which we all came to
regard ourselves as playing a role in the teaching, rather than just
in the assessment, of essay writing. This role would involve us in
thinking beyond the current research into argument. That is, it
would take us along an intellectual route that would lead us to
consider as motivated signs (i.e., signs with a history both personal and social) the essay questions we set, the critical works we
recommend, the discourses we use in feedback and assessment,
and so on.

This route would also lead to the rethinking of the curriculum of English studies in higher education, resulting in more

examination and discussion of writing about literature—published writing and student writing—and the theories on which it rests. I am suggesting that we avoid neat answers, and make efforts instead to see student essays not as things to be pigeonholed and graded, but as spurs to self-reflexivity for students and teachers. A student essay could then open up cracks in the apparent seamlessness of the taken-for-granted for students and tutors—a process that could take both forward into their own ZPDs.

Self-reflexivity is thus the theme I take up in these concluding paragraphs. Returning to Jessica's and Diana's essays, I now note an irony at the center of my discussion so far. I have pointed out that Jessica considers only texts from the periphery, and I have noted how Diana's essay fails to use Heller's text in the way it was expected. What I have ignored is the fact that my focus has resulted in my offering readings that do not do justice to my stated intention to bring the student into the picture—something I accused Mitchell ("Quality") of not doing in her recent work on argument. I implicitly treat Jessica and Diana, and also Jack, as the representatives of a particular view of how to write about a literary text, and I measure their essays against what I (in an attempt to identify with their examiners) think they should have written. That focus on what they "should have written" then helps me see how they might be helped to make progress as essay writers. This perception now leads me to look critically at my failure to note the fact that Jessica is a black woman from the Caribbean and Diana a woman writing about a novel that deals with social injustice to women.

Returning first to Jessica's essay, I now note the possible significance of the following sentences that I omitted in my earlier discussion of her text:

> It is important to critically address the stereotyped view of black people in the past because it is part of our history and if we ignore the stereotypes of the past colonial era . . . we will be accepting the colonisers' propaganda as true.

I had assumed initially that "we" and "our" were generic. Now I see another possibility: Jessica's "we" may mean "we black people." The following statements from her essay now take on special significance. They suggest that it is not only Lamming who has drawn on autobiography and family history. A large number of individuals internationally have had their lives damaged by colonization. Colonization not only affected their ancestors but also affects their descendants.

Bringing Diana's gender into the picture changes my perception of her way of writing. The "theatrical dramatization" of character and event, which I commented on earlier, now becomes a reminder that modes of criticism have themselves been seen as involving gender issues, a focus at the core of Heller's reading of *The Woman in White*. Furthermore, the interpretative, empathic approach that Jessica demonstrates, and that Mitchell ("A Level") would exclude from argument, is one of the forms of writing (autobiography is another) that women academics such as Miller and Ivanic would introduce into the university.

The politics of a student's positioning herself as a member of a particular social group in her writing about literature is clearly an important issue, especially in the United Kingdom, where an increasing number of women, "nontraditional" students, and those with non-U.K. backgrounds are enrolling in undergraduate courses. There is a danger, though, that in attempting to be sympathetic to student backgrounds we teachers may fall into the trap of stereotyping students in ways that we, but not the students, see as positive. I can, for example, recall a student who was annoyed at being encouraged to write about the literature of her country of origin. While the teacher thought he was being hospitable to the student's culture, the student felt that she had been slotted into an outdated national identity. This was understandable since she had been living in the United Kingdom for sixteen years. International students have identified another example of stereotyping, pointing out that teachers can be unaware of the complexities of students' relation to the dominant cultural and political ethos of the countries from which they come. Women students have also felt stereotyped on being asked to write in a personal style and to include autobiographical details. They have argued that they are happier with the conventional way of writing and do not feel that it excludes their voices as women.

These student comments have alerted me to another possible significance in Jessica's use of the pronoun "we." "We" may contain within it an ambivalence, a tension between "we British" and "we who are black." This reminder of the complexities of students' individual histories, and of their positionings in relation to the texts they read, takes me back to "interest," the concept I have borrowed from Kress's essay "Representational Resources." Its significance is now amplified. Accommodating the many factors coming together to make a text as it is and not otherwise, the term "interest" warns me that I should not see my responses to student essays as the only possible, or necessarily the best, readings.

"Interest" is also relevant to this chapter's concern with the shifting meanings of "argument" and the terms that cluster synonymously around it. In commenting on individual essays, I have traced how argument needs to become chameleonlike in the university, taking on different hues to match the differing conceptions of literature and literary criticism encoded in the essay questions assigned. Looking back to the theoretical framework I outlined earlier, I now see that what has finally emerged is a much more complex view of argument: argument as inseparable from interest. That is, argument is the student's remaking of the essay question as she brings together whatever resources of knowledge, feeling, and expression she regards both consciously and intuitively as relevant. The message I derive from this is that I need to help novice undergraduates to hear the voices of past experience so that the new voices of the university can become audible by recognizable echo or by contrast. This means, however, that I need to try to hear my own voices and to be aware of the ambiguities that may lie within them and within argument as interest.

Replacing the meanings encoded in argument at A-level with an appreciation of different critical approaches may initially seem confusing to new students. But as Graves put it succinctly in his poem "In Broken Images," a trust in "clear images" (which derive their clarity from an unquestioning reliance on the received) must yield to a confidence in "broken images" as the beginning of a "new understanding of my confusion."

Back to the Future

In the opening paragraphs of this chapter, I stated that I would finally enlarge the real-world frame that I had chosen for this discussion of student writing by returning to the topic of government goals and initiatives. Now, however, my perspective is different. While the introduction to this chapter emphasized my rejection of "elite instincts" and focused, like the chapter as a whole, on the importance of helping all students move on, I now aim to highlight both the problematic and the promising aspects of the recent initiatives of the Quality Assurance Agency.

The QAA's role is the enhancement of the quality of teaching and learning in the universities. Echoing the government's emphasis on the need for an employable pool of graduates, the QAA has stated that all undergraduate curricula should develop students' "key" skills, which, of course, include writing. The downside to this requirement is the increase in courses in writing that focus, as in the United States, on general academic writing skills. On the other hand, however, QAA initiatives are beginning to integrate writing more consciously into departmental curricula and teaching—what the United States calls "writing across the curriculum."

This will, I hope, result in more collaboration between writing teachers and teachers of the disciplines. This collaboration can lead to new approaches to writing that go beyond general writing skills and the assumption that academic writing has to be either "taught" or "caught" (as the study skills and acculturation orientations have it). Paradoxically, then, it might come about in the United Kingdom that the move toward greater regulation of the university curriculum will have positive consequences.

My concluding paragraph brings me back to the individuals who attend U.K. universities. It is not only students from underrepresented groups who are now encouraged to enroll in U.K. universities; there are also an increasing number of international students. In other words, the student population of U.K. universities is increasingly diverse in terms of the participants' linguistic, educational, and sociocultural backgrounds. It is a diversity that reminds me how important it is to increase my understanding of other countries' educational systems and dilemmas. Reading my fellow contributors' chapters has given me insights and possibilities that I aim to use to my students' benefit.

Notes

1. In the United Kingdom, a tutor is a full member of the teaching staff who, like professors in the United States, is also expected to carry out research. A tutor may be a lecturer, senior lecturer, or professor. In the United Kingdom, the term "professor" is reserved for the most academically distinguished member(s) of a department.

2. The Quality Assurance Agency is a body concerned with the quality of the courses offered by universities.

3. Universities in the United Kingdom are run, with only a few exceptions, by the national government, and undergraduates can receive government funding that pays most of their expenses.

4. A-level teachers use a common syllabus, which means that they prepare the students for the examination using certain criteria, not that they cover certain material in a certain order as in the United States.

5. Female Gothic refers to the use of conventions such as female victimization and subversiveness as primary themes in melodramatic novels of the late nineteenth century.

Works Cited

Andrews, Richard. "Learning to Argue." *The Quality of Argument: A Colloquium on Issues of Teaching and Learning in Higher Education.* Ed. Mike Riddle. London: School of Life Long Learning and Education, Middlesex University, 1997. 9–15.

———. *Teaching and Learning Argument.* London: Cassell, 1995.

Ashcroft, Bill, Gareth Griffiths, and Helen Tiffin. *The Empire Writes Back: Theory and Practice in Post-Colonial Literatures.* London: Routledge, 1989.

Bakhtin, Mikhail M. *The Dialogic Imagination: Four Essays.* Ed. Michael Holquist. Trans. Caryl Emerson and Michael Holquist. Austin: U of Texas P, 1981.

———. *Problems of Dostoevsky's Poetics.* Ed. and trans. Caryl Emerson. Theory and Hist. of Lit. Series 8. Minneapolis: U of Minnesota P, 1984.

Barry, Peter. *Beginning Theory: An Introduction to Literary and Cultural Theory.* Manchester, UK: Manchester UP, 1995.

Barthes, Roland. "From Work to Text." *Textual Strategies: Perspectives in Post-Structuralist Criticism.* Ed. Josué V. Harari. Ithaca: Cornell UP, 1979. 73–81.

Birch, David. *Language, Literature, and Critical Practice: Ways of Analysing Text.* London: Routledge, 1989.

Bourdieu, Pierre. *The Logic of Practice.* Trans. Richard Nice. Stanford: Stanford UP, 1990.

Brooks, Cleanth. *A Shaping Joy: Studies in the Writer's Craft.* London: Methuen, 1971.

Carter, Ronald A. "Poetry and Conversation: An Essay in Discourse Analysis." *Language and Style* 16 (1983): 374–85.

Clark, Katerina, and Michael Holquist. *Mikhail Bakhtin.* Cambridge, MA: Belknap/Harvard UP, 1984.

Collins, Wilkie. *The Woman in White.* 1861. Ed. Harvey Peter Sucksmith. Oxford: Oxford UP, 1973.

Connor, Steven. "In Exemplification." *The State of Theory.* Ed. Richard Bradford. London: Routledge, 1993. 35–54.

Daniels, Harry, ed. *An Introduction to Vygotsky.* London: Routledge, 1996.

Dirlik, Arif. "The Postcolonial Aura: Third World Criticism in the Age of Global Capitalism." *Critical Inquiry* 20 (1994): 328–56.

Donald, James. "Beyond Our Ken: English, Englishness and the English Curriculum." *Dialogue and Difference: English into the Nineties.* Ed. Peter Brooker and Peter Humm. London: Routledge, 1989. 13–30.

Foucault, Michel. "The Order of Discourse." *Untying the Text: A Post-Structuralist Reader.* Ed. Robert Young. Boston: Routledge & Kegan Paul, 1981.

Graves, Robert. "In Broken Images." *Robert Graves: Selected Poems.* Ed. Paul O'Prey. Harmondsworth, UK: Penguin, 1986.

Green, Bill. "A Dividing Practice: 'Literature,' English Teaching and Cultural Politics." *Bringing English to Order: The History and Politics of a School Subject.* Ed. Ivor Goodson and Peter Medway. London: Falmer, 1990. 135–61.

Hall, Stuart. "When Was the 'Post-Colonial'? Thinking at the Limit." *The Post-Colonial Question: Common Skies, Divided Horizons.* Ed. Iain Chambers and Lidia Curti. London: Routledge, 1996. 242–59.

Heller, Tamar. *Dead Secrets: Wilkie Collins and the Female Gothic.* New Haven: Yale UP, 1992.

Hounsell, Dai. "Essay Writing and the Quality of Feedback." *Student Learning: Research in Education and Cognitive Psychology.* Ed. John T. E. Richardson, Michael W. Eysenck, and David Warren Piper. Milton Keynes, UK: Society for Research into Higher Education and The Open UP, 1987. 109–19.

Ivanic, Roz. *Writing and Identity: The Discoursal Construction of Identity in Academic Writing.* Amsterdam: John Benjamins, 1998.

Kress, Gunther. *Making Signs and Making Subjects: The English Curriculum and Social Futures.* London: Institute of Education, 1995.

———. "Representational Resources and the Production of Subjectivity." *Texts and Practices: Readings in Critical Discourse Analysis.* Ed. Carmen Rosa Caldas-Coulthard and Malcolm Coulthard. London: Routledge, 1996. 15–32.

Lave, Jean, and Etienne Wenger. "Practice, Person, Social World." *An Introduction to Vygotsky.* Ed. Harry Daniels. London: Routledge, 1996. 143–50.

Lea, Mary R., and Brian V. Street. "Student Writing in Higher Education: An Academic Literacies Approach." *Studies in Higher Education* 23 (1998): 157–72.

Leavis, F. R. *The Living Principle: English as a Discipline of Thought.* London: Oxford UP, 1975.

Lessing, Doris. *The Golden Notebook.* London: Flamingo, 1962.

Medway, Peter. "Into the Sixties: English and English Society at a Time of Change." *Bringing English to Order: The History and Politics of a School Subject.* Ed. Ivor Goodson and Peter Medway. London: Falmer, 1990. 1–46.

Miller, Jane. *Seduction: Studies in Reading and Culture*. London: Virago, 1990.

Mitchell, Sally. "A Level and Beyond: A Case Study." *English in Education* 28.2 (1994): 36–47.

———. *Improving the Quality of Argument in Higher Education, Interim Report*. London: School of Education, Middlesex University, 1996.

———. "Quality in Argument: Why We Should Spell Out the Ground Rules." *The Quality of Argument: A Colloquium on Issues of Teaching and Learning in Higher Education*. Ed. Mike Riddle. London: School of Life Long Learning and Education, Middlesex University, 1997.

———. *The Teaching and Learning of Argument in Sixth Forms and Higher Education*. Hull, UK: University of Hull, 1994.

Olsen, Tillie. *Silences*. London: Virago, 1978.

Richards, I. A. *Practical Criticism: A Study of Literary Judgment*. London: Routledge and Kegan Paul, 1929.

Riddle, Mike. "Introducing the Colloquium." *The Quality of Argument: A Colloquium on Issues of Teaching and Learning in Higher Education*. Ed. Mike Riddle. London: School of Life Long Learning and Education, Middlesex University, 1997. 1–7.

Scott, Peter. *The Meanings of Mass Higher Education*. Buckingham, UK: Society for Research in Higher Education and The Open UP, 1995.

Showalter, Elaine. *The Female Malady: Women, Madness and English Culture, 1830–1980*. New York: Pantheon, 1985.

Stern, P. Van Doren, ed. *The Portable Poe*. New York: London, 1957.

Toulmin, Stephen, Richard Rieke, and Allan Janik. *An Introduction to Reasoning*. 2nd ed. London: Collier Macmillan, 1984.

Trow, Martin. *Problems in the Transition from Elite to Mass Higher Education*. Berkeley: Carnegie Commission on Higher Education, 1973.

Turner, Victor. *Dramas, Fields, and Metaphors: Symbolic Action in Human Society*. Ithaca: Cornell UP, 1974.

University of London Examinations and Assessment Council (ULEAC). *Teachers' Guide, GCE A Level English Literature 9171.* London: ULEAC, 1994.

van Leer, David. "Detecting Truth: The World of the Dupin Tales." *New Essays on Poe's Major Tales.* Ed. Kenneth Silverman. Cambridge: Cambridge UP, 1993. 65–91.

Vygotsky [Vygotskii], L. S. *Thought and Language.* Ed. Eugenia Hanfmann and Gertrude Vakar. Cambridge: MIT P, 1962.

Wollstonecraft, Mary. *Vindication of the Rights of Woman: With Strictures on Political and Moral Subjects.* 1790. Ed. Ashley Tauchert. London: Dent, 1995.

The Lycée-to-University *Progression in French Students' Development as Writers*

CHRISTIANE DONAHUE
Université de Paris/Northeastern University

In a recent interview, French Minister of Education Claude Allègre was asked why French students, who are so advanced compared to U.S. students at the end of their respective high school years, are apparently so far behind three years later at the end of their first cycle of university studies. He replied,

> It's obvious. [U.S.] postsecondary undergraduate education is less specialized than ours. In France we have undergraduate cycles [curricula] in psychology, in sociology, in philosophy, in history, etc. In the United States, the humanities first [undergraduate] cycles are more general. In France, we teach science like a race towards mathematization—physics is a caricature. . . . France, so proud of its culture, "deculturizes" its students with simultaneous overly precocious specialization and too much separation between disciplines. (77)

U.S. sociologist Marianne Debouzy quotes a French university professor who wonders "why brilliant young men [sic] coming out of American universities have a freshness and an enthusiasm, a dynamism, an efficiency ten times superior to their French equivalents who, generally, know a lot more than they do" (qtd. in Debouzy 26). On the other hand, French teachers and writers lament the chaotic written documents and work methods of these same "brilliant" U.S. students, and French university students resist mightily any hint of Americanization of their university system. In addition, French students, from Rollo

May's young scholar in *How the French Boy Learns to Write* (1913) to today's university exchange students, have a global reputation for knowing how to write and for possessing that elusive ability, "une méthode de travail." How can we account for these apparent extremes?

The rapid specialization Allègre mentions does not include continued writing instruction—"French class"—in most university majors. Not that writing instruction per se figures very much into the last years of high school—the *lycée* years—either; in fact, after the French equivalent of their junior year in high school, few students will take "French" or receive writing instruction again. And yet writing has an omnipresent role in the exam-driven French educational system. This makes its relative lack of instruction in secondary and postsecondary studies all the more striking.

When I first began the cross-cultural research that has led to this study, I thought that eighteen- and nineteen-year-old students—in France, those finishing secondary studies, and in the United States, those beginning their first year of college—should be at approximately the same stage in educational, and therefore in writing, development. But in fact it is at this point that the differences turn out to be the most evident.

For U.S. students, entering the undergraduate cycle of schooling (particularly in four-year programs) represents a paradigm shift from secondary studies. It is a major social and academic transition, and, more specifically, a major transition in terms of writing, an introduction to "academic discourse" as defined by the university and, even more, by the first-year writing course. First-year writing programs talk of initiating students into the new discourse community of the university, empowering students with the ability to code-switch, or building students' awareness of various disciplinary discourses. These discussions are not new, and in fact much recent scholarship has provided insightful critiques of the community metaphor (see Part 2). But as valid as the critiques may be, the metaphor itself is still helpful in demonstrating some key differences between U.S. and French approaches to education and specifically to postsecondary composition instruction.

For French students, entering the university cycle of studies is not a "rupture" or entrance into a "new" academic community;

it is a continuation of work begun in the last few years of the *lycée*. The postsecondary studies in France are a cycle of increased social autonomy and considerably less structure or "hand holding," with much the same lack of support, dispersed academic units, and scattered networks of resources as described by David Foster for Germany (see Chapter 4), but the nature of academic expectations about student writing does not radically change. French scholar A. Culioli emphasizes the "French inability to conceive of post-secondary education except in its relationship to secondary education" (qtd. in Chiss and Puech 13). In fact, as U.S. students at age eighteen enter a new cycle and begin to master new approaches to writing, most students in France are *finishing* a cycle, proving their mastery at writing in order to continue in their previously chosen track of studies.

In this overall progression, the major shifts in French students' development as writers and learners occur at the entrance to the *lycée* cycle (at about age fifteen) and then not again until the entrance to graduate studies at masters' and doctoral levels. The writing that students must learn in the *lycée* years—four essential essay forms, the *commentaire composé*, the *étude d'un texte argumentatif*, the *dissertation*, and the *discussion*, all described in Part 2—are the fundamental forms they will need through the first years of university study, although the *dissertation* will be most important.[1] In marked contrast to the shifts described for other countries in this collection, the characteristics of these French forms will remain the same from the final three years of secondary education through the first years of university study:

- ◆ an easily recognizable and repeatable external structure
- ◆ the absence of first person even as students express opinions
- ◆ a strong reliance on paraphrase without citing
- ◆ frequent explicit transitions
- ◆ a statement of "the problem" and "the plan" at the beginning
- ◆ a thesis statement at the end
- ◆ support for claims and assertions through short examples from literature, sociohistoric events, or current events

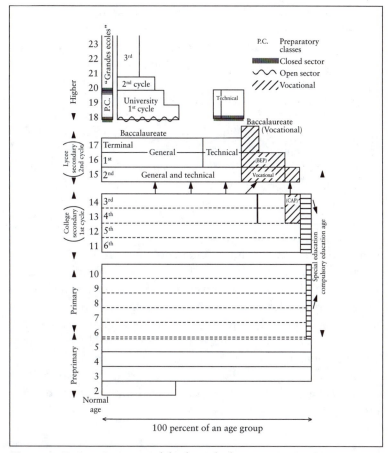

Figure 4. *France: Structure of the formal education system, 1990.*

The only significant change during this period will be the increasing length and development expected in university writing.

In fact, the notion that learning to write for school represents entering a specific discourse community could better be applied to the French student's entire schooling process, starting in kindergarten *(école maternelle)*, than to a particular shift from *lycée* to a university environment (see Figure 4). From the early years until the doctoral cycle, learning to write is intimately linked to the larger community of French culture, to general cultural literacy, and to academic discourse. Moreover, as Susan Wall points out, the tendency in U.S. composition studies to identify "discourse communities" as a discovery that students make when they enter university-level studies obscures the fact that U.S. students, like French students, learn and write academic discourse long before they arrive at the university. In addition, the "community" of the *lycée* is openly exam based, an admitted "gatekeeper," a means to an end. The exam is the path to avoiding "selectivity," the perpetuation of class differences through unequal access to advancement; the principle is, anyone can take the test, anyone can succeed.

I argue that a range of philosophical and institutional factors account for the kinds of writing taught in France and the roles that writing plays. To understand the place of writing and its pedagogy in the French system is to understand a complex weave of historical, political, sociological, and institutional factors in some ways similar to those Americans face, and in some ways quite different. Understanding those issues can help us see that U.S. assumptions are not universal, that "good writing" is indeed largely a culture- and language-based phenomenon, and that monolithic, univocal composition pedagogies are not necessarily unilaterally beneficial. I believe it is important for U.S. readers to better understand the strengths and weaknesses identified by teachers and scholars in the exam-driven French educational system as they seek to help their students grow and develop as writers.

Part I: The French Educational System

Traditionally, the French system is built on an ideology that strives to avoid selectivity at all costs, at least until the university. At the start of a child's education, he or she must have equal access to the same tools and experiences, and one standard must be used to judge his or her work. The national exams at the core of every stage of French education are the accepted basis for that one minimum standard; this kind of standardization drives several of the educational systems studied in this collection, including the Chinese, German, and English systems.

Because the French exams are heavily essay based, writing ability is one of the keys to advancement. As a student progresses, his or her individual success as the result of standardized opportunity determines access to various programs: elite and general university programs, professional programs, and vocational/technical programs. Essential institutional structures and hierarchies have not changed much in the past twenty or thirty years. A 1975 guide prepared by the U.S. Department of Education, *France: A Study of the Educational System of France and a Guide to the Academic Placement of Students in Educational Institutions of the United States* (Wanner), could just as well have been written this year with few changes.

In particular, any reforms suggesting selectivity or restricted access to education can create public uproar. One of the causes of the famous May 1968 riots, for example, was the student perception that government reforms were moving to "Americanize" the universities, making them expensive and deeming financial criteria as important as intellectual criteria (Debouzy 28). Reforms have been aimed at making some parts of the educational experience even more uniform.

National education is alternately described in France as "sacred" or a "national monument." It is the second-largest single employer in the world. The French provide education, equally funded and equally supported, for their children—all children. The preuniversity centralization of curriculum and methods is understandable in an exam-driven system. It is reasonable to think that if all students are to have a fair chance at success, they need an equivalent education. While Americans may balk at such standardization as "undemocratic," overly rigid, or contrary to our cherished interpretation of democracy as individual freedom, French teachers consider our highly uneven elementary and high school education and our university admissions procedures—not to mention our tuition—extremely haphazard and undemocratic by comparison. The United States has been described by many of my French colleagues as a society that operates at two speeds, the wealthy speed and the poverty-level speed, and our educational system is often cited as the most glaring example of such economic discrimination.

But in spite of a nationalized education system, the diverse geographic distribution of the most underserved populations does create strong socioeconomic differences. For example, a recent report issued by the government affirms, "a child who attends first grade in an underprivileged suburb has practically no chance of ever getting into one of the elite university tracks" (Attali par. 1). Such class differences are the subject of studies in France as often as racial differences are the subject of studies in the United States. In addition, the French resist any depiction of their educational system as unified, homogenous, even centralized. Michel Crozier insists,

> Behind the norms and the official bulletins, in spite of the frightening theoretical uniformity which constantly surprises foreign observers, in spite of the considerable efforts made in the past few years to homogenize the system and to impose a uniform *collège* experience, French *collèges* are as diverse as it is possible to imagine. (qtd. in Ballion 45).

These challenges to the French educational system have a direct impact on writing instruction. Language issues are central to debates about assimilation, whether focused on immigrant minorities or on underprivileged or working-class children within a dominant school culture. We see these issues raised in every country discussed in this collection: South African students coming from inadequate secondary schools; Kenyan students dealing with first-, second-, and even third-language barriers; Chinese students learning the language of the elite; British and German working-class students being far less likely to enter the most advanced academic tracks.

In addition, language issues are central to the underlying assumptions an exam-driven system makes about cognitive development, social equality, and the nature of exam-verified knowledge. These factors play a key role in the practices and pedagogies of writing instruction in France.

An Overview

This report focuses on the secondary and postsecondary academic years, the *lycée* and the university. But the educational experience at these levels is grounded in a centralized and comprehensive elementary education. *Lycée* and university studies come after a student's mandatory schooling experience in France, which, as in the United States, typically ends at age sixteen.

The formal school years are numbered in reverse in France, going from "preparatory" classes, "elementary" classes, and "intermediate" classes to the equivalent of junior high school, *collège* (grades 5 to 3), and finally the senior high *lycée* years (grade 2 to grade *terminale*) (see Table 1). Every French student receives at least these twelve years of formal schooling if he or she chooses. In addition, all children in France may begin kindergarten as early as age two in "maternal classes" designed to socialize them to schooling and, in particular, to reading and writing. At three years old, 98 percent of French children are in school, compared to 33 percent of U.S. three-year-olds (National Center for Education Statistics 67).

TABLE 1. French Educational System: Education from the *Lycée* to the End of the First University Cycle

	France	United States
tenth grade	enter *lycée (seconde)*	sophomore in high school
eleventh grade	*lycée, première*	junior in high school
twelfth grade	complete *lycée (terminale)*	senior, complete high school
thirteenth grade	enter DEUG or first year of *prépa* or first year of BTS.	enter B.A. program, first year
fourteenth grade	complete DEUG or BTS or second year of *prépa*	university sophomore
fifth grade	enter/complete *licence* (equivalent B.A.) or enter first year of Grandes Ecoles or enter first year of teacher-training institute (IUFM)	university junior

NOTE: These are not the only postsecondary educational choices, but they are the ones relevant to this study.
DEUG = Diplôme d'études universitaires générales
BTS = Brevet de technicien supérieur (advanced technical school)
prépa = Classes préparatoires aux Grandes Ecoles
IUFM = Institut universitaire de formation de maitres

The curriculum in France is highly centralized throughout the school years up to the postsecondary level. Students from kindergarten through the *collège* years follow a state-mandated program, which generally includes lists of materials to cover, works to read, work habits to learn, and skills to demonstrate. In the preschool years, for example, the National Center of Curricula's specific goals for native-speaking French children include understanding decontextualized messages (reception activities), paraphrasing orally and memorizing songs and other short texts (production activities), and distinguishing between types of texts by their exterior aspect—newspapers, books, posters (metalinguistic activities) (Chartier 178). This centralized curriculum requires formalized writing activities and text recognition even for preschool children. These activities for native speakers are central to their education throughout the formal schooling process.

Curricula and course work are standardized throughout the school system. In the *collège* years, students can choose their foreign language courses but otherwise share a curriculum. Even during the *lycée* years, each course in a given track remains standardized in preparation for the BAC *(baccalauréat)* exam series. The programs for each school year are provided to teachers and available to parents in the form of the government-supplied *Instructions Officielles,* which detail each year's program elements. The curriculum is so centralized that parents can receive lists of texts and supplies for the coming school year at the end of the current one and go to any local supplier to buy them. Early July (before families leave on vacation) and early September are bad times for casual book shopping in France! One enterprising establishment recently started order-by-phone textbook services, complete with free delivery.

The end of the first year of the *lycée* signals the beginning of a student's path to specific university studies; therefore students choose a relatively narrow area for their last two years of secondary studies. This transition comes much earlier than in Germany or South Africa, where the beginning of postsecondary studies is clearly a shift to specialization. Course work differs among *lycée* specializations in France, not only in weekly hours per subject but also in a system of weights for different subjects. Each semester is marked by take-home written papers and *devoirs sur table*, exams written in two- or three-hour periods at school. The emphasis is on on-the-spot writing, as is the case in China (see Chapter 1), although the written products are generally more developed. Students write regularly in every subject, including math and science. In math class, they must justify their methodology and their results; in science class, they document processes and explain outcomes; in history and geography, they write research reports and analyses, and so on.[2]

The BAC exam comes in three versions—the general academic series (with the "S" [scientific] as the most prestigious, a phenomenon that seems to be reproduced in other educational systems, such as China's), the technology series, and the professional series. The general series leads to university studies, the technology series to further studies in technical fields such as engineering, and the professional series to a cooperative arrangement of study and internship leading to employment. Students can shift only "down" in this system, from the most difficult programs in math and science to the less difficult literary program, for example, or from the academic series to the professional series.

The BAC exam is in many ways comparable to exams at the end of advanced studies in the U.S. system, such as the comprehensive exams for master's degree programs, and to the *Abitur* in Germany and the A-level exams in England. It includes two-to-three-hour sessions for each subject, with both written and oral components. The BAC exams are graded by teachers at high schools other than the students' home schools in order to ensure maximum standardization.

A crucial element of the BAC is the written French exam, to which the literature and writing curriculum for the previous two years has led. The forms of writing practiced for this exam are the same as those expected on other parts of the BAC, such as the sections on history or philosophy. The *dissertation* model mentioned earlier, for example, might ask students to discuss a quote by Marguerite Yourcenar; the philosophy exam might offer a quote by Aristotle or pose an "ageless" question such as "Are we our body, or do we 'have' a body?" Either way, the structure of the response will be the same.

Passing the general BAC, the literary-scientific series, guarantees a slot in the liberal arts or scientific tracks of the university system. In fact, the BAC is considered both historically and culturally the first university degree, *le premier grade universitaire*. Even though students are still in high school while preparing for the exam, they are considered members of the university community on passing the BAC. Official government literature and student-generated information on Web sites such as Phosphore refer to students in *terminale* as though they are already university members, giving pointers on registration, university course curricula, and program choices. Preliminary university studies are a right and a logical continuation for BAC holders, and the French *lycée* and university are generally not discussed as independent units of education (Allègre 76).[3]

Steady increases in the number of students choosing the track leading to the BAC have produced a growing number of students who pass the BAC exam every year.[4] Many researchers now talk of the *"nouveaux lycéens"*: students arriving at the *lycée* in far greater numbers, choosing the technical tracks more often, and acting more as savvy consumers—active participants who make demands and consider success on the BAC exam a right (Bautier and Rochex 109). This trend is one of the important differences between education in the United States and that in France; whereas in France a typical student's goal is to take and pass the BAC, in the United States, the typical student's aspiration is to get into the college of his or her choice.

As a natural extension of the *lycée* years, approximately 47 percent of eligible students choose to take the first two years of the general French university program. The *lycée* is in fact a preliminary part of the university system. Postsecondary studies are unilaterally referred to as "the BAC plus . . . ," depending on how many years a student chooses to pursue after the BAC:

◆ BAC plus three university years for a *licence* (the equivalent of a bachelor's degree)

◆ BAC plus five years for a *maîtrise* (master's degree)

◆ more years for a doctorate

At the university, students' course work is generally inflexible, with few electives—the specialization criticized by both

Allègre and the Attali report. The end-of-semester exams are centralized and blind: students report to amphitheaters to take them,
and fill out their identifying information on a part of the exam
the grader does not see. These exams are generally single-ques-
tion essays on which students work for two to three hours. Many
classes require essays throughout the semester as well, both in-
class and take-home, just as in the *lycée*. There are, however, no
semester-long projects or extended seminar papers like those in
Foster's description of Germany's university system (Chapter 4),
and the semester-end exam is the last opportunity for students to
complete the course, although failed exams can be retaken once
in September.

University studies are also the extension of the *lycée* years in
a social sense. Students generally do not leave home for the first
few years of postsecondary studies. Isolated campuses in rural
settings and dormitories are almost nonexistent. In fact, when
the government tried to create U.S.-style campuses in the late
1960s, the campuses failed. Students felt isolated, cut off from
the social and intellectual life they felt existed in the cities of which
most French universities are an integral part (Debouzy 28).

On the other hand, university students are left to their own
devices academically far more than in the United States. They do
not have advisors, they often wait in lines for hours only to discover they are not in the right place, and they do not have the
help of professors' office hours or access to support systems—
tutoring centers, writing labs, and so forth.[5] The Attali report
cites students who arrive at the university with no sense of the
appropriate specific major for their interests and abilities, and
points out that the first cycle (D.E.U.G.) results in failure for
many students:

- 34 percent abandon university studies after the first year
- 40 percent still haven't obtained the two-year degree after three or four years
- only 28 percent actually finish the first degree in the normal two years

Exam-verified knowledge becomes the focus of these later

years, and writing is the assumed tool for both acquiring and demonstrating that knowledge. The general feeling is that students have the right to expect that after twelve years of schooling they will have learned all they need to know for the first years of university (Barré-de Miniac 13). If they haven't, they will feel the lack most at the graduate level.

Students' career destinations after the BAC continue to reflect the hierarchical outcomes of written examination results. Students with the best academic records are recommended for tracking into the Grandes Ecoles, schools with reputations the equivalent of our Ivy League schools. These are usually tuition-free, and students who agree to teach or work for the state for ten years after graduation get a stipend. Again, rigorous exams determine actual acceptance.

Students who plan to take these exams first complete one or two additional years of general studies in the postsecondary track of *classes préparatoires (prépas)*, a track intended to prepare students for the entrance examinations for the Grandes Ecoles. The *prépas* are actually taught in the *lycée* and are not an official university program. But because they are intended as intensive preparation for the Grandes Ecoles examinations, they offer more consistent feedback and guidance on students' writing performance than does university course work itself. The *préparatoire* years thus serve as a rigorous initiation of sorts into the kind of work the Grandes Ecoles will expect of students.[6] And the credits earned in the *prépas* may be applied to university programs leading to the *licence* if the student does not qualify for the Grandes Ecoles. Thus more and more students choose to enter the *prépas* after the *lycée*, most switching to a specific university course of study later.[7] They seek general preparation not limited by the restrictions of a major. In a humanities *prépa*, first-year students study philosophy, history, French, Latin, Greek, two modern languages, and geography (Wanner 142). By contrast, in a first-year university program for majors in *lettres*, the courses might include rhetoric, narratology, French language and linguistics, literature, the intellectual history of civilization, a modern language, and Latin (*Livret Pédagogique de Saint-Quentin-en-Yvelines* 4).

Students who graduate from the Grandes Ecoles are generally destined for university teaching positions or government research posts. The highest scorers on the Grandes Ecoles final exams pursue university posts, the next highest teach in the *prépas*, and the lowest scorers teach *terminales* courses in the *lycées* or teach in the technical universities. High scorers on the exam taken by teacher-training students also receive *lycée* posts, while the lowest scorers teach at the junior high level of the *collège* (Ropé 86–87).[8] This hierarchy demonstrates the omnipresence of the exam model at every level of French education, as well as the underlying assumption that the highest-scoring teachers are best suited for the higher school levels. As Françoise Ropé suggests, the basis for this assumption is the notion that teaching is founded on the transmission of knowledge, and those who score the highest on the exams must know the most (86); this is the same assumption that handicaps writing programs in the Kenyan system (Chapter 5). Part 2 examines how these assumptions have resulted in a lack of composition instruction in the *lycée*.

The written exams are thus the heart and soul of the French system, as well as the basis for its antiselection ideology. From the *lycée* on, the exam system encourages autonomous writers who learn to assess scholastic writing assignments and to associate them with preordained structures. Students who must pass three-hour written exams in which they organize, draft, and polish an essay about literature, history, or an argumentative essay need to be able to produce it without revision, without peer review, without a teacher's intervention. This kind of on-the-spot writing, quite similar to the exam writing Xiao-ming Li describes for the Chinese postsecondary entrance exams (Chapter 1), drives writing pedagogy. On a practical level, given the amount of reading and exam preparation they must do each academic year, teachers and students simply do not have the time to work through the writing process in ways familiar to U.S. teachers. Students need to be autonomous writers in order to be successful on the BAC exam and in postsecondary studies.

This emphasis on examination writing helps explain the relative lack of research into writing pedagogy. Institutional constraints, created by the official curriculum's focus on preparing students for exams, encourage teachers to see innovative research about teaching writing as uninteresting or simply not useful. Writing research is being done today largely on strategies for teaching underprivileged or underprepared students. Unless the national education system turns away from the prevailing examination model, that isn't likely to change any time soon (Dabène, Frier, and Visoz 91).[9]

Students faced with the master's thesis and the doctoral *dissertation* have a fairly high rate of withdrawal, attributed to their lack of preparation for such a long piece of work (Barré-de Miniac 12). Perhaps even more important, students preparing to be teachers in the graduate-level teacher-training institutes do not take writing courses, not even to prepare for the various competitive exams. As a recent study shows, they are not particularly competent writers themselves in the areas of form, structure, punctuation, transitions, aesthetics, tone, and methods for emphasizing key points (Balcou 223).

Little research has been undertaken to determine why students are failing at any of these postsecondary levels—least of all, to determine whether their writing skills and abilities might play any role in students' difficulties. The Attali report, some one hundred pages long, recommends ways for the university to better help and involve students, but it does not once mention teaching writing. The report does insist on the need for reform that would include adopting the model used in the *classes préparatoires* for all students and offering methodological support for the transition from secondary studies to postsecondary studies. Because *prépa* instructors do work with students on their writing, this statement seems to recognize the current lack of attention to writing.

The Academic "Community" in France

Clearly, the exam in the French system, much like the Chinese university entrance exam and, to a lesser degree, the A-level exams in England, acts as the openly acknowledged gatekeeper for each new academic level, each new academic "community." In France, however, the exam operates at several gatekeeping points, not just at the point of secondary-postsecondary transition.

The metaphor of community has been important to the evolution of U.S. discussions about writing pedagogy and has directly affected how we think about teaching composition. Language use and writing are considered the key modes of access to the discourses of academic communities. Yet any academic community is largely an imaginary geography. Don Bialostosky suggests that a particular community changes at different times and in different circumstances (11–12); French philosopher Frédéric François emphasizes that the nature of community *is* its interior differences, which allow it to function. Others point out that the invocation of "community" can silence dissent. Nedra Reynolds reminds us that "community" is a particularly American construct that does not always export well (24). But the construct still has an analytical usefulness, allowing us to study the *lycée*-to-university "transition" as a process of intellectual, social, and linguistic continuity rather than rupture.

Patricia Bizzell has described the features that characterize disciplinary discourse: the shared style conventions, the preferred syntaxes, the commonplaces, the acceptable proofs, the common stock of words and even of arguments, the ethos specific to a given discourse (36). Cheryl Geisler has argued that academic expertise is both rhetorical and content based. As students come into contact with the conventions of a new community, they slowly develop an awareness of the signs, the metadiscourse, the other elements that indicate that certain perspectives are related to certain ways of learning and writing (7).

French students' general awareness of discourse communities is developed during their high school years. Their choice of a track at age sixteen largely determines the discourse communities they will enter in the *lycée* and at university. French students tend to identify themselves with a specific "mode" of thinking and writing in the *lycée* years (I am in the "S" track, I am scientific, logical, math-minded; I am in the "L" track, I am literary, I can relativize ideas, I am not stuck in the concrete; I am in "G," I am a musician, a performer. . . .) and with the level of prestige the track draws.[10] In fact, if we are to assume that students in educational systems worldwide do undergo initiation into a specific discourse community at some point in their move toward advanced studies, that initiation begins in France as students prepare to take a specific version of the BAC exam—literary, scientific, technical, professional. And as students progress to higher levels in a chosen track, the role of language and writing splinters and diversifies. Students in literary and scientific tracks learn to negotiate heavily traditional writing-based community expectations; students in technical or professional fields move toward new forms of writing that emphasize utilitarian goals.

For French researcher Michel Brossard, however, the French focus in all domains on skill-based "correct language use" as a condition of access to a discourse community runs counter to the official interpretation of examinations as instruments of democratic accessibility to education (Pollet and Rosier 66). Linguistic and cultural tensions show themselves at the *lycée* level in a schism developing between the idea of general culture *(culture générale)* as the pathway to democratic assimilation, and a push for radical change to address the needs of today's student populations. The *Instructions Officielles* for the national curriculum require that every student be taught a *culture générale* based on a Great Books approach to the best works of French culture and French civilization. But like Americans, the French are finding that traditionalist approaches are not effective for many students, especially immigrants and those in underprivileged suburbs and rural areas. This tension between selectivity and access manifests itself in issues relating to students' development as writers. Should schools socialize students into the dominant *beau langage* of highly literate French? Is there room in an exam-driven system for teaching writing as a process, for reading outside of the recommended list, or for encouraging a community of writers who collaborate and share, when in fact the best exam scores lead to the best jobs?

Research in writing is still largely focused on younger students. Elisabeth Bautier, in particular, emphasizes that "language . . . is a mode of socialization, a way of being and of understanding the world" (*Pratiques* 22). Building on Basil Bernstein, Pierre Bourdieu, and William Labov, she describes the "discursive behaviors" that working-class children do not necessarily know, and points out the alternative ways in which these children "read" academic situations and tasks (17–18). In French scholarship about teaching, however, the role of writing is generalized into the role of language development. Students' early efforts at writing are nurtured to help all children grow as school writers and thus have access to success.

Part 2: Characteristics of Student Texts

The essays that students produce in the French system are a concrete manifestation of the system's goals, priorities, and pedagogies. They demonstrate what students retain of the "official" version of writing, what they are taught, and how they interpret it. They also reveal what seems to be most specific to the French educational system. In Part 2, I look at student writing, in particular one university student's essay. In Part 3, I explore the specific pedagogies that have influenced that student writing.

Analyses of culturally influenced essay strategies must be made first and foremost in light of the kinds of tasks students must undertake. The student essays analyzed here were often responses to excerpts of argumentative texts or to quotes, with specific instructions about content and approach, such as, "In your essay, present an opposing argument for each of the five points Pascal makes, and offer specific new examples." An appropriate response to such a question will not include personal arguments, nor will it include arguments in support of Pascal. The same is true of student essays that rely heavily on paraphrase; if the assignment asks, "What does the author mean?" (a frequent assignment cue in France), students will likely paraphrase substantial sections of the author's work.

Other key variables can also affect analysis. Assumptions about truth claims implicit in a given prompt or text affect students' approaches to writing. Also significant is the fact that no student chooses to be a student writer; the writing is required. Even students who choose to go to the university are not "writers" in the sense that they make free decisions "to write." In addition, writing elements differ in different school situations. Students in their first year of technical studies at a French university will be encouraged to be organized and clear in their writing rather than to elaborate on examples. Students' inclinations to interpret examples or to simply cite them, to write canonic introductions or to choose creative ones, are linked to both institutional practices and to learned responses—routines called in to play, as David Russell would say.

Subject matter is also key to student response. Subjects create what Frédéric François calls "affinities" with certain examples or ways of developing ideas; for example, students asked to write about death are more likely to call on cultural commonplaces about the subject, whereas students who are asked to write about gender roles in society are far more likely to call on personal experiences with gender differences. There is perhaps a reason that so many student essay introductions begin with "In our society today, . . ." when we have asked students to identify social issues or to discuss social ills.

All of these variables show that any collection of essays on different countries' practices and pedagogies must avoid explicit comparison of "academic writing" as a generalized discursive act. Whether within or between countries, different situations and different goals produce different student texts. A case in point: in Chapter 1, Li cites the diversity of forms of writing considered "academic writing" at the university level in China. The same is clearly true in France, although within a given field (humanities, technical, professional) the set of forms available to students might be less diverse.

In any case, certain strategies are more likely to be used in French essays than in U.S. essays. These strategic patterns are shared by both *lycée* and university writing, and seem to highlight the explicitly "school-based" nature of French student writing, its openly schooled quality—a writing that Li suggests is not "real" writing.

The descriptions of student essays presented here are based on a dual qualitative-quantitative study carried out in France over three years. Three hundred expository student essays from nine institutions, approximately 50 percent *lycée* and 50 percent university, were analyzed using quantitative methodologies for select strategies, including use of the first person pronoun "I," placement of the thesis, external formatting, and use of explicit connectors.

Forty of these essays were analyzed using linguistic close reading techniques. Working from the assumption that student writing is "real" discourse—complex, rich, and valuable—and that researchers can use the linguistic tools and the critical theory criteria generally reserved for literary analysis to read and interpret student writing, this qualitative approach was designed to explore the underlying rhetorical strategies and perspectives at work in each student text. Each essay was examined for use of first, second, or third person; methods of persuasion as influenced by cultural and institutional expectations; types and frequencies of examples; overall organizational modes; textual heterogeneity from movements among various microgenres; approaches to introduction and conclusion; placement of thesis; intertextuality; and interaction with the wording of the assignment.

These elements were considered in light of four key theoretical perspectives:

1. The situation in which student writers find themselves as they transition from secondary to postsecondary studies can be described using Mary Louise Pratt's metaphor of a contact zone, a sociocultural space of interaction and struggle in which not all participants have equal footing and diverse language priorities influence what is acceptable, who can speak, and how the world is defined. Students use various literate arts—discursive tools—to integrate themselves, more or less, into these spaces.

2. The discursive negotiation students are carrying out in their texts is built on the already-said and the to-be-said described by Mikhail Bakhtin in his dialogic model of the ways in which utterances function. The analyses of student texts show how a student text is dialogic, and with whom.

3. French linguist Frédéric François's theory of *reprises-modifications*, discursive movements that simultaneously take up ideas and modify them in re-presenting them, can help elucidate the finite ways in which students actually construct texts. These *reprises-modifications* are the fiber of all discourse,

the dynamic movements with which a speaker or a writer appropriates language and reproduces meaning, modifying both in the process.

4. Student texts are heterogeneous documents that slip among genres and textual subject positions. In the social constructionist tradition, the analysis did not seek to identify "the" student writer, his or her voice, but rather the textual Subject as he or she was constructed in and by the assignment, the requested genre, the general situation, and the student's history as a writer.

Mayeul de G., First-Year University Student

In order to bring to life French student writing strategies and to show student writing as it presents itself after a year of university studies, in this section I foreground one university student's essay. The student cited here, Mayeul de G., wrote his essay in a first-year university French class.

Mayeul's characteristic ways of developing his essay were learned during his *lycée* years of study. His essay reveals a university student who has successfully assimilated the forms expected of the French students (the paper received 13 points out of 20, about a B), but who has been able to move beyond strict formula. His progression, however, as discussed in Part 3, is not clearly related to any pedagogy or curricular influence. How he progressed once his French writing classes all but ended in first grade *(première)* is not clear. What *is* clear is the rootedness of his essay's structure in the tradition of French exam forms.

The assignment question to which Mayeul responded was: "What does the author Joël de Rosnay mean when he writes: 'Managing one's life means arriving at a certain form of liberty, of autonomy'? Do you think that this conception is desirable and possible? Give your reasons, supporting them with precise examples." This assignment, which came after students had read de Rosnay's short piece, calls for a heterogeneous document, an essay that interprets ("what does the author mean . . ."), evaluates ("is this desirable, possible"), and persuades ("give your reasons," "give precise examples"). The nature of the question poses a particular problem for student writers. It asks them to evaluate, and yet there isn't much in de Rosnay's claims that requires evaluation, since most people wouldn't oppose the notion that "managing one's life" is a good idea.

Mayeul begins his essay with canonic page formatting for a French essay: the introduction is set off from the body with a double line, and each major section is clearly separate from the next with spacing. French scholastic essays, always handwritten, are formatted to expose the structure: the introduction and conclusion set off by double spacing, the "hinge" sentence in the middle set off by spaces, individual paragraphs staggered by *alinéas* (starting new ideas within paragraphs with a new line).

Most introductions in the texts I analyzed presented what is called the "problematic," the question the essay proposes to answer, generally rephrased from the wording of the assignment. The traditional introduction also included the "plan," a specific statement about the direction of the essay, the two major lines of argument—but not the thesis. The idea is to indicate direction without giving away the actual main point. This is generally accompanied by the metadiscursive "we," for example, "We will first consider in what ways author X might be right, and then the ways in which his argument might be modified. . . ." At the end of the essay, students almost always introduce some version of personal opinion, such as, "Even though the author makes a good point, in the long run he does not adequately account for all the options. I believe that . . ." This particular structure is the cornerstone of French student writing, the "thesis-antithesis-synthesis" structure both required and recognizable in all student essays except the *commentaire composé*. But at the university level, students branch out from this basic structure to a variety of modified forms and specialized structures, such as the *synthèse de documents* in technical fields and the *rapport de stage* (internship report) in business programs.

Although the particular structures are specific to France, this kind of academic writing is similar to that which appears in other systems presented in this collection: the "systematic study of established knowledge about a topic, and the incorporation and synthesis of diverse sources of this knowledge into an authoritative viewpoint" described by Foster (Germany, p. 216) and the "eight-legged essay" structure described by Li (China, Chapter 1), for example.

Mayeul begins by rephrasing the assignment, a typical move for French essays, but with a twist. In his plan, he says, "We will first explain what the author means by 'managing one's life,' which mechanisms are hidden under this term. Then we will see whether this conception is still valid today and most of all whether it is the best way to live our lives today." Even with all of its formulaic trappings, the student's implied criticism (which mechanisms are hidden, whether this is the best way) is an unexpected displacement of the scholastic tradition. The student absorbs and modifies the proposed theme, introducing his style (in Starobinski's definition of style—what a writer does in the margin of liberty offered by language and convention).

The essay thus calls into question the validity and quality of de Rosnay's proposal, and this questioning is developed further with the theatrical dialogue in the next paragraph: "What, you say, is it possible that someone else is deciding my life for me?" We see the student's perceived relationship with his reader in this imaginary dialogue; the reader is sketched at least partially as a noninitiate, and the student creates a position of authority for himself in his role as interpreter and guide, one who sees the obvious and recognizes the hidden.

The essay comes full circle in the conclusion, returning to the introduction with the perspective of an argument/evaluation completed: "Managing one's own life can only be imagined, because it is not achievable. Too many factors in our lives today influence our behavior." These signs of the essay's "schoolness" are underscored by the explicit connectors: "effectively," "in spite of everything," "in these two cases," "in addition," "on the other hand." The student also connects his ideas throughout the essay with the repetition of "managing one's life" at strategic points.

Explicit connectors are essential to French students' writing, so much so that misguided students sometimes begin their essays with phrases such as "in addition." Mayeul's interpretive role is underlined in the explicit proposition, "Let's first try to explain what the author means," which is repeated two times and taken up again later in the text with "according to the author." Even though he stays close to de Rosnay's excerpt in his wording and references ("according to the author," "the author says that"), Mayeul establishes his perspective with his own examples, each one presented with the metadiscursive "we," as in "we will now see." At the same time, this essay is explicitly "scholastic" in its metanarration of the textual movements: "Here, the word 'management' is a bit crazy"; "as we just saw"; "to answer the second [part of the] question." These references to the development of the essay are seconded by the several uses of "we" as a scholastic technique, with the personal "we" standing in for "I." This particular use of "we" is generally associated with scientific theoretical discourse in academic situations.

In the body of the text, this coming and going among explicit positions continues. The metadiscursive "we" and the personal "we" are mixed, and the addition of the pronoun "one" makes the text sometimes difficult to follow. Anything that might be considered subjective is often dissimulated by using the French equivalent of passive voice, the "on" pronoun, much more frequent than our "one," in fact, and much more slippery because it is able to represent "I," "we," or "they" without warning.[11] One striking characteristic of French student writing is the almost total absence of "I" other than in its formulaic concluding role, and reliance instead on this slippery "we" associated with academic and sometimes scientific writing.

This use of "we" decreases as students enter the university level, although not in Mayeul's case. French theorists propose that this "we" represents the community targeted by the essay, but I believe it is simply a strategy that permits the presentation of the writer's own point of view without using the forbidden "I," much like U.S. students' use of "one." The lack of distinction on students' part about the various ways to use "I" and "we" is typical of the essays in this study. The only normed use of "I" is, as mentioned earlier, at the end of the essay in the synthesis paragraph, which presents statements such as "I therefore think that . . ." But even this varies depending on the subject matter, the teacher, the institution, and its population. Perhaps the most intriguing use of these various positions in Mayeul's essay is his play at one point on all three (I, we, *on*) in a single sentence. That said, the "we" of his conclusion is much more personal, a direct appeal: "we need to improve our daily lives," "live as we want." This tone of direct address creates a feel at times of real "play" with the reader.

Mayeul also successfully develops movement between the declarations of his point of view and the specifics that develop those declarations. Consider this paragraph:

> From this point on, managing one's life would consist of getting beyond life's restrictions, dominating them, surpassing them. In the morning, if a worker doesn't take his train in the morning he'll arrive late. He can escape this restriction by taking his car. He will still have to arrive on time but his car operates under his orders. The definition of the ideal mode of life would be "to live according to one's choices."

The paragraph has no explicit "for example" or other explicit connectors, but its narrative thread in the example creates an alternative coherence. The modes of expression and even the time frame change abruptly with the shift to the morning train example. The hypothetical "if" shifts the grammatical mode of the paragraph and simultaneously changes us from the domain of abstractions to the domain of possibilities.

Another interesting characteristic of Mayeul's essay is the tendency to rephrase the text read for the assignment without explicit crediting the author. Paraphrases in French essays are striking because they go uncited and often "undigested." U.S. writing teachers would consider French student work plagiarism in many cases. Although Mayeul does occasionally say, "The author says . . . ," generally he uses no documentation, and he paraphrases closely what he does re-present. French teachers' heavy reliance on assignments that call for summary, coupled with the lack of instruction in documentation, invite this kind of rephrasing—acts of appropriation that help students make sense out of the text. Each appropriation of an idea from the excerpt is followed by an example from the student; this movement is predicted by theorists such as David Bartholomae, who talks about students' need to take what is said and make it their own, sometimes at first simply by literally repeating it; the act of interpretation begins, according to Bartholomae, with the act of speaking the other's words ("Wanderings" 93). In fact, it is very much the kind of dialogue with assigned texts that Bakhtin predicts in his exploration of individual utterances as links in the chain of discourse, dialogic moments in which the already-said and the to-be-said frame the moment of saying. Students such as Mayeul are making their way, or negotiating, as Suellen Shay and Rob Moore describe their South African students doing (Chapter 6), when they take on the role of historian in order to find an authoritative voice among the multiple voices presented to them. French students are, again in a movement shared with the South African students described by Shay and Moore, close borrowers of the original texts from which they work.

In fact, no writer ever "just" paraphrases. Every paraphrase is an act of interpretation, not merely a convention for working with texts. Paraphrases are academic negotiations, interactions with texts that can't be entirely displaced, because the assignment calls for working with them. In this student essay, both Mayeul and de Rosnay are speaking, although the turns taken are not always clearly marked. Mayeul does displace de Rosnay with his own examples, generally introduced with "we."

The examples in Mayeul's essay are not personal, true to French interdictions about using personal anecdotes. The text circles around propositions about dependence, independence, autonomy, and interdependence: "a network of interdependence," "management happens through autonomy," "the trap . . . is in dependence." These threads of meaning help the writer modify his point of view as the text progresses, with explanatory tentatives, oppositions such as management/autonomy, and specific examples clarifying his interpretations of de Rosnay. Because by and large there are only "subject matter" courses in French university studies, the examples used in French essays are specific to the assignment. In economics or history essays, the examples are from the course work and readings; in philosophy essays, the examples include *faits divers* or personal/societal examples; in French essays, the examples are literary, again directly influenced by the course readings. These examples come from the excerpt in the assignment or from class discussion; they are Bakhtinian movements, built on the already-said that students have encountered in school and in general life situations.

French student essays appear to appeal to reason and logic or to readers' emotional connection to the issue, rather than to the authenticity or sincerity of the student author. This is understandable given the institutional push to dissimulate the subjective "I" and avoid personal examples as unreliable. With a pedagogy similar to the one described by Mary Scott for England (Chapter 2), French writing teachers push their students to move from the everyday experiences they have as individuals to the "distance . . . provided by the sociohistorical context" (p. 94); at the postsecondary level in particular, for France as for England, "a personal experience both is and is not personal in that it has to be transformed into a general comment within a shared community of values while not ceasing to be an individual interpretation" (p. 103).

On the other hand, student writers do not seem to make a distinction between personal opinion and academic argument, even though such a distinction is emphasized by the textbooks and the *Instructions Officielles*. In fact, French students' essays present personal opinion as much as the U.S. student essays I have read; they simply make more of an effort to dissimulate that opinion. Most student essays are simply a series of claims presenting the writer's point of view about the issue at hand, supported by paraphrases or "reprises" of the point of view presented by the assignment—what François has called *reprise-modification*. Following Stephen Toulmin's model, we could say that they do not supply the "data" or "grounds" for their claims. But they do take ownership, to varying degrees, of the material they paraphrase.

In another example of *reprise-modification,* Mayeul's essay is built on the commonplace that "we think we have free will, free choice, but in fact we don't."[12] The writer represents himself as the subject who is able to take the long view, balance the various interpretations, and suggest a "thesis" at the end. Indeed, the essays in this study generally embody a liberal-leftist-humanitarian perspective supporting better education, middle-of-the-road solutions, and personal improvement. There is nothing surprising about this reliance on *prêts-à-penser,* the necessary forms of thinking on which a given age builds its operating principles. For

Mayeul's essay, the statement that we can't just let anarchy rule, that there must be some form of social control, is not new, but it is the only workable response in a situation in which no one has asked him to talk about managing his *own* life.

This combination of commonplaces, liberal traditions, and reasonable conclusions creates texts that rely on "argument by acceptability," as Swiss philosopher J. B. Grize would say. Mayeul's point of view is constructed through a series of declarations about the theme of liberty and autonomy. The point is not being "argued" in the traditional sense so much as deliberated through various definitions picked up from de Rosnay and other texts, and by identifying de Rosnay's perspective with his own, brought to a "reasonable" conclusion. From the start, the tone of the essay suggests a subject position of control, the "knowledgeable voice" that will interpret de Rosnay for the readers. The student speaks "for" us, he knows our problems, he can propose the "best" way for all of us to live. At the same time, he does not hesitate to show his own writing and thinking processes by using parentheses to indicate reformulations or reconsiderations of some statements.

On the whole, Mayeul's essay demonstrates the French student writer's respect for the conventions of form, structure, and development, while going beyond some of those conventional approaches by reinterpreting the assignment question, playing at times with the reader, and using some unusual coherence techniques. He is comfortable enough to modify his own point of view throughout the text. He has developed these techniques over his *lycée* and first-year university studies, and they will serve him in both exam and take-home essay situations.

Of course, Mayeul's relative success is not necessarily representative of university students' experiences as a whole. French teachers share with U.S. teachers the tendency to complain about the deficiencies of "students today." Even at the university level, professors interviewed for the Ropé study cited their students' "total lack of culture" (44), and teachers at each educational cycle or level point to the previous cycle as the cause of students' inadequacies. These complaints have encouraged some research attention to students' writing difficulties. Several recent studies, for example, have linked incoherence or "coherence ruptures" in student writing with poorly structured assignments and with the importance of teaching successful writing strategies (Brossard et al. 73).

Part 3: Writing Practices and Pedagogies in the French Educational System

How does a student like Mayeul learn to write in the manner just described? When and where did he learn to structure his essay, to invite his reader in, to avoid personal examples, to appropriate a text read in class and respond to it? Why doesn't he cite sources? Why doesn't he call on his own experience to answer the question? Where did he learn to develop his thesis throughout the text and present it at the end of his essay as his conclusion? The pedagogy associated with writing preparation in the French system is embedded in a cumulative systemic expectation. On the one hand, as Christine Barré-de Miniac says, writing is from the first years of schooling "the object of teaching, a teaching and learning tool, the object and subject of knowledge, a method for testing levels of mastery of knowledge, a component both omnipresent and multifunctional in the school setting" (13). On the other hand, French researchers point out that writing isn't taught as such but is presented as an almost magical synthesis of other subsets of language mastery such as spelling, vocabulary, and syntax; it is the "unteachable paradox" (Reuter 53). Yves Reuter proposes that writing instruction begin with students at the *collège* level because after this level, as they enter the specialized track they will pursue in later studies, it is assumed that they know how to write (13).

A major expectation built into the education system is that earlier masteries should make success possible at higher levels. In the later years of schooling—*lycée* and then university—students like Mayeul should be "writing their way into" the new academic communities by succeeding on the requisite exams. The forms, rhetorical skills, and frames for thinking learned in the *lycée* are intended to serve until the graduate cycle of study, as Dominique Bucheton points out (160). Students in *seconde* (tenth grade), for example, might write about Emile Zola's Dreyfus affair speech; in *première* (eleventh grade) they might write about Marguerite Yourcenar's ideas on class and culture; Mayeul's first-year university French course wrote about Joël de Rosnay's discussion of managing one's life; in a *prépa* class, students might write about Pascal's two kinds of humanity. The key difference? The students in *seconde* will turn in a 400-word essay, students in *première* an essay of about 800 words, and the postsecondary students roughly a 1,500-word essay. The basic approach, the subject position offered by the assignment and adopted by the student, and the structure and the strategies do not dramatically change.

One indication of the French attitude that "by now, they should have gotten it" at the *lycée*-university level is the lack of research attention to student writing at the upper levels. Ropé reports that most studies of student texts focus on earlier years of schooling, with recent attention being paid to the *collège* years. This research focuses on the teaching of grammar, language acquisition, and textual strategies for coherence and topical elaboration. The scholarship about writing in education journals focuses on teacher training or on the finite issues of student difficulties with the cognitive phases of writing, most frequently as they relate to forms of creative writing (83–86).

An analysis of the *lycée*-to-university progression in writing must begin with the writing instruction that takes place before the *lycée*.

What Gets Taught in the Pre-Lycée Years?

In French culture, writing is tied to the act of handwriting. The continued use of fountain pens, the resistance to computer-written essays, the emphasis on penmanship, even the handwriting analysis frequently required in the hiring process, are signified in the term for student writers: *apprenti-scripteur*—apprentice (hand)writers. From the time French students learn to write, they are writing "something": a story, a summary, a response, a *dictée*. Bucheton points out that in the elementary grades, French teachers need to work with the ways in which the knowledge and culture of schooling interact with the "already-there," that is, the students' relationship with writing already constructed by their experience—a relationship rooted in the social and familial and in early schooling (Bucheton 159–60). First the focus is on *dictées* and on stories told orally to the teacher, who transcribes them. Students also write short narratives and short fiction stories, describe the rules of a game, summarize short texts, rewrite texts from one genre to another (a letter becomes a poster, for example), and revise drafts of their work. Already in the primary grades there is heavy emphasis on the reading-writing connection and on the study of "text" and text construction as the primary way to learn to write. Students are also encouraged to write for pleasure; the "playful" quality of assignments is noticeable.

In the fifth- to third-grade years, emphasis shifts to the *devoir d'idées* or *rédaction*, the first written work requiring development of an argument or a thesis. Students continue to work with narrative and storytelling, but these forms are gradually phased out in favor of the more "intellectually rigorous" work of the *rédaction*. The underlying cognitive assumption is one Americans would recognize: students can learn the subjective expression favored in narrative and storytelling, but they must be pushed toward the more complex tasks of persuasive or informative texts. Throughout their schooling up to the *lycée*, students complete texts with gaps, work with one or two sentence-level elements concurrently, and are drilled in spelling and grammar—*orthographe*. In French, spelling is actually much more a morphological-grammatical issue than it is in English.

Clearly, the view of language learning as a parts-to-whole process accounts for the sentence-to-paragraph-to-full-text approach in French language pedagogy. Reuter relates "progress" in writing to reduction in errors, and glides over the fact that a focus on grammar is not a focus on teaching text construction. And yet current research in pedagogy, particularly with respect to teaching academic argument and critical thinking, questions this very approach. Alain Boissinot, tracing the history of rhetoric in the French classroom, points out that this linear progression from small units to large units is neither effective nor productive. In France the filtering of theory into practice is slowed by the added layer of the *Instructions Officielles*, whose authors are slow to respond to research in language and writing pedagogy.

Given the antiselective, egalitarian ideology underlying French schooling, teachers wait until students are in the *lycée* years to begin teaching the four essay forms students need for the BAC exam.

What Gets Taught in the Lycée Years?

In the *lycée* cycle, writing is omnipresent; students like Mayeul have spent hours writing in preparation for the BAC exam essays. Almost all testing takes the form of essay exams. These written documents are graded for content, clarity, and correctness, the features on which the BAC exams themselves will be evaluated. Teachers also frequently assign oral reports in the belief that when students prepare oral presentations, they develop the organizational and critical thinking skills necessary for oral and written communication.

Lycée students use highly formulaic forms, genres with specific conventions based on literary methods and approaches. Presenting material familiar to both students and teachers, these forms will carry students through their university first-cycle studies:

1. The *dissertation* or persuasive essay related to a reading (a subcategory is the literary essay, which literary critic Gerard Genette has called a "scholastic discourse about literary discourse"); a nonliterary example would be, "At the end of her text, Marguerite Yourcenar affirms that she gives little attention in her relationships with others to class and cultural differences. Do you think that in the world of 2002 one can easily overcome class and cultural differences? Offer a well-developed argument with examples." This is the type of essay Mayeul developed.

2. The *discussion*, a persuasive essay presenting an argument without using outside reading, generally a response to a quote; for example, "Dr. Klein has said that animals are vital to our existence. Develop an argument agreeing or disagreeing with her statement."

3. The *commentaire composé*, the infamous French close reading of a poem or an excerpt from another literary work,

generally not more than one page and always canonic—Zola, Racine, Molière, Hugo; for example, "Discuss the literary elements of humor in the excerpt of Pierre Desproges's *Superfluous Dictionary for Use by the Elite.*

4. The recently added *étude d'un texte argumentatif,* a close reading of short nonfiction excerpts that are less canonic than their literary counterparts, although authors such as Pascal or Montaigne are the most frequently used. A recent question asked students, after they had read Emile Zola's *O jeunesse,* about the Dreyfus affair: "What do you think is the great need, the great challenge facing your generation?" This form of question is becoming much more common at the *lycée* level, while the *discussion* is being relegated to third-grade studies.[13]

All four of these forms are given to students in take-home and two- to three-hour in-class versions. The final texts are three to five pages long handwritten. Most *lycée* students write often. The subjects, generally drawn from the previous year's exams, invite repetition of similar kinds of writing, so that each essay type is practiced. Students' writing experiences will begin to vary, however, after the *seconde.* They will spend more or less time on essay assignments depending on their track, and in the last year of school, French as a subject is relegated to a few hours a week because students have taken the French portion of the BAC before their last year of secondary studies.

As was clear from my analysis of a student essay, actual essays are highly structured in certain basic patterns, particularly the "thesis-antithesis-synthesis" model. Reuter points out that the dominance of this model demonstrates a lack of "textual theory" about student writing in France (54). But other models do exist, including the *commentaire composé,* which can be organized thematically or by literary strategy, and the "list" structure, wherein five or six points are made about an argument, ending with the "thesis."

Textbooks and the *Instructions Officielles* offer students other modes of organization such as the comparative or analytic mode (cause-consequence). Boissinot points out demonstrative structures, expository structures, and dialogic structures also available for textual development, even though these do not appear often in students' writing. Such disparity suggests a gap between what linguistic and pedagogical theorists support and what teachers in a rigidified school system are doing.

Essay structures come with specific methods of introduction and conclusion. For example, an *étude d'un texte argumentatif* will introduce the subject, repeat the quote or other parts of the assignment wording, and then present the problem to be addressed (usually in question form) and the "plan": "First we will consider . . . and then we will consider," as in Mayeul's essay. A *commentaire composé* will begin with a general statement contextualizing the theme, the work, the life of the author, and so forth, followed by a specific presentation of the text to be studied (title, author, genre, etc.), and then will present the "plan": the key axes of the student's analysis of the text (see Table 2).

TABLE 2. Introduction Formula According to French Writing Manuals

	Introduction to an *étude d'un texte argumentatif*	Introduction to a *commentaire composé*	Introduction to a *dissertation*
Setting up the situation	Presents the context of the argument being analyzed: situation of production, type of text	Situates the text being analyzed in a literary, artistic, or historic context	Generalizes from the *dissertation* topic to a larger theme; the approach to the subject must be progressive
Problématique	Reminds readers about the argumentative thesis of the text being analyzed; reformulates this thesis	Defines the angle or approach chosen for studying the text, evoking theme, tone, author's intentions, etc.	Rephrases all or part of the quote used as a prompt; clearly formulates the general issue raised by the topic
Announcing the plan	Announces the axes of organization in two or three questions	Proposes a series of three or four possible readings that will be verified in the development of the essay	Draws conclusions about the *problématique* while proposing two or three lines of reasoning, each of which will be a major part of the essay
Approximate length	Between 5 and 10 lines	About 15 lines	About 15 lines

Interestingly enough, U.S. studies by Nancy Sommers and Muriel Harris have pointed out that a key difference between student writers and "expert" writers in U.S. writing is the experts' primary objective of finding form, or structure, for their ideas—a framework. Their second priority tends to be finding recognizable transitions, ways to "resolve dissonance" for their imagined readers. So in fact French students are learning at least some of the strategies that U.S. expert writers report as most useful. At the *lycée* level, however, these structures and forms are often fairly empty. In the student essays I read, the form often seemed more important than the development of ideas.

Intertextuality (in its simplest sense of reference to other texts) is almost always restricted to a list from the *Instructions Officielles*. The 1998 *Instructions* include, for example:

> Authors from the sixteenth and seventeenth centuries: Montaigne, Pascal, Corneille, Molière, Racine; from the nineteenth century, a novel by Balzac, Chateaubriand, Flaubert, Gautier, Hugo, Maupassant, Merimée, Nerval, Nodier, Stendhal, or Zola; poetry from the sixteenth, the nineteenth, and the twentieth century, and perhaps a few works from a selected list of twentieth-century authors such as Cocteau, Anouilh, Gide, Giono, Ionesco, Malraux, Pérec, Saint-Exupéry, and Vercors. (Ministère de l'Education Nationale 25–26)

Students use texts outside of such lists cautiously, always keeping in mind what BAC exam readers might find acceptable. They are not encouraged to displace the language of the literary texts they read, but instead to explain, honor, and exploit the value of those texts. When they quote from the texts, it is to underscore the value of the original thought. This focus on the literary appears in other school systems explored in this collection, such as the appreciation and close reading commentary Li describes for Chinese students (Chapter 1), for example, and the English focus on the literary text as described by Scott (Chapter 2). Work with nonliterary texts, on the other hand, invites more of the *reprise-modification* found in Mayeul's essay: the paraphrases, often without citation, and the commonplaces are typical of a French student's response to an argumentative text. Even the assignment invites modification of the ideas presented in the initial text prompt, explicitly asking the student to interpret de Rosnay's point of view and then to work with it (is it feasible? is it desirable?).

Although *reprise-modification* is a subjective act—an appropriation of academic texts—student essays are not supposed to be "subjective," which was clear from Mayeul's avoidance of personal examples. (My analyses, however, have shown some non-normed uses of "I" creeping into students' essays that are *not* actually discouraged by the *Instructions Officielles*.) The prohibition against using "I" seems to have developed as a generally accepted convention without clearly traceable roots. The rules against using "I" are specifically spelled out in textbooks, along with warnings about using personal examples. One textbook says, "the personal example is only a particular case which can not be generalized." This source goes on to propose that "concrete non-personal examples of particular situations" have the advantage of being precise, real, and irrefutable (!), that statistics as argumentative support give "rigor to the demonstration," and that cultural signifiers such as history, literature, and the arts are "the reflection of rich and varied human experiences, constituting a quasi-infinite reservoir of examples related to every academic domain" (Crépin, Desaint Ghislain, and Pouzalgues-Daman 195). On the other hand, the first-person pronoun "we" (which might seem to be quite personal or at least subjective to U.S. writers and readers) is ubiquitous. Mayeul's frequent use of "we" is typical of French student essays.

Literary studies, literary texts, and even literary examples in non-literature-related essays are the citations examiners most value. Reuter attributes this to French history; as of the 1800s, literary texts became a primary way for schools to develop French nationalism, and such texts remain integrally identified with French culture and values (54). Multiple studies in France have shown not only that literary studies are preferred by French teachers, whose degrees are almost always in French literature, but also that when these teachers grade BAC exams, they systematically give higher grades to students who choose the literature questions over the nonliterature questions (Armand 68)—a preference not unlike that reflected in U.S. English department schisms between rhetoric and poetics. A recent study of student teachers preparing to begin *lycée* careers in teaching French revealed that these students chose the field because they loved literature. Many reported feeling underprepared to teach anything about language and, in particular, about writing (Elalouf 64).

In contrast, most research on language, reading, and writing is located in the *sciences de l'education* and *sciences du langage* departments of major universities. The competitive exams for teachers include a section on stylistics, generally considered part of the linguistics field. Although some linguistics analysis is included in French literature courses, the most popular approaches are thematic (studying the intent of the author) and sociohistoric (studying the codes, norms, and ideologies of periods and contexts). This focus explains the heavy emphasis on similar topics in *lycée* courses (Ropé 42–43).

The impact of structuralism on current French language pedagogy is a complex matter. Structuralist linguistics is considered the French department's heritage, the visible and transmissible subject matter; it has become the disciplinary paradigm (Chiss and Puech 6). This influence is visible in the focus in the early grades on teaching grammar and sentence construction as the foundation of effective composition. At its inception, structuralist analysis set itself in opposition to the belles lettres approach, against bourgeois notions of "taste" and "the beautiful." The structuralist approach was appropriated as a means of resisting dominant cultural ideology, thus offering all students, regardless of background, the tools for textual analysis (Ropé 46). This view still underlies writing about literature in the French *lycée* today, shaping analyses of argumentative texts even though the structuralist approach is no longer taught at the university level to aspiring teachers.

French pedagogy also emphasizes the concept of "argument." In fact, the emphasis on "argument" seems to be particularly European, as we can see from its role in England and in Germany (see Chapters 2 and 4, respectively). Teachers emphasize expressing an opinion as an important form of argument, but clearly they seek personalized response without "uninformed personal opinion" (Chapter 2, p. 98). In their years of study leading up to the *Abitur*, German students are drilled in question-response patterns that are based on supported interpretation and argumentation; teachers play devil's advocate and encourage students to see issues from multiple perspectives (see Chapter 4). French theorists specifically construct other versions of argument as a formal proof or formal reasoning, or in terms of Toulmin logic, Chaim Perelman's new rhetorical strategies, or Grize's natural logic. The "opinion" argument, as constructed by textbooks and teachers, is personal; textbooks generally affirm that subjective opinion can be separated from objective argument. According to the textbooks, an essay presenting an opinion uses various techniques in order to manifest the presence of the author—direct address to the readers, adjectives that express approval or disapproval, and other expressions of degree of conviction ("doubtless," "perhaps," "certainly"). This type of essay was the most frequently used approach in the student essays I studied. It is also the only essay form about which any discussion of intended audience occurs. The other essay forms seem to presume an audience of the exam reader, who French students are told to imagine as "the indeterminate reader who is at least of average competence and for whom the student is at least a partly interchangeable writer" (François).

The textbooks also present the "true" argumentative text as that which is developed on the basis of "argument techniques," which consist largely of acceptable examples and logical connectors that create argument patterns (see Table 3). Of course, U.S. students will find these persuasive strategies as familiar as do French students, but the strategies seem more important than the logic itself in some French student essays. Other coherence techniques, such as the use of linear progression (and then . . . and then . . .) for creating patterns of coherence, do not occur in French students' argumentative texts. This might be partly because the use of "I" is strictly reserved for introductory or concluding formulae (In this essay, I will . . .), making narrative structures that often rely on "I" more difficult to use. This might also be related to the more emphatic separation in the French classroom of argumentative and narrative genres.

Boissinot explores this issue in his extensive treatise on teaching argument, *Textes Argumentatifs*. He maintains that the narrative-to-argumentative progression underlying the French school system's understanding of student writing development is based on an erroneous assumption that children must learn to tell stories before they begin to develop arguments. Boissinot, arguing that this progression is unsupported by research, outlines what is taught to French students (see Table 4). While teachers might expect students in the higher grades to mix these genres, French students will generally try to achieve the pure genre.

Another intriguing feature of French students' writing is the formatting of their essays, as Mayeul's essay demonstrated. Essay structure is evident simply by looking at the essay's spatial organization on the page. The introduction and conclusion are separated from the rest of the text by a double space; the "hinge" sentence in the middle of the essay (for example, when an essay shifts from thesis to antithesis) is set off by double spacing; and the main paragraphs are not subdivided but rather segmented by *alinéas:* at each new idea in a paragraph, the student returns to a new line, giving the paragraphs a jagged right edge. These formatting elements demonstrate the understanding of "flow" underlying

TABLE 3. Textbook Presentations of Logical Relationships, Logical Connectors, and Functions

Logical relationship	Logical connectors	Function
Addition or gradation	and, plus, in addition, first, then, finally, not only, but even more . . .	Adds an argument or an example
Parallel or comparison	in the same way, just as, even as . . .	Establishes a relationship between two facts
Concession	even though, doubtless, in spite of, although . . .	Observes facts or arguments opposed to the thesis while maintaining one's own opinion
Opposition	but, on the contrary, on the other hand, however, even if, even so . . .	Opposes two facts or arguments to foreground one of them
Cause	because, in fact, given that, on the pretext that . . .	Allows development of the origin or reason behind a fact
Consequence	so, therefore, from that, from that point on, so that . . .	Allows a statement of result, the outcome of a fact or an idea

French writing practice. As in the student essays, these formal techniques carry directly over to university written work; there is little rupture between the two cycles, contrary to the clear differences reported for every other country discussed in this collection. In fact, the university writings examined for this study reveal most of the same techniques used by *lycée* students. The primary differences are in topic, length, and frequency of explicit connectors.

What actual methods do teachers use to help students develop these techniques? Given that French students write often, the French system certainly shares the U.S. composition philosophy, "the more you write, the better you get." But it does so without focusing on the U.S. principle that "the more you revise, the better your essay will be." The individual essays students write, as described earlier, are not developed through revision, editing, or drafting. Students might prepare the essay's all-important organization in class with the teacher and discuss in class different ways to develop the subject. Peer collaboration and review have become essential in the earlier grades, but they are not part of the writing culture at the *lycée* level and are unheard of at the university level. Drafts for teacher review and feedback are not assigned. Occasionally at the *lycée* level a teacher might ask students to review their work for grammar errors, and the rare teacher actually asks students to correct and revise already-graded essays in hopes that future essays will improve (Morand-Fehr). Another common activity is to present both good examples and poor examples of essays from the class after they have been graded. A frequent *lycée*/university activity is to provide a *corrigé* for the assignment, a step-by-step breakdown of what students should have done to successfully answer the question.

TABLE 4. Narrative/Argument Distinction Taught to French Students (Boissinot 36–37)

Narrative essay structure:
initial state→transformation→final state
Argumentative essay structure:
thesis the reader doesn't accept→argument process→thesis the reader is moved to

Reuter's summary of French instructional strategies is helpful:

◆ writing is taught by using student papers as examples of the best and worst approaches to a given assignment;

◆ writing is taught by imitation-osmosis, without technical, precise analysis, and without necessarily linking the subject of a lesson about writing to actual difficulties encountered by students;

◆ writing is taught by returning to the "same" assignment-type more than once at regular intervals, and often a return to the same organizational approach to the assignment. (Reuter 18; trans.)

These approaches help French students learn a variety of school-based genres, whereas U.S. students who revise single essays tend to learn one paper or genre at a time. Even U.S. research has been inconclusive about the value of revision (see, for example, research by Muriel Harris and Linda Flower and John Hayes); the lack of a "culture of revision" in French pedagogy is not necessarily an impediment to students' development as writers.

Indeed, in the French approach there is an openness to the work of prewriting before and during the act of "putting into words" one's ideas. Witte calls this the writer's "pre-text," the mental construction of the text prior to transcription. He points out that "a writer's linguistic representation of the intended meaning . . . [is sometimes] manipulated mentally" (qtd. in Harris 97) and can actually approximate written prose. So the question might be, is the process of making meaning tied to "putting into writing" or to "putting into words"? Two things facilitate mental work in the French classroom: the extended discussions prior to writing assignments and the repetition of writing assignment forms. Even in preschool activities students practice a form of pre-texting, as students not yet able to write tell their stories to teachers, who transcribe them.

What French teachers and the *Instructions Officielles* call "teaching writing" more often relates to reading and understanding text construction. Although French writing tasks may sound composition oriented ("teaching students to develop and write a comparison essay"), the tasks themselves are clearly reading based.

Reuter, for example, proposes a unit on writing that involves "collecting and analyzing texts, classifying types of texts, identifying texts which don't belong to a group, giving students texts with sequences out of order and asking them to reestablish the order," and so on (123). In textbooks studied for this project, however, chapter exercises required students to identify strategies such as exemplification, writing an introduction, or developing an argument in a given text, rather than having them produce their own writing. One *lycée* textbook asked students to identify examples used in various excerpts, then "write a paragraph discussing the examples used by Taine to show the double characteristic of the fantasy author: observer of men and observer of animals." In another example, a *collège* teacher's sequence of activities in teaching story writing involved three hour-long classes, focused first on identifying the elements of narrative texts and reordering parts of a narrative that had been mixed up. The final assignment, with no other preparation, was to write a short narrative.

Because the structure of most assigned school essays is already in place, students and teachers focus more on the development of individual ideas and arguments. The essay forms and development plans are so conventional that once the correct form is chosen, what remains is for students to develop their points within that structure, especially examples. Isabelle Delcambre, one of the few researchers to focus on *lycée* students' writing, has argued that in French students' essays, the example *is* the argument. The *lycée* student texts I have read in France have almost all been constructed within each paragraph by alternating claims and examples.

To summarize, the techniques and strategies students learn during their *lycée* studies:

♦ are primarily designed to help them analyze and understand text construction

♦ focus on preestablished forms and structures, connectors, and other specific coherence cues

♦ build a sense of argument as a movement between pros and cons (on the one hand, on the other hand) developed as a series of claims, each supported with an example (preferably literary; rarely personal)

◆ encourage a close relationship between the text read for the assignment, the wording of the assignment, and the student's written response

What Is Taught at the University Level?

As in Mayeul's text, university-level student essays use the same strategies as school essays: multiple connectors and other explicit coherence devices, formulaic structures, and an impersonal tone. The quantitative analysis done for this study showed that university essays tend to use more examples and be less dependent on the mechanical or superficial use of connectors. But this shift in depth is not specifically taught, leaving us to wonder: Does it occur simply because the better students have self-selected to continue their studies? Or because the course content is more detailed and more challenging, and so the students' essays reflect that development? Nothing in the French literature or the discussions I've had with university-level instructors appears to explain the shift.

Generally speaking, the forms students are taught at the *lycée* level are the forms expected to carry them through their first cycle of university studies, the undergraduate level leading to a *Diplôme d'etudes universitaires generales* and then the *Licence*, which is equivalent to the U.S. bachelor's degree. Of the four *lycée* forms, the *dissertation* and, to a lesser degree, the *commentaire composé* or other close-reading task will be the two dominant university writing forms. Marie-Christine Pollet and Jean-Maurice Rosier report that in the university tradition the implied expectation for student writing has been either to "do the same thing [as in the *lycée*] but better," or to "present roughly the same material as in the secondary cycle but in postsecondary form" (65). In Mayeul's essay, for example, the interaction with an imagined reader, his twist on the assignment, and his hypothetical examples are all elements more likely to appear in a university essay than in a *lycée* essay.

Students write in all of their university courses, although they often do not do extended, independent, or research-based writing until the *licence* cycle or perhaps the *maîtrise*, in contrast to the practice in Germany (Chapter 4) or in South Africa (Chapter

6). There is an implicit continuity not only from secondary to postsecondary studies but also between the generalized "academy" and specific disciplines, at least for the first years of university study. Highly specialized discourse is reserved for *maîtrise* and *doctorat* levels.

Students average two or three take-home assignments and two or three essay exam sessions per semester. The take-home papers jump in length, from the *lycée* average of three to six pages to the university length of five to eight pages, still handwritten. The essay exams are substantial and demanding. The exams are blind; all of the students in various sections of a given course report to exam amphitheaters, and students' names are often not on the actual exams. Most sessions last two to four hours, and students work on only one or two questions in that time, synthesizing material learned in a course into a coherent whole focused on a particular aspect. Here are examples of questions in three disciplines:

- *Culture générale:* "Can I blame the uncertainty of the future for my own lack of responsibility?"

- French: "Discuss the epic characteristics of Fenelon's *Telemaque.*"

- History: "Taking into account the inheritance of the first twenty years of [the twentieth] century, analyze the social, demographic, and cultural transformations which have affected French society since 1945 and show the limits of those transformations."

As different as these questions might seem in terms of content, the questions all invite a structured response that will include an introductory overview, organization in either a list or "on the one hand/on the other hand" structure, and a conclusion presenting the student's thesis.

Even the exam for prospective French teachers well advanced in their university studies is based on the formula developed in the *lycée* years. Ropé describes its components as strictly rule based:

The material presentation has its rules: distinguish clearly with white spaces the parts of the essay, and the paragraphs by *alinéas*; underline the titles; make no spelling mistakes. The

> rules of composition are equally strict: the introduction is decisive; after the preamble, it reproduces the quote proposed in the assignment, situates it in its context, analyzes the key words to lead to a problematization which proposes a plan of reflection about the topic. The essay's development must not be a catalogue of ideas but a thorough analysis of examples to elucidate the *dissertation*'s main point. The conclusion must tie everything together, present the thesis, respond directly to the question of the assignment. (97–98)

These rules, identical to those for *lycée* essay writing, are based on the traditional rhetorical view that such a framework does not constrain thoughts but helps in the development of their expression.

As writers at the university, students are expected to continue using the forms, structures, and devices (e.g., transition words, introductory patterns) learned for *lycée*, but to "fill" those forms with more detailed and sophisticated content from course material and readings. The university-level papers in this study were generally more detailed than the *lycée* papers, with more examples related to class discussion and readings. These essays used more explicit connectors than *lycée* essays (about 49 per 1,000 words rather than 34), and these devices were far more likely to support substantive connections rather than "stand in" for such connections. University essays also had a subtle self-assurance, a feel of taking on the academic subject position expected of them.

But none of these developments can be attributed to any teaching being done at the university level. Students seem to exploit *lycée* forms and strategies for university writing tasks without any explicit instruction or teacher feedback. Perhaps this development can be attributed to self-selection; the better students, ones who had already mastered the *lycée* forms with some sophistication, have gone on to college, so the better students are writing university-level papers. But that seems too simple. Perhaps the more challenging nature of the course content itself calls for more sophisticated thinking on the students' part, allowing them to use earlier structures in new, more sophisticated ways. If that is the case, French pedagogy becomes even more intriguing for U.S. theorists and practitioners. Until more research is done, and until more investigation into both writing pedagogy and student success are explored at the university level, this element of students' development as writers will remain elusive.

A recent issue of *Le Français Aujourd'hui,* dedicated entirely to teaching French in the universities, shows that French scholarship and practice in teaching writing are poised to develop rapidly in the next few years. A volume of the research journal *Spirale* to be published in 2002 will be dedicated to "teaching reading and writing at the university level." The diversity of subjects in the articles each journal presents points to the underdeveloped scholarship, as does the fact that these are the first journals to develop the topic. One of the authors, Danièle Manesse, summarizes the issue: "the university is getting its turn at being confronted, after the *collège* and the *lycée,* by situations which simply are not under control: what to teach, how, and in what ways to such a diverse public" (97). In another article, Pollet and Rosier criticize the intense grading focus on language errors, the classroom focus on exercises in which students simply write to write, and the lack of work on conceptualizing how to help students (66).

Teacher-Training Complications

The writing skills students actually develop sometimes seem to conflict with the pedagogy governing writing instruction, while the assumptions underlying student writing tasks sometimes seem at odds with the ways writing is actually taught. French writing pedagogy at all levels is complicated by various pedagogical theories and their underlying linguistic or literary assumptions, creating conflicts in the ways teacher training is framed that are exacerbated by the lack of interaction between teachers and researchers.

French *lycée* and university teachers receive relatively haphazard training, particularly with respect to teaching language skills, before they begin teaching (Elalouf 5); much as Mary Muchiri points out for Kenyan teachers (Chapter 5), French teachers receive almost no pedagogical training in or theory about teaching writing. As much as the preuniversity cycles are centralized and uniform, the postsecondary cycles are highly individualized depending on the expertise of given professors and the interests of the particular university (Ropé 9). This is true for teacher preparation but also for the curriculum of any major in the general university system. French secondary and postsecondary teachers are thus preparing students for standardized exams without having received a standardized preparation for teaching and without having received a standardized preparation in the subject matter they will teach. In fact, the only true standardization factor is—not surprisingly—the national qualifying exam at the end of their teacher-training studies (the CAPES). The *annales* that come out each year, books with the previous year's questions, strategies for responding, and *corrigés,* become the quasi-official guide for classroom activities (Ropé 19; Plane). This reliance on *corrigés* and *annales* becomes in turn the method for teaching *lycée* students to write for the BAC. The *annales* for the BAC come out every fall and are studiously worked through, again and again, by students in *seconde* and *première.* The implication appears to be that teachers who are certified by passing exams, regardless of the lack of standardized preparation, will be able to teach students to prepare for exams.[14]

Universities offering the programs that future writing teachers are likely to take, the *sciences de l'education* (education), *sciences du langage* (linguistics), or *lettres* (literature) majors, build these programs based on the interests of the professors who teach them (Plane). In the 1970s, there was a strong link between the work of linguists and writing pedagogy, but several recent studies have shown that most future French teachers choose the *lettres* major, and so they study primarily literary texts and take a smattering of linguistics courses that haphazardly cover linguistics principles that might be helpful to their teaching, courses such as generative grammar, functional linguistics, textual grammar, or psycholinguistics with an emphasis on the cognitive processes involved in learning to read and write (Ropé 12). These four areas are the same areas in which the bulk of linguistics research related to writing takes place. As a result, the majority of French teachers equate teaching writing with teaching correct grammar and expression. And yet student teachers avoid "pure" linguistics courses to fulfill their core requirements, and few do their thesis on language-related issues (Elalouf 5–6). French writing teachers are rarely trained linguists from *sciences du langage* programs.

The same study shows that most beginning French *lycée* teachers choose the works they will cover from the *Instructions Officielles* based on the texts they studied themselves at the university, and most do not see much connection between the linguistics courses they took and the writing they teach (Elalouf 9). Linguistics and literature do not share departments in French universities, and because French university cycles are so quickly specialized, students focus on only their own majors. In addition, because students are not offered writing courses at the university level, most will end up teaching writing to their students from a distance of five to six years since the last time they took a writing course themselves. This might explain why 35 percent of them report feeling unprepared to teach language-related skills and, specifically, writing (Elalouf 71). In fact, many report being uneasy with writing themselves (Ropé 27; Plane).

Conclusion

Much of what has been presented here might seem to render the French education system vulnerable to what I call "composition theory colonization," the urge to begin exporting U.S. theories and methods to an apparently writing-theory-impoverished country. In fact, every system explored in this collection seems to invite intervention. Each country is at a point of self-aware critique, a turning point of sorts toward inventing new strategies and new practices to address the needs identified. Consider, for example, the gap described by Scott in Chapter 2 between preuniversity writing that asks for students to imagine themselves, their subjectivities, in one way, and university writing that calls on a different way of imagining personal response and argument. The nature of the shift to university approaches that "perceive and unsettle" assumptions clearly calls for theorizing. The modernization Li describes in Chapter 1 as driving Chinese universities' pedagogy and the dissatisfaction expressed by students seem to indicate that voices from composition theory might be more easily heard now than in the past in China. Shared problems with plagiarism and paraphrase—with students' understanding of what "original" might mean and how each student might claim the authority to speak in balance with the multiple voices already present—suggest that French and South African universities might benefit from extensive research into practices related to teaching students to read difficult texts and to write about them. "Let them read Bartholomae," we might say. And the apparently undersupported German students Foster describes in Chapter 4 would seem to be prime targets for writing workshops and writing-in-the-disciplines courses as they enter the sophisticated discourse communities of their fields; they also seem caught in a struggle to negotiate between their own authority and the authorities of the already-spoken, the rich intellectual traditions they have inherited. Yet merely to advocate U.S. pedagogical solutions for each of these challenges would be to ignore the complex institutional, cultural, and sociohistorical traditions that require their own sets of responses, their own applications of theoretical perspectives, and their own pedagogical innovations.

The French approach does indeed have problems and weaknesses; change is necessary. Bucheton points out that students graduate from *lycée* programs knowing how to write but with poor writing "self-images." They don't see themselves as subject-writers (160). The nature of the various exams students must pass in order to gain increasingly specialized passage to new academic levels clearly restricts the degree to which pedagogical innovation can take place. The political issues influencing school discourses, instruction, and students' assimilation into school culture are not likely to be resolved quickly, nor by importing other cultural perspectives.

French students seem comfortable with decisions about structure, flow, coherence, and appropriation of texts they read, and they understand how to develop a thesis, make a balanced presentation of perspectives, and develop persuasive examples. But they seem uncomfortable with connections to personal experience, narrative structures, and departures from formulaic approaches; they are far less likely to develop a strong opinion or provide evidence from outside the preestablished school or course parameters.

These tendencies seem contrary to the U.S. move away from the teaching of modes and forms in the past twenty years. Yet there are clear benefits to students' growth as writers in the French system. Expert writers generally focus on structure as a way into their topics, and the availability of explicitly taught forms frees students and teachers for exploration of topical content. In particular, students working through a series of written exams need to manage structures so as to respond explicitly and speedily to exam questions. Within such a system, the art of one-draft writing must be mastered. The focus on four essay types allows students to learn a different kind of revision, a progressive mastery of a given approach to an essay.

Major challenges facing the development of writing pedagogy in France are the lack of collaboration among the researchers and those planning the teacher-training curriculum, the content of the competitive exams, and the *Instructions Officielles* for *lycée* courses. Researchers in linguistics, education, and other language-related areas have proposed new approaches to teaching, including new methods and philosophies, but these innovations often are not appropriate for the rigid structures imposed by *lycée* curricula. Ropé cites teachers who "deplore the fact that they can not adjust their teaching based on recent scholarship, as they are held to traditional methods by the need to prepare students for the exams" (49). Universities that prepare teachers keep their students isolated in the areas of research their individual professors pursue; the exams dictate the content of at least part of students' programs at every level; the *Instructions Officielles* seem to ignore new teaching theories and the practical problems of day-to-day teaching, and so on. But the mere mention of reforming the exam (or eliminating it) brings out vitriolic responses, with would-be reformers accused of attacking the very core of national values.

My review of current composition theory in France shows a country poised to develop new methods and approaches rapidly in the next decade. Some developments have already been taking hold during the past ten or twenty years. One of the most pervasive U.S. influences has been the work of Flower and Hayes. First introduced in France by Claudine Garcia-Debanc (cited in Reuter 39–40), the cognitive model Flower and Hayes propose has been extensively applied (and often misapplied) to teaching writing in the earlier grades. As surprising as it may seem to Americans, much of the current process movement in France grew out of this work.

Another sweeping development in recent years has been the *atelier d'écriture*, the writing workshop. This development is widely attributed to U.S. teaching styles. In fact, when I tell people in France that I am an American writing instructor, they generally assume I teach this type of workshop. But the *atelier* is a creative writing workshop designed to "unblock" adult writers' inner creativity and abilities and to help them "play" with language. In fact, most *ateliers* have as a goal to get adult writers back in touch with the pleasure of writing, a pleasure that the *collège* and *lycée* years are often said to have stamped out.

At the *collège* level, more and more researchers and teachers are experimenting with the personal narrative, most often in the form of autobiography. The pedagogical journal *Cahiers Pédagogiques* recently dedicated an entire issue to personal/narrative writing, tangling with many of the same issues we face: Is it appropriate? Is it easier or harder to learn than other types of writing? Does it unfairly place students in compromising situations? and so on. Unfortunately, noticeably absent from the issue was any discussion of how personal narrative might or might not help students write for the BAC, one of the major unresolved issues in French scholarship.

Another innovation was a movement toward group work in some classrooms, shifting the emphasis from teaching to learning, to understanding how knowledge is being constructed. According to Reuter, this shift, designed to target students having trouble with the traditional modes of learning, allowed them to learn by doing, to work on written projects that did not have the usual predesigned contents and parameters (27). The group project movement did not become widespread, however. Its benefits included attention to the students and their modes of learning, an openness to the writing process and revision, and the opportunity to consider new theoretical frameworks. But for the French system, the limitations often outweighed the benefits. It was found most useful for developing longer written texts, but this isn't practical "for younger students who don't yet have the necessary writing skills, nor for *lycée* students because they need to focus on preparing for the national exams" (Reuter 28). In addition, teachers felt it restricted the variety of texts students might write because group projects slowed down students' writing process. Finally, and perhaps most interesting for our purposes, Reuter feels that leading group/process projects with students requires "a very high level of teacher ability, not only in terms of pedagogy but in terms of the problems he must be able to predict, without *preprogrammation*" (28). I believe that Reuter is correct, and that this is the same problem many U.S. high school and university teachers face when they first begin to teach more open-ended approaches to writing.

How might French teachers and researchers begin to effect the changes that will work for them? Among other influences, the strong linguistic tradition in French scholarship and pedagogy needs to find its own bearings, discover its own interdisciplinary connections leading to new pedagogies and practices. This movement is already in process; entrenched theoretical camps have begun to communicate with one another. Reuter has pointed out the need for research methods focusing on student writing development in the French educational system. Barré-de Miniac calls for the same interdisciplinary work in her pluridisciplinary exploration of various composition teaching practices. I believe that in the next few years several new programs might develop, including writing workshops for graduate students, addressing student needs within the current framework. French students are learning and growing as writers beyond the *collège* years, and without the kinds of explicit instruction Americans deem necessary. Indeed, as rigid as the notion of codified forms of writing appears to U.S. readers (on the assumption that this approach stifles students' adaptability as writers), most French students I have worked with in the U.S. university system have little trouble adapting to U.S. writing forms, with two notable exceptions: they seem very uncomfortable with the use of personal examples, and they resist putting their thesis statement anywhere near the beginning of their work. It is precisely these specifically cultural phenomena that show us that what we choose to teach, and how, is a value judgment—that writing development and pedagogy are always specific to particular learning cultures and their attendant conventions. They serve as initiations into "our" academic communities, not "the" academic community.

Notes

1. As this book goes to press, radical changes in the forms of school writing are being implemented in France, including the elimination of the *étude d'un texte argumentatif* and the *discussion,* leaving three forms: the *sujet de commentaire,* the *sujet de dissertation,* and a completely new creative form, the *sujet d'invention.* These changes have been implemented for the 2002 *baccalauréat.*

2. French students who choose to exit the system at age sixteen, ending their formal schooling with the *collège* years, receive a preliminary diploma after passing an exam. Students are in fact guaranteed the right to stay in school until they earn the lowest exam diploma, the pre-*lycée* vocational certificates: the Certificat d'aptitude professionnelle (CAP) or the Brevet d'études professionnelles (BEP) (Ballion 24). The students who continue for three more years will finish with the week-long interdisciplinary *baccalauréat* exam (the BAC).

3. Students can actually register for their first university year of study and courses during their *terminale* year in high school, and a slot is held for them pending BAC results (Morand-Fehr). The students are theoretically free to choose their majors as long as there are sufficient slots. But this apparent freedom is also limited. Students are geographically limited in their school choice, and most schools offer only some majors, effectively eliminating freedom of choice for many.

4. The few reforms over the past twenty years have been largely in response to changing demographics and a huge increase in the number of students attending school through the end of the *lycée* cycle: from 1960 to 1991, the number of students in the secondary cycle went from 800,000 to 2,300,000, tripling in those thirty years (Vasconcellos 53). In late 1950, 10 percent of the adolescents at the eligible age actually took the BAC exam; by 1988, 58 percent took it (Vasconcellos 54). The success rate of those taking the exam in the 1950s was only about 23 percent, but in 1997 it reached 79 percent. These increases are due partly to immigration but largely to a change in perception about job-based needs for a diploma and about students' right to higher education, and they are further complicated by racial tensions and political motivations.

5. I know of only one university that has begun to offer first-year support services to its students: the Centre du perfectionnement en langue française at the Université Libre de Briuxelles.

6. These years are called *khagne* and *hypohkagne*, for humanities students, *taupe* and *hypotaupe* for math/science students.

7. Indeed, far less than *one percent* of a graduating class actually makes it to the Grandes Ecoles. The other *prépa* students are generally granted credit toward a regular first-cycle university degree called a *licence,* the equivalent of our B.A. (Cusin-Berche). According to the National Center for Education Statistics, of the 39,000 students who choose this route annually—roughly 8 percent of a given graduating class—only a few are admitted. Based on my calculations from posted exam results in 1997, for example, only approximately 6 percent of the students who took the entrance exam for the four "Ecoles Normales Supérieures," prestigious schools for students who wish to become university professors or government researchers, were admitted.

8. This examination is called the CAPES exam (Certificat d'Aptitude au Professorat de l'Enseignement du Second Degré).

9. And yet attitudes are changing. In the last year alone, several new studies have been launched related to the reading/writing issue at the postsecondary level, and several researchers have focused on the various genres produced by *lycée* students.

10. The exceptions to this would be for (1) the students entering the Grandes Ecoles, for whom the notion of entering a new elite community is actually foregrounded during the post-BAC period, and who are initiated specifically, in the two years of preparatory study, into the different kinds of writing that will be expected of them, and (2) the students in technical postsecondary classes, who are explicitly initiated into technical communication in some programs.

11. The French *on* is actually not equivalent to the English *one. On* is specific to French, a "polyphonic person par excellence," because it can stand for any pronoun. The key is to be able to decipher whether, and to what degree, the speaker is included in the statement (Auricchio, Masseron, and Perrin-Schirmer 27).

12. I am using *commonplace* here as defined by David Bartholomae, "a culturally or institutionally authorized concept or statement that carries with it its own necessary elaboration" ("Inventing" 17).

13. In the past seven years, these forms have undergone more change than in the previous twenty. The *dissertation* is currently under fire and may be eliminated in the next few years. See note 1.

14. In the last two years, this tendency has begun to change. Teachers are now required to attend classes in pedagogical theory, they are asked questions about their pedagogy on the exams, and they spend one year teaching and being observed before they are permanently awarded a post.

Works Cited

Allègre, Claude. "Arrêtons la Course aux Maths!" *Le Nouvel Observateur* 3 Sept. 1998: 75–77.

Armand, Anne. *L'Evaluation du français à l'epreuve anticipée du baccalauréat.* Rouen: CRDP, 1992.

Attali, Jacques. "Pour un modèle européen d'enseignement supérieur." *Le Monde* 9 Sept. 1998. 12 May 1998 <www.emn.fr/fran/enseignement/Attali.html>.

Auricchio, Agnès, Caroline Masseron, and Claude Perrin-Schirmer. "La polyphonie des discours argumentatifs: Propositions didactiques." *Pratiques* 73 (1992): 7–50.

Bakhtin, Mikhail. *Speech Genres and Other Late Essays.* Trans. Vern W. McGee. Austin: U of Texas P, 1986.

Balcou, Maryvette. "Les professeurs des écoles en formation initiale et l'écriture." *Repères* 16 (1997): 221–39.

Ballion, Robert. *La démocratie au lycée.* Paris: ESF, 1998.

Barré-de Miniac, Christine, ed. "L'écriture—vers un projet didactique renouvelé." *Vers une didactique de l'écriture : Pour une approche disciplinaire.* Ed. Christine Barré-de Miniac. Paris: INRP, 1996. 11–18.

Bartholomae, David. "Inventing the University." *Background Readings for Instructors Using the Bedford Handbook for Writers.* Ed. Glenn Blalock. Boston: St. Martin's, 1994. 14–26.

———. "Wanderings: Misreadings, Miswritings, Misunderstandings." *Only Connect: Uniting Reading and Writing.* Ed. Thomas Newkirk. Upper Montclair, NJ: Boynton/Cook, 1986. 89–117.

————. "Writing with Teachers: A Conversation with Peter Elbow." *Cross-Talk in Comp Theory*. Ed. Victor Villanueva. Urbana, IL: NCTE, 1997. 479–88.

Bautier, Elisabeth. *Pratiques langagières, pratiques sociales: de la sociolinguistique à la sociologic du langage*. Paris: Harmattan, 1995.

Bautier, Elisabeth, and J. Y. Rochex. "Apprendre: des malenten-dus qui font la différence." *La Scolarisation de la France: Critique de l'Etat des Lieux*. Ed. J. P. Terrail. Paris: La Dispute, 1997. 105–22.

Bialostosky, Don H. "Liberal Education, Writing, and the Dialogic Self." *Contending with Words: Composition and Rhetoric in a Postmodern Age*. Ed. Patricia Harkin and John Schilb. New York: MLA, 1991. 11–22.

Bizzell, Patricia. *Academic Discourse and Critical Consciousness*. Pittsburgh : U of Pittsburgh P, 1992.

Boissinot, Alain. *Les textes argumentatifs*. Paris: Bertrand Lacoste, 1992.

Brossard, Michel, et al. "Role du contexte dans les écrits scolaires." *Vers une didactique de l'écriture: pour une approche disciplinaire*. Ed. Christine Barré-de Miniac. Paris: INRP, 1996. 71–84.

Bucheton, Dominique. "L'Epaississement du texte par la ré-écriture." *L'Apprentissage de l'écriture de l'école au collège*. Ed. Jacques David and Sylvie Plane. Paris: PUF, 1996. 159–79.

Chartier, Anne-Marie. "La formation initiale en didactique." *Repères* 16 (1997): 162–80.

Chiss, Jean-Louis, and Christian Puech. "De l'émergence disciplinaire à la didactisation des savoirs linguistiques." *Langue Française* 117 (1998): 6–21.

Crépin, F., C. Desaint Ghislain, and E. Pouzalgues-Daman. *Français, Méthodes et Techniques*. Paris: Nathan, 1996.

Cusin-Berche, Fabienne. Personal interview. 20 Aug. 1998.

Dabène, Michel, Catherine Frier, and Michèle Visoz. "La construction du sens dans l'activité de lecture: Recherches empiriques et formation initiale des enseignants de français." *Etudes de Linguistique Appliqués* 87 (1992): 51–64.

Debouzy, Marianne. "The Americanization of the French University and the Response of the Student Movement, 1966–1986." *American Studies International* 27 (1990): 23–36.

Delcambre, Isabelle. "Enquete autour d'un objet didactique: La notion de circuit argumentatif." *Pratiques* 96 (1997): 63–79.

Elalouf, Marie-Laure, et al. *Enseigner le français: la formation linguistique des professeurs de lettres en question.* Amsterdam: Editions De Werelt, 1996.

Flower, Linda, and John R. Hayes. "A Cognitive Process Theory of Writing." *College Composition and Communication* 32 (1981): 365–87.

François, Frédéric. Personal interview. 16 Aug. 1998.

Geisler, Cheryl. *Academic Literacy and the Nature of Expertise: Reading, Writing, and Knowing in Academic Philosophy.* Hillsdale, NJ: Erlbaum, 1994.

Grize, Jean-Blaise. *Logique naturelle et communications.* Paris: PUF, 1996.

Harris, Muriel. "Composing Behaviors of One- and Multi-Draft Writers." *Background Readings for Instructors Using the Bedford Handbook for Writers.* Ed. Glenn Blalock. Boston: St. Martin's, 1994. 86–111.

Livret pédagogique du département des humanités, U.F.R. de Saint-Quentin-en-Yvelines. [Student handbook.] 1996/1997.

Manesse, Danièle. "Pour appeler á d'autres numéros sur l'enseignement du français à l'université." *Le Français Aujourd'hui* 125 (1999): 95–101.

Ministère de l'Education Nationale, Direction des lycées et collèges. *Instructions Officielles: Français, classes de second première et terminale.* Paris: CNDP, 1998.

Morand-Fehr, Christine. Personal interview. 2 Sept. 1998.

National Center for Education Statistics. *Education in States and Nations: Indicators Comparing U.S. States with Other Industrialized Countries in 1991.* Washington, DC: National Center for Education Statistics, 1996.

Perelman, Chaïm, and Lucie Olbrechts-Tyteca. *The New Rhetoric: A Treatise on Argumentation.* Trans. John Wilkinson and Purcell Weaver. Notre Dame, IN: Notre Dame UP, 1969.

Plane, Sylvie. Personal interview. 14 June 1998.

Pollet, Marie-Christine, and Jean-Maurice Rosier. "Le français à l'université: Contre le fétichisme langagier." *Le Français Aujourd'hui* 125 (1999): 64–69.

Pratt, Mary Louise. "The Arts of the Contact Zone." *Ways of Reading.* 5th ed. Ed. David Bartholomae and Anthony Petrosky. Boston: Bedford, 1999. 527–43.

Reuter, Yves. *Enseigner et apprendre à écrire.* Paris: ESF, 1996.

Reynolds, Nedra. "Composition's Imagined Geographies: The Politics of Space in the Frontier, City, and Cyberspace." *College Composition and Communication* 50 (1998): 12–35.

Ropé, Françoise. *Savoirs universitaires, savoirs scolaires.* Paris: L'Harmattan, 1994.

Russell, David R. "Rethinking Genre in School and Society: An Activity Theory Analysis." *Written Communication* 14 (1997): 504–55.

Sommers, Nancy. "Revision Strategies of Student Writers and Experienced Adult Writers." *Background Readings for Instructors Using the Bedford Handbook for Writers.* Ed. Glenn Blalock. Boston: St. Martin's, 1994. 86–94.

Starobinski, Jean. *La relation critique.* Paris: Gallimard, 1970.

Toulmin, Stephen. *The Uses of Argument.* Cambridge : Cambridge UP, 1958.

Tozzi, Michel. "Français-Philosophie: Une approche interdidactique." *Le Français Aujourd'hui* 109 (1996): 99–108.

Vasconcellos, Maria. *Le système éducatif.* Paris: Editions La Découverte, 1993.

Wall, Susan. Personal interview. 21 May 1997.

Wanner, Raymond E. *France: A Study of the Educational System of France and a Guide to the Academic Placement of Students in Educational Institutions of the United States.* Washington, DC: American Association of Collegiate Registrars and Admissions Officers, 1975.

Making the Transition to University: Student Writers in Germany

DAVID FOSTER
Drake University

A German university professor, asked whether he would be willing to permit a visitor to study his students' writing in an upper-level seminar, replied that it really "didn't make sense." After all, he said, all you have to do is look at how the system works to prepare students to write. It is a question of the proper form, he continued; students writing papers in upper-level seminars will naturally base their writing on what they have already learned about form in beginning courses. And this is taught by practice, he concluded, with each student required to write research papers beginning with the first courses they take at university.

Like this teacher, many teachers in German universities find it hard to talk about how students learn to write successfully in the university. In their perspective, writing is a fundamentally transparent activity. It cannot be discussed apart from the work of learning within students' academic disciplines. In the course of the project reported here, when I tried to explain my background as a U.S. writing teacher, I usually drew blank looks and puzzlement at first. Why are you interested in writing? Our students are students of the subject, they said, not students of writing—historians (sociologists, literary interpreters), not writers. You really want to ask how we teach our subjects, don't you? Because we don't teach writing.

This chapter explores what this might mean—how students who are not "taught" writing learn to be academic writers within the German university system. Indeed, in German universities writing is learned and practiced entirely within the disciplines, not parallel to or outside them as in the composition courses of U.S. universities. Students in this study typically majored in two or three academic fields, usually one primary and two or more secondary concentrations. Entering directly into their chosen courses of study, students are expected to plunge right in to the reading and writing of their major disciplines. Of course, much of this writing consists of taking examinations, at which students are well practiced by the time they enter university. As in the French system, examinations dominate the writing landscape in German secondary schools. The habit of writing frequent examinations culminates decisively in the secondary school leaving examination (the *Abitur*) that qualifies students for university in their chosen fields.

But when they enter their major fields at university, German students find that exam-writing abilities, though necessary, are not sufficient for success. Another, very different kind of writing is required, for which they are generally not prepared: seminar research papers. Students typically enroll in seminars in each major discipline at least once each academic year. Writing a substantial research paper is the primary task of most seminars. Researching and writing these papers, students must, as Stuart Greene suggests about U.S. students, "enter an intellectual conversation . . . [and] rethink, perhaps transform, their understanding of what it means to write in school" (189). Unlike U.S. students, however, German students must begin this conversation immediately because they enter university as majors in specific disciplines. While U.S. students begin their studies with some version of first-year composition as well as general education requirements, German students begin with a direct plunge into disciplinary study and apprenticeship. My findings in this study suggest that this pressure to begin performing as apprentice scholars/writers in disciplinary seminars creates significant dissonance for German students in the transition to university. Some academic departments offer introductory courses in the skills needed to research, develop, and write seminar papers in their disciplines. But the evidence of this study suggests that such efforts are not widespread in German universities. Of the five humanities and social science disciplines represented by students in this study, only one—political science—offers systematic introductory help to students as writers in their first semester at university. A German educator asserts that German universities are generally "silent about the process of writing academic texts. They offer no help in developing students' school preparation . . . to deal with complex academic texts at the university level" (von Werder 2).

Students must begin designing and composing research papers in several disciplines simultaneously, without passing through the buffer zone of general studies and general writing instruction offered by U.S. universities. Faced with writing papers with substantial scholarly references in the first semester, students recognize quickly that they must develop new masteries as writers. They must learn to use what I call an "incorporative rhetoric," drawing together the authoritative voices and perspectives of their disciplinary discourses. But to be successful at this, they must simultaneously learn to master other elements of their writing environment as well. The structured, teacher-centered environment of the *Gymnasium* (the academic high school leading to university) gives way in university to scattered resource networks, confusing layers of bureaucracy, and dispersed academic units. Students must learn to work within new institutional and material spaces and accommodate a new time frame—based on wide freedom and autonomy—for planning, research, and composing activities. If students are to write successfully within this new environment, they must build new habits and attitudes as writers, including an independence unknown to U.S. university students, especially the habits of self-directed, long-term goal setting for seminar study and writing.

In this study, I use the term "authority" to indicate the complex range of masteries that students need for success as writers at university. Authority has been defined in various ways in writing research. For example, it may be said to express itself through the completed student text—a successful research paper, for instance. In this perspective, a student's authority as a writer could be construed as the mastery of task interpretation, planning and composing strategies appropriate for the disciplinary discourse in which the paper participates. And indeed, most studies of students' writing development focus on texts and writing strategies. But for the students in this study, mastering the forms and processes of academic discourse is necessary, but not by itself sufficient, for success in university writing. Writing is a profoundly situated activity. The work of writing for the German students in this study is strongly shaped by complex institutional and material contexts of academic life. University writing for them requires new forms of institutional accommodation, work orientation, and self-awareness. To better account for these dimensions of writing, it is necessary to broaden the construct of writing authority to include elements beyond the mastery of discourse forms and strategies. A wider view of writing authority should include assessment of important elements of setting and environment: institutional and curricular structures; faculty-student relations; time and space configurations; resource networks; and work-family dynamics. The authority a student writer will need to develop for success in an institution should be conceived as a fluid, multilayered set of masteries that may alter with any change in one or more of the elements of the writing environment.

This essay focuses on some noteworthy elements of the authority students must develop as writers as they make the transition from *Gymnasium* to the two universities represented in this study. Using a wide range of evidence—narratives of participating students and teachers, curriculum and teaching materials, and observations of their learning/writing contexts—I describe the writing environment in *Gymnasium*, identify the difficulties students face as writers in the transition to university, outline crucial elements of the university scene of writing as these students describe it, and analyze their strategies for adapting to the challenges of this environment. By means of this analysis, I want to offer a broad, multilayered account of the construct of authority that emerges for the student writers in this study.

Authority as a Theoretical Construct

In recent studies of students' writing development, the transition from school to university is defined primarily as a matter of novices entering new discourse fields. Gaining authority as a student writer at university is represented as an apprenticeship process in which the composing and knowledge-building strategies of particular academic discourse communities must be mastered. In her study of academic literacy, Cheryl Geisler defines the nature of the authority that apprentice writers seek as "expertise" in the discourse of a particular domain or disciplinary field. To conceptualize this transition, she builds on Bereiter and Scardamalia's distinction between "knowledge-telling" in school writing and "knowledge-transformation" in academic writing at university. Because school writing is limited to knowledge-telling, she argues, students at university must learn "to negotiate three distinct worlds of discourse: the *domain content world* of logically related truths, . . . the *narrated world* of everyday experience, . . . and the *rhetorical world* of abstract authorial conversation" (240). She describes apprentice writers' problems in mastering academic discourse in terms of the difficulties they encounter negotiating these worlds: students are "caught in between" the demands of domain and rhetorical "spaces," she suggests, as they plan, write, and revise (184). Studying both school and university writing and students' behavior as writers, Geisler creates an important model and critique of the apprenticeship pattern through which U.S. students learn academic literacy.

This study and others like it define the authority of student writers primarily in terms of their discourse activities and the tasks and forms of disciplinary genres. Authority and expertise are conceived as the mastery of genres and conventions appropriate to disciplinary discourse. Some researchers, however, have tried to account for the influence of wider institutional, social, and personal conditions on students' development of writing mastery. Stuart Greene's study (1995) of the planning/writing strategies of first-year students, for example, explores students' task representations and composing strategies in a beginning university writing course. Focusing on how students construct their writing tasks, he traces in depth the "processes of composing" of two students as they "struggle with conflicting discourses . . . [and] construct their own experiences and advance their own rhetorical purposes as authors" (188–89). Greene also suggests the importance of "social, historical, and cultural contexts that influence the development of . . . rhetorical behaviors" (213), and analyzes the impact of students' ethnic and family backgrounds on their understanding of their writing tasks. These elements of apprentice writers' environments are important in assessing the forces that shape their development. But there are other elements of setting and environment that also inevitably have a role in shaping students' work as writers: for example, institutional and curricular structures; time and material space configurations; faculty-student relations; interactions with other students (in classrooms or personal encounters); as well as living environments, access to resources, and work or family dynamics that influence the work of writing.

A broad description of the authority needed by student writers must take into account the situatedness of all learning and communication. In their study of apprenticeship learning, Jean Lave and Etienne Wenger suggest that in order to understand "the whole person" within his or her environment, the inter-connections of "agent, activity, and the world" must be assessed as they "constitute each other" (33). In recent years, various approaches to the study of writing's situatedness have emerged. One such approach deriving from activity theory is invoked in genre studies. David Russell's (1997) treatment of genre through "activity theory analysis" exemplifies this approach. Drawing on Cole and Engeström's formulation of activity theory, Russell argues that writing must be studied as an element of an "activity system," an "ongoing, historically-conditioned, dialectically structured . . . human interaction" (510). Russell disallows the traditional analytic habit of separating the activities of writing from their contexts, instead viewing "context" holistically as "an ongoing accomplishment, not a container for actions or texts" (513). In Russell's view, the dancer cannot be separated from the dance: "the activity system [itself] is the basic unit of analysis" (510), so that a given behavior or text must be situated in relation to influences that shape it.

Another approach to analyzing the complex situatedness of learning/writing may be found in Paul Prior's notion of "laminations," the layered interaction of multiple activities and contexts in students' work. For students, says Prior, "activity is laminated" and "multiple activities co-exist, are immanent, in any situation" (24). "Whereas one or more of these activity footings (e.g., school learning) may be relatively foregrounded at any one time," he continues, "the background activities (e.g., of home, neighborhood, work) do not disappear" (24). "Situated explorations" of writing activity are necessary, says Prior, in order to recognize complex interconnections among the conditions and constraints of a writing environment. From this perspective, a broad definition may be inferred of the various authorities students must develop in order to write successfully in the transition to university. They must simultaneously attempt to master domain subject matter, genre discourse strategies, curricular and institutional expectations, and the time frames and material spaces of institutional environments. In this perspective, important differences in the writing situations of U.S. and German students become clear. Such differences are particularly visible in curricular and institutional structures and in the time and material spaces of their environments. The German students in this study must learn to function productively within widely dispersed academic bureaucracies (much more decentralized in German than in U.S. institutions) and negotiate the ambiguity and confusion of loosely structured reading/writing tasks in seminars, without the mediation of the general writing instruction U.S. students receive in first-year writing courses. Further, while U.S. students must negotiate specific time schedules in producing texts within semester deadlines, German students writing in seminars must learn how to research and write lengthy papers on their own after courses are over, in the time periods between academic semesters. For German students, the contrast between *Gymnasium* and university scenes of writing is sharp and sometimes disorienting. German students' previous writing experiences in the *Gymnasium* emphasized controlled, well-defined writing in supervised classroom work. The masteries necessary for students' success as autonomous writers at university differ markedly from those needed for the tightly structured work of the *Gymnasium*. These differences are the source of considerable dissonance for the German students in their transition to university. To better understand this transition, it is necessary to look first at how this study was constructed, then to examine the learning/writing cultures of the schools and universities in this study.

Methodology of This Study

The data for this study come from a sampling of students, *Gymnasium* teachers, and faculty at two universities in two distinct regions of Germany. To provide a distinct focus for this study, only students from selected humanities and social science disciplines are included. The universities represent two types of German institutions in two regions: North Rhine-Westphalia and Saxony-Anhalt. The University of Münster in North Rhine-Westphalia is a traditional university from an "old" state in the west; the University of Magdeburg in Saxony-Anhalt is a small comprehensive university (reorganized after the two Germanys reunited) from a "new" state in the east. Of course, there are hundreds of German universities, with many variations among them, so while the two universities in this study are indicative of some of this variety, they are not necessarily typical of all such institutions. There are striking similarities in the narratives of students and teachers alike, however, which suggests widely shared commonalities in the experiences of students and teachers from both regions.

The study data come from several basic sources: from students' narratives of their experiences as writers in the final years of *Gymnasium* and their first few years at university; from *Gymnasium* and some university teachers' descriptions of their goals and methods related to student writing; and from institutional and ministry documents such as curricular materials, program requirements, and policy guidelines. Interviews were conducted primarily during the 1996 summer semester and the 1997–98 academic year. In initial interviews lasting up to two hours, students described their personal writing histories, covering their *Gymnasium* experiences, their development as writers in university, and the contexts of the institutions and educational system they participate in (see Appendix 1). Teachers and faculty members explored their goals and strategies concerning student writing development (see Appendixes 2 and 3). Subsequent contacts and follow-up interviews were used to gather additional materials and clarify responses.

Students in the study were enrolled either in the traditional degree for the humanities and social sciences, the M.A. *(Magister),* or in a parallel track (the *Staatsexamen*) leading to teacher certification in the field.[1] Student participants in the study were drawn from volunteers indicating interest in the project. Participants were selected from a variety of majors within the humanities and social sciences, ranging from the first semester through the thirteenth semester. A total of eighteen students participated, eleven from Münster (eight women, three men) and seven from Magdeburg (five women, two men).[2] The two-to-one proportion of women to men, representing the gender ratio on the original list, reflects several factors. One is the gender balance in the various disciplines: in the humanities, for example, women considerably outnumber men. Another is the preponderance of women in all the pedagogical components of the disciplines represented here. *Gymnasium* teachers and university faculty were selected to represent a variety of disciplines and (in the teachers' cases) schools in the areas of the participating universities.

The German School System

The two regions and their respective schools and institutions have different historical and cultural backgrounds. Yet they are bound together by long-standing educational traditions and by strong structural ties within the federal educational system. Germans do not hesitate to say that there is a "German system of education" across the unified Germany of today. The generic diagram in Figure 5 of the school-university continuum looks basically the same for all German states.

Historically, education in Germany is based on early selectivity and differentiated goal orientation. There are multiple pathways to vocations and degrees through varying lengths and outcomes of schooling (Golz; Anweiler). All children attend the first four or five years of elementary school together. After the fourth year in most states, the schoolchild (at the age of ten or eleven), the parents, and the teachers must together choose the path to further education. There is a general schooling option often leading to an apprenticeship *(Hauptschule)*, a more focused option leading to vocational/technical studies *(Realschule)*, and a *Gymnasium*.

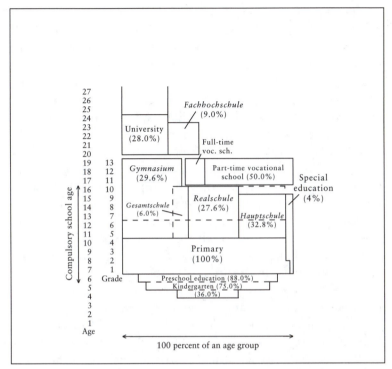

Figure 5. *Germany: Structure of the formal education system.*

Gymnasium is the main avenue to the examination called the *Abitur*, and only by "making the *Abitur*" can students attend university.[3] The academic track in most German states takes thirteen years from elementary through *Gymnasium* levels, so students are at least nineteen years old if they go to university straight from *Gymnasium*. German men must serve a year in the army or in national service *(Zivildienst)*, normally before university, so most men are at least twenty years old when they enter university. Over the last few decades, the percentage of students entering *Gymnasium* to earn an *Abitur* has been increasing. Recent figures suggest that roughly one-third of German school students graduate from a *Gymnasium* with an *Abitur*. Approximately three out of four of these *Abitur* holders go on to university at some point (Anweiler 53–54).

Thus a university education is the right of a particular group of students: those who are selected for the university track early in their schooling and who successfully complete the leaving examination at the end of their schooling. Because the selection decision comes relatively early in the schoolchild's life, it is not an easy one for many families. The decision is not a top-down administrative process but a collaboration between student, parents, teachers, and administrators to try to reach a mutually agreeable resolution. The children and their families must think a long way into the future, develop at least provisional academic or vocational goals, and choose the appropriate schooling. A number of states require a trial period at the fifth- and sixth-grade levels during which students have to prove an aptitude for studying in the type of school they have chosen. To be sure, students may change school types after the trial period—and also at later points in their education—but they are required to "prove aptitude" to do so (Golz 22). Crossovers—for example, changing from a vocational to an academic *(Gymnasium)* track—are possible, but they require concerted effort and intensive goal reformulation to accomplish.

The *Abitur* consists of a series of written and oral examinations extending over several days, taken usually during or after the final semester in *Gymnasium*. The written exams last several hours each day; the oral exams are shorter, an hour or so each. Students typically choose to be examined on subjects (called the *Oberstufe* in most states, *Kurstufe* in a few) they have concentrated on during the final four to six semesters of *Gymnasium*. Students must then write their *Abitur* exams in some of these chosen areas, with other areas also required for some breadth. For humanities and social sciences, these examinations consist of three- or four-hour essays on each of several days. When students receive a passing grade for their *Abitur,* they may choose to enroll at any university offering the major subjects they seek. In high-demand fields such as medicine, law, and some sciences, enrollments are limited, but in most humanities and social sciences subjects, students with a successful *Abitur* will be able to enroll at the university they choose.

The Schools and Universities in This Study

Westfälische Wilhelms-Universität Münster is a large research university of 50,000 students, publicly funded like all universities in Germany, in the northwestern city of Münster, a city of 280,000 north of the Ruhr industrial area and not far from the Dutch border. It is in the state of North Rhine-Westphalia (NRW), whose capital is Düsseldorf and whose economic base is the Ruhr area. The city of Münster and its surroundings are white collar and professional but packed with enough churches, castles, and historical sites to make it a major tourist center—"a city of churches and pubs, civil servants and students" in the words of the university's brochure. Brick bike paths are wider than sidewalks, and students ride and stroll the intersections with the careless preoccupation of those who know they own the streets. The university is one of the largest in Germany, with studies in virtually every academic and professional area, attracting students primarily from northwestern Germany but also from other western regions as well. It has an extensive research emphasis, wide-ranging degree programs at all levels, and heavy enrollments in the humanities and social sciences. Though not as old as the universities in Freiburg, Heidelberg, and Göttingen (for example), it is solidly traditional in its organization and faculty-student relationships. Academic units are separate fiefdoms, often with their own libraries and facilities, and students identify more with their disciplinary faculty and departments than with the university at large.

Otto von Guericke Universität and the city of Magdeburg offer a striking contrast to the burgherish appeal of Münster. Magdeburg is about the same size as Münster but a world apart culturally. It is the capital of—and the only major city in— the state of Saxony-Anhalt (SA) in the east central region of Germany. This largely rural state had a precarious economy during East Germany's years as a separate country, and today it has the highest unemployment rate of any German state: about one in five have no job *(Westfälische Nachrichten)*. Much of its industry has disappeared. The long blocks of drab beige office buildings that had served as a major administrative center for the East German Communist Party were emptied and left to deteriorate after reunification. Now the city is completing the task of rebuilding: the great cathedral is getting a facelift, the city center is being rebuilt, the heaved paving stones in the streets are slowly giving way to better road surfacing.

The recent history of the university mirrors that of the city. A center of engineering education since the nineteenth century and throughout the history of the German Democratic Republic (GDR), Otto von Guericke University has now been reshaped as a small comprehensive university of 6,000 students, anchored still by engineering and technological studies but also offering arts and sciences, law and medicine. It has a recruiting program complete with glossy publications that would do a competitive private college in the United States proud. Most of its students still come from the immediate area, however, and they reflect the attitudes and cultural patterns of the region's recent history. The faculty and organization of this newly reshaped university also reflect the impact of unification. As with all the universities of the former GDR, Magdeburg's faculty was reorganized by the state education ministry after reunification. Faculty deemed too ideologically "bent" were forced out, replaced by professors mostly from the west—again as happened everywhere in the new eastern states. The new faculty members from the universities of West Germany were often put in positions of power over surviving East German faculty members. Tensions were fierce, of course, though they are slowly fading as the new arrangements mature. Students faced their own dislocations in *Gymnasium* and university as the ideological directions of their studies altered, sometimes literally overnight, from GDR communism to federal republicanism. The University of Magdeburg is now developing a new set of traditions and purposes strongly linked to those of the west.

The Role of Testing in Upper Secondary Years

At the beginning of the *Oberstufe* years—the final two years of *Gymnasium*—students choose several subjects for concentrated study, on which they will then write their *Abitur* examinations. In these years, students build the test-taking mastery needed for the *Abitur* tests. The urgent focus on testing has a simple motivation, of course: if you pass the *Abitur,* you can go to university; if you don't, you can't. It sounds simple, but the effects of various program structures and grading systems on student motivation make this a rather complex rite of passage for university-bound nineteen-year-olds. In both North Rhine-Westphalia and Saxony-Anhalt, the *Abitur* consists of three four-to-six-hour written examinations and an oral of one-half to one hour, taken over the course of a week or two. Each examination represents the culmination of a particular course of study in the *Oberstufe* semesters: if students concentrate on German literature, history, English, and math, they take those subjects on the *Abitur.* The questions are set by a regional board of teachers and administrators and may be read by teachers from the students' own schools as well as from other schools.

With the sustained practice offered in the *Oberstufe* years, students in this study report no real difficulties in writing interpretive-analytical essays good enough to satisfy the *Abitur* examiners. But in both states in this study, earning a good grade on the *Abitur* is more than a matter of writing the final examinations successfully. *Abitur* grades combine marks on the written tests themselves with performance in the course work of the *Oberstufe* period. So students motivated to earn high *Abitur* grades must perform well not only on the tests but also in courses throughout the *Oberstufe* period leading to the tests.[4] Indeed, motivation for academic achievement among these students is a complex individual matter. Some need good grades to qualify for the relatively uncommon privately funded scholarships; most who work hard in the pre-*Abitur* semesters do it because, as a third-semester history major from Münster put it, "I wanted to do well out of personal pride."

The masteries necessary for writing successful examinations are therefore crucial to students who want a successful *Abitur.* The connections between learning, writing, and test-readiness in *Oberstufe* study are clearly spelled out in the education ministry guidelines of the two states in this study.[5] In the NRW guidelines for humanities subjects, the linkage between writing, learning, and test-readiness is forcefully stated in a section entitled "Learning Assessment Goals." All writing is seen as a means of assessing students' readiness for the *Abitur* examinations: there is an "indispensable congruence between the educational process and the leaving examination" (*Richtlinien: Deutsch* 135).[6] The writing in each course must "verify the student's readiness for the *Abitur* and the general readiness for university" because "every *Oberstufe* course, including its forms of learning assessment, offers a systematic preparation for the *Abitur* examination" (*Richtlinien: Geschichte* 100).

Various writing activities are described in terms of their importance in assessing students' learning progress: tests, protocols (written summaries of lessons and classroom discussions), and analytical/interpretive essays in and out of class. Methods for "Correcting and Grading" the tests and essays are spelled out, identifying logic, structure, grammar, style, and spelling as focal points. The term "error" is to be understood as covering "faults" in what is written as well as the "absence" of that which should have been written (*Richtlinien: Geschichte* 118). The guidelines instruct teachers to discuss writings with their "correction markings" in class by means of transparencies. All marks are to be made "in red" in margins; students are to be told to leave margins wide enough for this purpose.

By the time they sit for the *Abitur* exams, then, students have become deeply familiar with its forms and topics. Teachers have drilled them in typical questions, with the scope and writing time increasing as the *Abitur* nears. Questions typically present a text—a poem, prose passage, historical document—and ask students to carry out the same tasks of analysis and interpretation they have intensively practiced. In his final school year, says a seventh-semester Magdeburg student, "we did write in the class; these were mostly tests." He wrote them, he continues, with the attitude that "there were people who want something from me and I have to just make something to get my mark—the best one that's possible . . . just to have a very good *Abitur,* and that's it." A *Gymnasium* teacher from North Rhine-Westphalia says that "the writing in the *Oberstufe* eventually . . . serves the purpose that the student learns to perform what is on the *Abitur.*"

Thus the test-related writing of this period serves to naturalize the writing required by the *Abitur* examinations, encouraging students to see the *Abitur* as the appropriate culmination of the writing mastery they have spent years developing.

Building Rhetorical Authority in *Oberstufe*

Despite the classroom emphasis on test-related composing, *Gymnasium* classrooms are not depicted by students or teachers merely as scenes of knowledge-telling. To be sure, students from both regions report doing some writing that was primarily reproductive: "in religion and biology we had to repeat and write down what we heard," reports an eighth-semester Münster student. And a seventh-semester Magdeburg student says that "you had to be able to deduct the main information from a text and to write something about an opus or a scene [of a literary text]." But students in both areas portray themselves as agentive in their speaking and writing, encouraged by teachers to shape their own textual interpretations and analyses as well as personal opinions in writing and discussion.

Teaching students to develop independent interpretations of texts and issues is an official learning goal in the school systems of both states. Guidelines from both North Rhine-Westphalia and Saxony-Anhalt education ministries assert the importance of students articulating their own opinions in writing and discussion. The NRW guidelines for history assert the importance of "independent thinking" and urges teachers to "give students the opportunity to express themselves," particularly those "who in classroom lessons are reticent or self-conscious" (*Richtlinien: Geschichte* 110). The SA guidelines for German emphasize the need for "independence and originality of contributions" (*Rahmenrichtlinien: Deutsch* 80–81). Students from both regions indicate that they are pushed to articulate textual interpretations as well as logical arguments about issues arising in discussion and writing. A young Münster student says that "analyses of literature" and "analysis of historical texts in history" were the most common writing tasks for her, occurring "mostly when you write the tests." She adds, "I had them as homework" also, which she and her classmates brought into class and submitted for general discussion. Magdeburg students use the same terms to describe their main tasks: "In the 11th and 12th year it was almost all interpretation; it was the most frequent form of writing," says a fourth-semester Magdeburg student. An SA teacher confirms this emphasis on interpretation and argument as the primary tasks of *Oberstufe* writing: "Interpretation is the universal tool to pass the *Abitur* in German. In history it is the argument. If [students] want to pass the *Abitur* they must learn interpretation and argumentation."

The rhetorical mastery developed through interpretive writing and discussion is, as Christiane Donahue points out, a fully school-based authority framed within the academic discourse in question. Students' rhetorical horizons are certainly school-bound; they do not report being asked to do wider research in scholarly literature beyond available classroom or school library materials, or to account for disciplinary voices beyond resources provided by schools and teachers. They describe their classroom settings as participatory, topic focused, and orally demanding, with individual student writing often singled out by teachers for critiques of structure and logic. A sixth-semester Münster student remembers her daily class meetings as often too filled with discussion for there to be much time for writing; instead, they did shorter writings at home and brought them to class for discussion and critique:

> During the lessons we hardly ever wrote, just talked and dis-
> cussed different matters. But then we sometimes . . . got a ques-
> tion in written form for homework, and then had to read it out
> the next day and discuss it. It was always related to the topic we
> were dealing with and the question was given [by the teacher].

Students thus portray themselves speaking and writing within a well-defined rhetorical situation consisting of trusted classmates and a familiar teacher.

But this rhetorical setting is not limited to the analysis and interpretation of texts. Students from both regions note that teachers also encouraged them to build arguments based on personal opinions about current issues. The fourth-semester Magdeburg student quoted in the previous paragraph says that

> there was another form of assigned writing *[Aufsatzform],* where a common issue, for example AIDS, was the topic, and then an argumentative structure for or against was developed. This was the second most common form of assigned writing.

A sixth-semester Münster student describes opinion-formation activity in similar terms:

> In German [class] . . . the question would be something like, are you of the opinion girls and boys should have sports together. Where you have to find different arguments pro and contra and come to a conclusion. I would start off saying what my opinion was, and then give reasons and draw conclusions.

In some *Oberstufe* classes, teachers stimulated the play of opinion as a dialogical rhythm in order to encourage students' mastery of the rhetoric of argument. A ninth-semester Münster student describes his favorite teacher in *Gymnasium* compelling students to articulate opinions by often changing his own statements and forcing them to react. In this way, he says, "we had to discuss the question and not write something down which was dictated," but "think about it and bring [it] into a new written structure and a new form":

> The teacher gave us a question, and his opinion, and then he began to discuss. Then he said, oh no this isn't my opinion, my opinion is this. So there were some of the pupils on his side and some on the opposite, and it was interesting to see how some of them tried to bring their opinion on the right side. At the end of the lesson, he said, OK, neither right or left is right, my opinion is really this. So we were [again] on the wrong side, and he did this many times. So we learned to think about what we had to do, and how to get our own opinion, and not to say what he wants to know.

These accounts suggest persistent classroom pressures on Münster students to build an authority based on mastery of argumentative strategies that may be brought into play in a variety of discourse settings.

While both Münster and Magdeburg students represent interpretation and opinion formation as important, the grounding of the rhetorical authority implicit in Magdeburg narratives differs to some degree from that represented in the Münster narratives. Several older Magdeburg students describe the contrast between the newer interpretive freedom that emerged after reunification and the earlier ideological foundationalism of the East German school writing and discussion. A seventh-semester student whose education and work experience spanned the entire reunification process talks about his experiences as he began *Abitur* preparation in East Germany before reunification: "There were books already written about the books we were reading in class. So the teachers mostly referred to those books . . . and there was standing, more or less, the truth." As a result, in class discussions "the teacher . . . already had her own opinion about [an interpretation]. And when it [student opinion] was slightly different, she just said, oh, that's not right." One popular text in German classes during the days of the GDR, says this student, was *Professor Mamlock* by Friedrich Wolf.[7] "There were just the conclusions which were given, and I just tried to harmonize them," he continues. Writing a test about this book,

> I just had a few ideas about it . . . they came intuitively to my mind. . . . [But] when I got afraid about getting a mark, I just looked up . . . in the back of the book [where] we could use kind of an interpretation already given. [So] I just mixed it up with the things I wrote down and which were written there [in the back]. And I got a mark of one afterwards [the highest grade].

One SA teacher summarizes this climate with a colloquialism current at the time: GDR students, he says, trained to learn by the "open mouth"—that is, to learn material and repeat "just what is written in the text." Another Magdeburg student, a seventh-semester political science major whose schooling also spanned the period of reunification, describes a culture of ideological correctness in GDR classroom discussions. He describes the impact of "the change" on his writing:

> After the wall came down in 1990 we got the freedom to have an opinion of our own. For the first time we were allowed to write

exactly what we thought, without given opinions that we had to follow. And this change became visible in the texts *[Aufsätze]* we wrote. For the first time did we have the feeling of having an opportunity to write what we had always wanted to say.

Remembering what it was like to speak and write tethered by the one-right-answer rule, this student celebrates the feeling of liberation he experienced in the postreunification *Oberstufe* classrooms.

After reunification, the right-answer texts and the teachers who used them quickly disappeared from schools in the "new states" of the east. But the version of interpretive authority described by the SA students in this study differs in emphasis from the interpretive freedom described by NRW students. While in the SA narratives the ideological constraints of the East German system era have disappeared, they seem to have been replaced by a standard of validation requiring interpretations and opinions to be tightly grounded in textuality—in what is written. Developing "one's own ideas" from a text appears, in the SA narratives, to be a text-centered process—a kind of textual, rather than ideological, foundationalism. Indeed, an ambivalence about the role of personal viewpoints in schoolwork may be discerned in the SA curricular guidelines cited earlier. In the guidelines for German, even while the independence and originality of students' work is rated important, a warning is also given about the unsuitability of personal opinion in assessing students learning: "political and ideological views as well as personal opinions *[persönliche Meinungen]* are not proper subjects of evaluation" in oral and written work (*Rahmenrichtlinien: Deutsch* 80). SA teachers and students note this cautious attitude toward personal opinion and interpretation in their postreunification classrooms, indicating that students' personal views were developed, but were and still are required to be tightly grounded in textual awareness and referencing. An SA teacher of German says that in German class

the students are given a text they have to work on. . . . The students are asked to write down their opinions regarding certain issues; they are asked to use their own arguments for or against the issues they find in the text. And, sadly enough, this is no free discussion, which I always regret a little. . . . Now the discussions are always linked to a text, in one way or another.

Confirming this view, students note teachers' insistence that discussions be framed by and grounded in the text at hand. A fourth-semester student records her impression that

> [the teachers] want to hear our own perspectives, but always in connection with those of the authors. That is, one can't write one's own opinion separate from the text, but must always establish the connection to the text, and to the argument of the author, that is, assess it from this perspective.

A seventh-semester student emphasizes the conditions under which a student's view can differ from the teacher's perspective: "You always have to view [your opinion] in relation to the text in question. . . . . You always had to stick to the text and you had to prove [your statements] within the text." In the postreunification classrooms represented by these students, "what is written" seems to form the basic warrant for interpretive authority. The interpretive foundationalism implicit in these statements may be attributable at least partly to the habit of ideological absolutism ingrained in the SA school culture by East German pedagogical practice. Yet the evidence here is only suggestive; further study is clearly needed. I observe later in this chapter that there is some evidence in the Magdeburg students' narratives that the foundationalist bias in their school reading/writing practices carries over into the writing they do at university.

In summary, the scene of writing in the *Oberstufe* years in both states in this study may be characterized by the following features:

- ◆ a sense of cohesion through shared critiques of written and oral work and daily trust-based student-teacher, student-student classroom interaction

- ◆ a shared, clearly focused writing purpose deriving from the *Abitur*-orientation of tests and shorter writings

- ◆ an intensive focus on topic fields relevant to students' *Abitur* subjects

◆ a sense of rhetorical authority shaped by interactive discussions of students' opinions, analyses, and interpretations within the rhetorical scene of the *Gymnasium* classroom

The Shock of Discovery: Entering a New Writing/ Learning Culture

Entering university, students must acculturate themselves to a very different learning environment. Some of its features are readily recognizable in the U.S. university setting. Instead of the tightly structured, interactive classrooms of *Gymnasium,* featuring shared study goals governed by trusted teachers, German university students (like university students in most countries) must join classes with students whose backgrounds and goals diverge widely, and work with teachers who embody discourse communities with complex, unfamiliar expectations. But in the matter of both autonomy and time-space configurations, German students face a situation very different from that of U.S. students. The students in both universities in this study must adapt to a challenging autonomy in material and institutional elements of the university environment. The traditions in both universities spring from common historical roots that have outlasted the differences developed during the period of the separate Germanys. The East German educational system itself was, after all, only an interlude in the long history of German school and university education.

The characteristics of the new scene of learning and writing at university include:

◆ wide autonomy in choosing the occasions, time frames, deadlines, physical sites, and working rhythms for writing

◆ immediate immersion in the discourse of specific knowledge communities, with professors (rather than examiner-teachers) as readers

◆ use of an incorporative rhetoric rather than a rhetoric of personal argument to establish authority in disciplinary writing

At university, students' relationship to the curriculum is more ambiguous and undirected than in *Gymnasium*. Time guidelines for completing courses of study are general and seldom enforced in many disciplines.[8] Neither university in this study requires that students earn credit for courses in which they enroll; that is, they can attend, listen, take notes, and participate in discussion without earning credit, or they can attend and, by taking a test or (in seminars) writing a paper, earn credit. They may stop attending when they choose; the university imposes no penalty. If they do not write the research paper in a seminar, for example, they simply get no credit and must reenroll in the same or a similar seminar later—if it is a requirement. The university is only concerned that they complete requirements in the right sequence. Nor does either university in this study keep the kinds of records found in U.S. universities—summaries of courses taken, attempted, passed, failed, or left incomplete. Only students themselves keep a cumulative record of the credits they earn each semester.[9]

Students in the humanities and social sciences typically enroll in several lecture courses and several seminars each semester, knowing they will not complete them all for credit. During the semester, they choose which lecture courses to earn credit in by taking the required exams; they also choose which seminars to complete by writing a paper. Individual conferences with the teacher are usually required—but only of those students planning to write a paper. Others, attending only to read the material and listen to discussions, normally have nothing required of them. Thus seminars in particular confront students with a dangerous autonomy as writers. They must decide which courses to write papers for—depending on such things as their need for credit in a specific course or the workload they want to maintain in a given semester.

Each choice is fraught with consequences: students may choose not to write (thus deferring the completion of requirements but perhaps enhancing disciplinary knowledge), choose to begin a paper but not to finish (thus expending time and energy without gaining official credit), or choose to finish and submit for credit (thus setting a long-term writing task for themselves). If they receive credit but a low grade, they may choose not to ask the instructor to sign the credit form, but instead request permission to write the paper again, or simply give up and retake the course later. An experienced (and jaundiced) Münster student sums up her early encounters with the system:

> STUDENT: When you come to a professor, you have to have a really clear question. If you just come in and say, I have to write a [paper] but I really don't know about what, they just send you out again, because they say you have to have clear ideas when you come in here. . . . But if you have an idea, well, I think I can write about this but I am not sure, they will say, yeah, but cut it down a bit or it needs a bit, then they send you off again. . . . Either you finish it and hand it in or just give up.
>
> FOSTER: And if you give up, what is the consequence?
>
> STUDENT: You don't get your credit *[Schein]*. So you have to repeat the course or choose another course next semester to get your credit.

The seminar tradition thus entails both freedom and responsibility. At some point in each semester, students must begin building the university version of the house that Jack built: they must choose the course to pick the topic to write the paper to earn the credit to make some progress in their major.

When they arrive at university, facing (usually in the first semester) their first seminar paper, students discover what they have gotten themselves into. The regular reinforcements of *Gymnasium* are gone—the daily interactions of friends and trusted teachers within a familiar classroom setting, and the strong goal orientation of *Abitur* preparation. For university they must not only write within specific discourse communities requiring a new kind of rhetorical authority, but also develop a new kind of situational authority to deal with the dangerous freedoms of the university environment. These forms of authority, rhetorical and situational, are reciprocal and interconnected; one can't be learned without the other.

The rhetorical authority students must learn at university is grounded in *wissenschaftliches Schreiben,* which is best translated as "academic writing."[10] The phrase suggests a more essentialized and normative construct in German academic discourse than the same term implies in English-speaking systems. This construct is used by every professor, instructor, tutor, and student in every discipline represented in this study. It signifies the systematic study of established knowledge about a topic, and the incorporation and synthesis of diverse sources of this knowledge into an authoritative viewpoint.

For students at university, *wissenschaftliches Schreiben* and its companion phrase *wissenschaftliche Arbeiten* (academic work) signify various strategies by which students research, assimilate, and incorporate knowledge sources into their writing, especially seminar papers. Like writing textbooks for U.S. students, generic handbooks devoted to *wissenschaftliches Schreiben* are widely available for German students.[11] One textbook, for example, asserts that *wissenschaftliches Schreiben* is universally required in academic work: "syllabuses require it of school students, examinations and study sequences require it of university students" (Peterßen 11). In this textbook, it is characterized as both "process" and "product." As process, *wissenschaftliches Schreiben* handles "a theme, a problem in the academic form and manner, that is, according to academic standards and principles, with academic methods and techniques" (Peterßen 11). As product, it consists of "texts composed with academic rules and formats" (11). Like other textbooks of its kind, this one contains chapters on finding a topic, searching for materials, organizing and assimilating information, and detailed citation rules.

Making the transition to this new way of writing is difficult and often frustrating for students. As one history professor from Münster puts it,

> in *wissenschaftliches Schreiben* what is important . . . is bringing together material, to know how material may bear on my argument, how to place them in a text, how to produce a text. That is, to follow a certain logic and line of argument, to formulate the argument and develop the text that develops the argument in an intelligible way. But the kind of subject that goes beyond what is taught in *Gymnasium* is crucial.

To be sure, some elements of *wissenschaftliches Schreiben* are introduced in the *Oberstufe* curriculum, as the guidelines from both states in this study suggest. SA guidelines, for example, state that *Oberstufe* writing should require some "independent scholarly work," including finding and summarizing sources, catalog and database searching, and citing and paraphrasing. But students in this study—unlike the French students studied by Christiane Donahue (Chapter 3)—report that the test-oriented writing of *Oberstufe* does not prepare them for the scope and complexity of the synthesizing labor entailed in seminar papers. Donahue reports that the test-oriented writings done by French school students in preparation for the BAC (the *baccalauréat* leaving examination) persist in similar forms at university. German students encounter a very different kind of transition. The uncertainties of topic development and the incorporative energies required to locate and integrate the multiple secondary sources of a seminar paper are specific to the university seminar setting.

Students and faculty in this study indicate that teachers generally help students formulate their topics and identify readings, but they do not give feedback to students during the writing or revising stages of students' work. One professor of social sciences who has taught in both western and eastern universities in Germany suggests both why he helps students as they draft their texts and why he believes most of his colleagues don't: "I go through their papers and would take two or three pages and make a careful editing and help [those] who have difficulties to put it into paragraphs, and then I would do some comment at the end . . . focusing on the content . . . and style of writing." He believes, however, that his concentration on individual students' writings is not typical of German faculty generally:

> I cannot remember any single case that my colleagues would do what I do, take the first written statements, these homeworks of second semester that I would go through and would give them written and oral reactions to. The professor cannot earn any merits there because we don't have an assessment of the university professor as a teacher.

Such institutional pressures—familiar in most U.S. universities— help shape faculty views of their roles in working with student writers.

Students identify the writing required in seminar papers as the single most difficult learning/writing challenge at university.

Differences in the ways students in this study report learning academic writing do not correlate with region or discipline, but instead differ widely among departments and individual university teachers. Some students in this study report receiving systematic instruction about writing in their major disciplines; some report none. One published survey of a small sample of German universities indicates that about half of the universities surveyed report some formal instruction in *wissenschaftliches Schreiben* within the curricula of individual disciplines (von Werder 2–4). The report identifies only "five university rectors [among surveyed institutions] who can name a university teacher concerned directly with research in *wissenschaftliches Schreiben* as a pedagogical technique" (von Werder 6). But the majority of students in this study say that instructors expect them to learn and use academic writing techniques more or less on their own, as part of their responsibility from the beginning of university study.

Developing Rhetorical Authority: Incorporating Disciplinary Voices

Students hear university teachers say to them (as a political science instructor from Magdeburg reports himself saying),

> You want to tell me your opinion? I don't want to hear your opinion! In *Gymnasium* the teacher wants to know what *you* think. Here I want to know what the authorities you have read are saying and how you would respond to *them!*

Suddenly, thoughtful reasoning isn't enough to please the instructor; beginning with their first seminar writings, students must incorporate the voices and ideas of published scholars in their discipline. Of course, developing this kind of rhetorical authority is an important element of writing development for university students in most educational systems, as David Bartholomae's description of U.S. student writers trying to "invent the university" suggests:

> Every time a student sits down to write for us [professors], he has to invent the university for the occasion. . . . The student has to

> learn to speak our language . . . to try on the peculiar ways of knowing, selecting, evaluating, reporting, concluding, and arguing that define the discourse of our community. Or perhaps I should say the *various* discourses of our community. (134)

Students must "take on the role—the voice, the persona—of an authority" in order to attempt to write "in the privileged language of university discourse" (138). But this was a more immediate and acute challenge for the first-year students in this study than for first-year U.S. students. No first-year composition courses are available to help German students adapt their rhetorical strategies gradually to academic writing. Beginning in the first semester at university, the students in this study had to embed their own voices in disciplinary discourse, quoting, citing, and documenting established scholarly views in seminars in each of their major disciplines. To be sure, they learned in *Gymnasium* that they are agents of discourse—that they must write and speak convincingly to skeptical others. But to write seminar papers at university, they discovered that they must navigate across a far more diverse and complex rhetorical terrain than in *Gymnasium*. In this new territory, personal views—however well thought out—become less important. What becomes more important is the ability to integrate views of authoritative others skillfully and coherently into a more complex, multivocal perspective.

Learning how to bring together published scholarly voices from the discipline into one's own writing is seen by students in this study as the most difficult challenge they face as writers new to the university. Students tend to portray this challenge in two ways. One describes the incorporative effort as a hurtful loss of personal identity. An eighth-semester Münster student articulates her struggle this way:

> First you have to choose literature, and you have to read, and if you have the thoughts of another person who has made these thoughts, you have to make footnotes . . . you have to *belegen*, to prove where you have this thought from. . . . There is nothing you can do from your own thoughts. It is difficult to decide.

For her, the new rhetoric of incorporation demands a depersonalized, "objective" condition of knowing:

> There are no personality parts in *wissenschaftliche Arbeiten.* It
> has to be correct and understandable *[nachvollziebar].* It means
> that . . . in such a text, it isn't allowed to think in my opinion. . . .
> Another word would be objective. . . . In the university nobody
> asks you for the personal meaning of something.

Another experienced Münster student says that "what I object to
is that I am not given a chance to have an opinion that may differ
from what ten other researchers may have said." She feels silenced
by her struggles with an incorporative rhetoric:

> Basically what is asked of me is not to give an opinion but to give
> a review of what researchers have said. I think I have something
> to say and I want to know if what I have to say is important and
> I want a chance to find out if it's true.

A university professor of German acknowledges this attitude as
a common student response to the challenge of building authority
in disciplinary discourse. He says that "finding a point of view
and a voice are very hard for German students because they are
accustomed to think of *wissenschaftliches Schreiben* as a collation
of other peoples' views, objective and impersonal."

The majority of students in this study do not share this view
of incorporative rhetoric as a process of being silenced. Most say
that developing rhetorical authority as university writers is a
matter of learning to shape their own viewpoints within the
dynamics of incorporation itself. Here there is a difference in the
narratives of Münster and Magdeburg students, perhaps related
to the differences noted earlier between ways of grounding
authority in school discourse. Magdeburg students' narratives
tend to reveal a rule-centeredness, exposing the effort to integrate
others' voices as a process of mastering systematic rules. A second-
semester Magdeburg student, for example, says that her biggest
problem as a first-year writer is knowing "the rules for citation.
. . . Because we hadn't learned this in school. Simply that."
Framing the incident as a problem-solution move, she reports
consulting a professor after the *Referat* (oral report) stage, not in
order to ask about concepts or topic development, but to get
exact instructions on citation: "I have written a work, and during
the work I have a problem with citation rules. I didn't have a

problem with other things. If I did not know the solution, then I go to my professor," who provides her with the solutions that allow her to use the code properly.

A seventh-semester Magdeburg student describes a more complex process of rule-mastery. He describes his repertoire of text strategies:

> Professors demand . . . that we confront the scientific [*wissenschaftlich*] dispute [among our sources]. And they like it . . . if you don't focus on just one opinion but if you contrast some and come up with a kind of synthesis. Yes, thesis-antithesis . . . that is required.

He self-consciously uses the metaphor of the "red thread" to describe what he tries to do:

> You need to have a red thread [*rote Faden*] throughout the whole paper, as the saying goes. . . . So first you write down the main opinions, then you try to find counter-opinions . . . then you make the link. Then you find yet another affirmative opinion and then "he says the same." That builds up a whole chain then which you can finish nicely.

The image of the "red thread" suggests the kind of logical connectedness a good seminar paper is supposed to exhibit. This student enumerates the code terms he has learned to use to signify the impersonal logic of *wissenschaftlich* authority:

> We were taught not to use "I" or "one" in scientific texts. [So] I use expressions such as "From this it follows that . . ." On my first paper I wrote, "I hold the opinion" and that was marked as wrong. . . . Instead you use "It can be observed that . . . ", "From there it follows that . . . ", or "Thus, . . ." And honestly, it looks better when I write, "It follows that . . ."

This confident description portrays the incorporation of others' voices as a process of learning and applying stylistic strategies to achieve the authority appropriate to an academic writing task.

In contrast, Münster students tend to represent the development of an incorporative rhetoric as a balancing act played out through careful, sometimes risky textual moves. A sixth-semester

Münster student gives the following account of trying to articulate her own conclusions:

> STUDENT: That's very hard. Most of the time this is the most difficult part of the *Hausarbeit*. . . . I try to find my own opinion, which is new, really my own, but I might have read it somewhere. I can agree with it but it is not really my own opinion.
>
> FOSTER: So how do you find your own words?
>
> STUDENT: I can't say exactly, it just comes. . . . My own words often contain the ideas of the quotation, often the same words of it, but what I do is kind of brainstorming. . . . I must admit I use very much of the words in the source. If the words are hard words and don't fit into the style of my paper, so then I don't use it. But I must admit that sometimes I write down things I really don't understand. I slightly adopt it into my language and this is quite helpful.

This student's frank description of her hesitancy and risk-taking as she writes in an unfamiliar discourse field clearly reflects Bartholomae's characterization of students struggling to "speak [the] language" of academic discourse and "trying on peculiar ways of knowing." She knows that she is supposed to use the standard terminology of her discipline. But she also knows she does not have firm semantic control of this language. So she faces an unpleasant choice: she must either lapse into her own nonstandard vocabulary (somewhere on the border of the discourse field), or—to maintain her authority—use a term from the disciplinary discourse whose implications she doesn't really understand. Because she needs the feel of authoritative terminology in her paper, she chooses disciplinary terms even when she is uncertain of their meaning or context. This is the kind of semantic risk she believes she has to take to build rhetorical authority in her seminar paper.

A tenth-semester Münster student who is articulate about his own composing strategies describes a flexible, interactive relationship with the authoritative voices of his sources. As he ponders his own composing intentions, he says, he reads scholarly sources to find "similar approaches" to the perspective he is developing. He then describes the impact on his next composing moves:

> If there is a quotation I might use . . . that is quite nice, because it feels good to know you are not on the wrong track. So I mark this in the text so I might use it. My idea that I have already [developed] does not change completely, but my approach to the idea might change by reading through the text and finding quotations. Because I see, yeah . . . you can look at it from a different angle than planned, it's not the complete idea, it's the way I work with the idea.

This student emphasizes the global nature of his response to such encounters. Finding a relevant quote creates the possibility of structural rethinking:

> The last time that happened to me I changed the whole paper. I had it finished, and I had just found another essay dealing with the same idea as mine, and well, I read my paper and . . . wasn't happy with it. So I said [to myself], you can't put it like that, and I began writing from the start again, and in the end the approach I had in my ideas was a completely different one.

Unlike some students in this study, this student portrays his efforts to enter disciplinary conversation as an opportunity to renegotiate and rework the focus and structure of the paper. One of the most experienced writers in the study, he reflects an incorporative mastery developed from years of writing within the seminar system. But students indicate that such mastery is not the only form of authority necessary for successful university writing; they must also learn to negotiate the challenges of the environment that shapes them and their work.

Gaining Situational Authority: Free-Time Writing and the Challenge of Autonomy

The scene of writing at university presents a complex range of elements—student-faculty and student-student relations, curricular and institutional structures, and the material geographies of space and time. Of course, it is not possible here to consider all the relevant situational aspects of student writing in the universities represented in this study. One aspect stands out in these students' narratives, however, both because it powerfully affects their writing and because it differs profoundly from U.S. patterns: the structures of time and space that shape the planning and labor of student writers.

Students have wide latitude in choosing when and where to write seminar papers. A few professors require that papers be turned in at the end of the regular semester, as in U.S. universities. But at both universities in this study—as in most German universities—professors will take completed papers whenever students finish them—at semester's end, later during semester break, even after the next semester begins. The students in this study typically write papers in the time between semesters—either in the February-to-April period between winter and summer semesters, or in the July-to-October period between summer and winter semesters. At Münster, for example, the semester calendar is officially divided into two parts: the lecture time and the lecture-free time *(vorlesungsfreie Zeit)*. Lecture time is when classes meet —roughly the same as a U.S. semester, about three and a half months. It includes class meetings and a week or so of exams afterward, as in U.S. universities. The lecture-free time is an unfamiliar construct for Americans, however. This period covers all the time from the end of exams of one semester until the beginning of next semester's classes—what Americans typically think of simply as vacation. German students think of this as paper-writing time. Thus, for Münster students, all months of the calendar year have an academic signifier; no part of a twelve-month period is excluded from this schedule. It is during this free-time period that most students research and write their seminar papers.

The sometimes widely dispersed resource systems of universities represented in this study pose a challenge for students new to the decentralized pattern of German universities. The holdings of the main university libraries on both campuses, for example, are inconsistent and unpredictably cataloged, often of little use for seminar research in the humanities. Departmental and divisional libraries offer more sources for their majors but are sometimes closed for unpredictable periods during the free-time months when students need them. Moreover, departmental libraries often have different cataloging systems than the central university library. Municipal libraries, on the other hand, are usually open but typically have strict lending policies that limit research usefulness. But students may find useful resources in all places. To find resources, therefore, they may have to search in different sites for each seminar paper, sort through various cataloging systems, identify book and article availabilities, and build an ongoing research/composing schedule for the free-time period, when they will write. During the free-time periods, however, many students work as well as write, and conflicts are inevitable. Students must adapt each semester to different instructors' expectations, different topics, and different personal circumstances. If, for example, they write at home but need more source materials, they must plan to travel back to the university if departmental libraries are open; but such travel can interrupt any for-pay work schedule they may be following, which means they might have to choose between delaying the paper or forgoing additional income.

One writing handbook for university students, looking for some humor in the matter of free-time research and writing, imagines the following dialogue between friends about when to write a seminar paper *(Hausarbeit):*

FIRST STUDENT: I want to write my paper in the free time.

SECOND STUDENT: But you do have to get your course credit before this semester is completely over, otherwise you'll have problems with your financial aid.

FS: Well, the semester lasts until the end of September, so I can finish it then.

SS: But we want to have a vacation in September!

FS: By then I can finish the paper.

SS: But the teacher has to read the paper before you get the credit.

FS: No problem, I'll turn it in by the end of August.

SS: And what if the teacher goes on vacation in September?

FS: Then I'll ask him to date the credit certificate in September even if he reads the paper in October.

SS: Would he do that!?

FS: Petra says that he did it for Gaby. I have written others in the summer like this.

SS: But you haven't started this paper. You are taking a real risk. If you don't produce the credit dated by September, the people in the financial aid office will be merciless.

FS: No they won't. It's just that they have rules. I know that!

SS: Oh well, its your financial aid, not mine. (Bünting 179)

Financial aid rules notwithstanding, most students follow some version of this scenario in their planning. Indeed, this customary arrangement has the force of an unwritten contract between faculty and students. Students from both universities describe their understanding of the system in identical terms. One experienced Münster student explains the convention of free-time writing in terms of the need for focus and concentration:

> Usually the paper is just started when the semester is finished. During the holidays I just started to write and finish two months later from that time. . . . [I work on it] in three or four months [during the free time]. Some professors want it during the semester, but very few. You really have to concentrate on a *Hausarbeit*, you can't really do anything else during that time. . . .

A fourth-semester Magdeburg student exhibits a similar orientation toward free-time composing and delayed turn-in:

> Yes, the research paper is chiefly written in the vacation *[Ferien]*. During the semester, I think, I would have not time and really no desire. During the semester we have to do the oral reports and the semester examinations. So I always write it during the vacation. [Since] I don't live in the [university city] I would have to take the train back here. So I always turn in the paper at the end of vacation.

Faculty sometimes try to articulate their version of this flexible system, though usually not in writing. In an unusual effort to clarify terms, however, the following notice was pinned outside the office door of a faculty member at the University of Münster (see the note in its original German in Appendix 4):

Turn-in Date
for
Seminar Research Papers

is always the first day of the following semester.
    To go beyond the turn-in deadline:
Absolutely the last turn-in date is 1 November for the summer semester and 1 May for the winter semester. Prior written justification is required. Only valid reasons like a longer stay abroad or sickness count. This justification must be included with the finished paper.

The formality of set policy seems embedded in the language of this notice. The due dates are "always" on certain dates, reasons for late turn-in are "always required," and they must be "valid." By means of such qualifiers, a preexistent contractual understanding among all readers is implied. Yet there is much ambiguity in the subtext, recognizable only to those locally situated. For example, since the "first day of the following semester" is usually the October 1, there is a month's lapse between this date—the "Turn-in Date"—and "absolutely the last turn-in date." The second sentence liberally reinterprets the first sentence.

Indeed, this note in effect requires students to construct their own version of the contract by deciding which of its multiple terms they will follow. In this way, students must often negotiate and revise their situational authority from semester to semester. Yet this openness is not portrayed by faculty as a weakness either in professorial standards or student willpower, but as a function of student autonomy. Such an understanding may appear to those in a different educational culture as a grand dodge; after all, if no paper is due at any firm deadline, then both faculty and students are surely off the hook. But in fact this convention carries a subtle blend of responsibility and obligation. Students acquire the autonomy implied in this message simply by becoming university students. Their challenge is to build authority as writers in response to this autonomy—to be able to carry out successful planning, composing, and writing within an ambiguous environment of expectations. Above all, they must create their own circumstances of composing. In their narratives, students present the free-time period as a space within which strategies for writing success are developed. A tenth-semester Münster student describes his perception of the postsemester period as an integral part of university work:

> Normally we do [writing/revising] after the time the courses take place, so we have about two months to finish the paper. We normally have to hand them in by the actual end of the term, which is the end of September or the end of March. I don't think of this time as vacation. As long as I have to write a paper it's not a vacation. I can slow down my speed of work, and my way of working. I got used to [using my postsemester break], it is quite normal, I don't really think of it as a duty, I think it belongs to the semester, that it's OK for me, no problem.

For many students, the primary value of the delayed-turn-in convention is that it locates writing and revising within the private space of personal, nonregulated time. A seventh-semester Magdeburg student identifies his work pattern as ideally suited to free-time composing:

> I like it [writing] better in the time after classes are over, because then I have more time. I think you could not work as intensely during the class periods . . . because you have classes and lectures to prepare then. And I work best in the evening, after 8 P.M., sometimes I work until 2 A.M. . . . You can do this better during the "vacation" time, because you do not have to get up the next day to go to class. . . . And during the class periods you have some stress during the day, so I prefer the time between classes [*Vorlesungsfreie Zeit*—lecture-free time].

The delayed-turn-in convention, then, divorces the writing of seminar papers from other writing and learning tasks—reports and exams—undertaken during the regular semester.

It is this time/space autonomy that perhaps most clearly distinguishes the German from the U.S. scene of writing at university. While at semester's end U.S. students work within a tightly structured time frame to finish writing tasks, German students typically begin to write only after classes end. Such differences illustrate the situational variability inherent in efforts to assess students' authority as writers at university. For example, Stuart Greene's recommendation that instructors give students guidance "throughout the entire process of writing" (214) is bound to the U.S. situation. It is quite appropriate for U.S. students intensively completing their writing in the semester's final weeks, but it would be difficult for German students, who often go home to write and whose teachers are no longer available after classes end. The students in this study plan, compose, and revise over several months, all the while working at paying jobs, making family visits and vacation trips, revisiting libraries as needed, and completing papers in response to a complex range of personal and social factors. Such self-directed planning and composing is not easy for most students and very difficult for some. The psychological challenge of such autonomy is recognized by German faculty and students alike. One well-known writing textbook, for example, specifically addresses the difficulties in motivation and self-direction encountered by students facing academic research/writing tasks. The several editions of this textbook—*Keine Angst vor dem Leeren Blatt* (Kruse), roughly translated as "No Fear Before the Empty Page"—suggest the aptness of its assumption about students' felt need for help: it is sensible to combine the technical with the "emotional or motivational side of writing," says Kruse, because any student with "a deficit in technical writing skills" is also likely to have "emotional inhibitions" about writing that only the discovery of "the pleasure of writing and the experience of its creativity" can resolve (14). This challenge recurs each time students face extended writing tasks requiring long-term, persistent planning and writing.

For the students in this study, the challenge of autonomy embeds itself in their sense of agency as learners/writers. They indicate that their goal during the period when classes meet is to work through the semester's material and discussions, as a way of grounding their thinking about the topic they plan eventually to write on. It is this rationale that a fourth-semester Magdeburg student emphasizes as the crucial reason for writing papers after course meetings are over:

STUDENT: Normally I get ready to do the research paper at the end of the semester. First the seminar is completely finished, and afterwards one has worked out an overall view of the seminar work, then one writes the paper.

FOSTER: Not during the semester?

STUDENT: One can also during the semester, naturally. But really it is more sensible after the semester, after one has completely finished the semester, to write a paper.

This student's judgment that it is "sensible" to write during the free time clearly reflects her experience in negotiating the variables at play in planning and writing seminar papers. She values being able to develop a cumulative understanding of seminar issues during a full semester's participation and to shape a paper topic from this vantage point. It is a point few U.S. students can reach, forced as most are to begin planning papers early in a semester in order to complete them by semester's end. Institutional structures give U.S. students little choice, and successful writers learn to adapt to tight planning/writing schedules. German students also learn to adapt—to the challenging autonomy within which individual choice and persistent self-discipline become the traits adaptive for success.

Authority for German University Writers: Autonomy and Complexity

The evidence from this study suggests that we need to broaden the way we think about the authority students must develop as writers at university. The learning/writing work these students do is embedded in a complex, overlapping set of conditions that require multiple masteries for success. This work fully exemplifies Lave and Wenger's admonition that particular learning/writing strategies do not develop independently but holistically—that "activities, tasks, functions, and understandings do not exist in isolation; they are part of broader systems of relations in which they have meaning" (53). For this reason, I have framed the authority for student writers in this study as a multidimensional construct, entailing mastery of domain subject matter, genre and discourse strategies, curricular and institutional structures, and the configurations of time and space embedded in university settings.

In this final section, I want to note the most significant elements of this authority, connect them with the conditions of disciplinary apprenticeship and autonomy characteristic of German students, and draw comparisons with U.S. student writers. German students' autonomy in the seminar environment reflects a systemic assumption that students can succeed as self-directed learners/writers even in their early years at university. The transition from *Gymnasium* to university, however, requires that students adapt readily to a very different learning/writing environment. They must learn institutional expectations; discern institutional rhythms (topic conferencing, office patterns); locate resource systems (often dispersed among departmental, university, and regional libraries); organize peer-group activities (if required for seminar group reports); and develop planning/composing strategies for long-term, self-directed activity. As the free time between semesters begins, they often must continue resource searches even as they begin composing. In the between-semester times, they must complete this process by writing the paper and juggle study/writing loads with for-pay workloads (like U.S. students in summer).

The interactions among these factors in students' writing intensifies the challenge of autonomy, especially at certain moments in the writing situation. One such moment is the negotiation of the seminar paper topic with the instructor. This normally occurs at some point during the regular semester while the seminar is meeting. But several factors affect the level of closure that such negotiation may reach. If students are scheduled to give oral reports *(Referate)* during the semester (as they typically do in seminars), they frequently choose to develop the topic of the seminar paper from their report. When this is the case, students will have conducted an initial negotiation with the instructor, which may be elaborated and refined after the report into a specific paper topic. But classroom discussions and other students' reports may well spur some reshaping of the topic. The flexibility to revise and reshape perspectives both during and after the regular semester time span is an essential adaptive opportunity for students. But this flexibility may also bring a disadvantage. Students still shaping their paper topics as the semester closes must meet the professor in the free time for further approval, try communicating by mail or telephone, or face deciding whether to write without further consultation, if the instructor is no longer available. Faced with these choices, some students wait until the next semester before beginning to write, in order to gain the instructor's view of the topic. The expectations and customs that define this relationship are tacit and customary rather than statutory, and students must learn them through experience.

Students must also learn the genre roles and activities associated with specific disciplinary communities, positioning themselves as authors to practice the incorporative rhetoric of scholarly conversation. In *Gymnasium* they have learned to function as learners/writers within the school-bound contexts of personal interpretation and argument. Making the transition to university, they discover a new rhetorical territory in which personal perspectives are less important than conversations with authoritative voices in the discipline. Constructing such conversations requires identifying and interpreting authorities and integrating them in a shape that holds the "red thread" of logical continuity. While some students represent this new process as a loss or a silencing, most describe it as the challenge of making risky rhetorical moves toward the center of a disciplinary discourse, embedding new understandings in often unfamiliar codes and terms so that their writer's apprenticeship strengthens within the discipline. As students come to recognize that disciplinary knowledge is constructed out of the interplay of voices, they become more willing to join the discourse of their disciplines.

The contrasts between German students' early disciplinary specialization and U.S. students' delayed, sometimes dilatory entry into disciplinary discourse are striking. German students begin studying in a few specific disciplines in their upper secondary years, undergoing intensive study and practice test writing in preparation for the *Abitur* examinations in those disciplines. Although their writing is typically short timed writing that rehearses the format of the written examinations, it develops disciplinary issues and topics more deeply as the upper secondary semesters progress. The *Abitur* examinations represent students' personal engagement with disciplinary concepts and applications, and they are evaluated in terms of what they show about students' cumulative mastery of disciplinary knowledge. U.S. high school students, on the other hand, generally take a variety of courses in the final years of high school. Some may take several semesters of a particular subject if they happen to like it, and some will take Advanced Placement courses that offer written examinations at the end. The nature and extent of writing that U.S. students will do in their upper secondary years varies widely from teacher to teacher and school to school, but it generally does not feature extended or cumulative writing that probes well into specific disciplinary areas. Few U.S. school students will experience the cumulative challenge of extended, discipline-specific writing moving progressively across several semesters, culminating in a major written performance. Thus most U.S. students arrive at university without in-depth learning/writing experience in any discipline. And—given the ubiquity of general education as well as general composition requirements—most U.S. students will write tentatively for several semesters in a variety of genres and disciplines before beginning serious disciplinary study. In this way, the U.S. system defers students' entry into learning/writing apprenticeships in the disciplines, allowing them significantly shorter time to develop disciplinary-community memberships before completing undergraduate degrees.

These contrasts between German and U.S. students in the transition to university reflect the expectations of each national system in turn, and suggest that further study of these differences, and their effect on students' agencies as learner/writers, will be essential in developing further cross-national perspectives on writing development. Studying these complex issues within or across national systems requires a commitment to a broad research perspective that must seek common features while recognizing the uniqueness of local elements. It is a challenge especially appropriate to the new century, as more students experience the challenges of transition from school to postsecondary education in a climate of increasing international awareness.

Appendix 1

Questions for Student Writing History Interviews

1. What courses in *Gymnasium* required writing? What types of writing were required?

2. How did you learn to write these types of writing in *Gymnasium?*
   (class size, activities)

3. In *Gymnasium* how, where, and when did you write?
   (in school, at home, individually, in groups, assigned or self-chosen topics, etc.)

4. What kind of writing did the *Abitur* require? How did your writing in the *Gymnasium* prepare you for the *Abitur?*

5. How did you feel about yourself as a writer in *Gymnasium?*

6. What kinds of writing did you do in your *Grundstudium* courses at university?

7. In what ways did the writing you did for your *Abitur* prepare you for these *Grundstudium* writing tasks in the university?

8. In what ways were your *Gymnasium* writing experiences most helpful in your *Grundstudium* courses when you came to university?

9. In what ways were your *Gymnasium* writing experiences least helpful when you came to university?

10. What kinds of writing were you best prepared for when you came to university? Why?

11. What kinds of writing were you least prepared for when you came to university? Why?

12. What kinds of writing were you required to do in your *Hauptstudium* courses?

13. How well were you prepared for the writing in your *Hauptstudium* courses?

14. When and for what reasons do you decide to write a *Semesterarbeit* or *Hausarbeit?* When do you write this paper?

15. Could you describe the processes you use to plan and write a *Semester-* or *Hausarbeit?* Could you describe the strategies you use to incorporate secondary sources in your writing?

16. What parts of your writing planning, preparation, composing, and revising do you do individually? With others or with the teacher?

17. In what ways does the *Semester-* or *Hausarbeit* challenge you as a writer?

18. What kind(s) of readers do you envision when you write? Do you envision different kinds of readers for different kinds of writing?

19. How have your attitudes about yourself as a writer changed since you came to the university?

Appendix 2

Questions for Gymnasium *Teachers*

1. What kinds of writing do you think it is most important for your students to learn in *Oberstufe*?

2. What purposes are served by the writings which students do in *Oberstufe*?

3. How important are writing activities in comparison with oral contributions?

4. What writing activities do you emphasize in your teaching?

5. How much and what kind of writing do students do at home, and how much in school?

6. How do students receive topics for *Hausaufgabe* writing [writing at home]? Do you give them specific topics? Do students develop their own topics for *Hausaufgabe*?

7. How do you respond to students' homework writing, tests, and reports?

8. How important in your teaching are the ministry guidelines about writing?

9. In what ways do you differ in your teaching practices from the *Richtlinien* guidelines about writing activities?

10. How much freedom do your students have in writing their texts? What kinds of choices do they have?

11. In your opinion what are the connections between writing in the *Oberstufe* and writing the *Abitur*?

12. In your opinion what are the connections between writing in the *Oberstufe* and writing in the university?

13. In your opinion what are the most important outcomes of the *Oberstufe* education?

14. In what ways do you think students are best prepared as writers when they make the transition to university? Least prepared?

Appendix 3

Questions for University Faculty

1. What connections do you see between writing and the learning processes of your discipline?

2. What kinds of writing do you expect students to have learned in their *Oberstufe* studies? What writing abilities and writing preparation do you expect students to bring from *Gymnasium* to university?

3. In your experience, what kinds of problems do students have when they make the transition from *Oberstufe* to university as writers?

4. What kind of writing do you think is important for students to learn in the *Grundstudium* [first four semesters] courses in your discipline?

5. In what ways are students' writing abilities developed in the courses of study in your discipline?

6. How does your teaching build on students' existing abilities as writers? How do you seek to change and develop students' writing abilities in your courses?

7. What writing activities do you emphasize in your courses? Why?

8. How do you respond to students' shorter writings? Tests? Reports? Seminar research papers? What kinds of feedback do you give students for these types of writing?

9. What do you expect your students to learn in a seminar? How is students' writing tied in with these expectations?

Appendix 4

ABGABETERMIN
für Hauptseminarhausarbeiten

ist immer der 1. Tag des folgenden Semesters.
Grundsätzlich gilt für die Überschreitung der Abgabefrist:

Absolut letzter Abgabetermin ist für das Sommersemester jeweils der 1. November, bzw. für das Wintersemester der 1. Mai. Eine schriftliche Begründung ist vorher erforderlich. Nur triftige Gründe wie ein längerer Auslandsaufenthalt oder Krankeit zählen. Diese Begründung wird dann der fertigen Arbeit beigelegt.

Notes

1. In 1998 the federal government gave official sanction for universities to explore B.A. and B.S. programs as alternative curricular options in some fields.

2. From Magdeburg the following students participated: Janet Gressler—6th semester, political science/psychology (Gymnasium Oschersleben); Christian Hausmann—7th semester, political science/history (Gymnasium Stendal); Doreen Hausmann (no relation to Christian)—4th semester, sociology/education (Gymnasium Schönebeck); anonymous—2nd semester student; Michael Koliska—7th semester, sociology/English (Gymnasium Magdeburg); Odette Mannecke—4th semester, pedagogics/psychology (Gymnasium Halle); Livia Regel—3rd semester, English/sociology (Gymnasium Roßlau). From Münster the following students participated: Mona Brueing—10th semester, English/German/education (Gymnasium Paderborn); Janine Cramer—6th semester, English/history/education (Gymnasium Warendorf); Jessica Csoma—3rd semester, history/economics (Gymnasium Wolbeck); Lena Drosselmeyer—6th semester, theology/education (Gymnasium Holzminden); Andreas Francke—9th semester, public relations/political science (Gymnasium Morgenröte); Sandra Gulschinsky—7th semester, history/English/education (Gymnasium Lengerich); Andreas Kirsch—9th semester, history/mass media; Maria Kötter—13th semester, English/education; Alexandra Metz—8th semester, German/math/education (Gymnasium Wupperthal); Karla Stobbe—2nd semester, philosophy/law; Rolf Swadzba—10th semester, English/education (Gymnasium Ahlen).

Teachers interviewed include, from Sachsen-Anhalt, Magdebur, Ulf Brüdigam from Immanuel-Kant-Gymnasium Magdeburg and a group including Frau Kubon, Frau Hampel, Frau Jakuzeit, Frau Wiegand, and Frau Rößling from Hegel-Gymnasium Magdeburg. From Northrhine Westphalia: Dr. Alois Tomes, Gymnasium Lengerich; Lothar Esser, Gymnasium Lüdinghausen; Alexander Diesenroth, Studienseminar Münster.

University faculty interviewed include, from the University of Magdeburg, Dr. Walter Bauer, Prof. Dr. Ingrid Hölzler, Dr. Jürgen Martini, Prof. Dr. Wolfgang Renszch, and Prof. Dr. Fritz Schütze. Faculty from the Univesity of Münster include Dr. Arnulf Jürgens, Herr Markus Kötter, Prof. Dr. Klaus Ostheeren, Prof. Dr. Ulrich Pfister, and Dr. Willi Real.

Background information was provided by Herr H.-J. Gauss, Dr. L. Katzorke, Herr F. Minogue, and Herr A. Steger, all of TU Chemnitz; Prof. Dr. G. Bach, Prof. Dr. E. Haueis, and Prof. Dr. Steinig of PH Heidelberg; Prof. Dr. J. Ossner, Prof. Dr. J. Redling, Prof. Dr. W. Peterson, and Prof. Dr. Tillman of PH Weingarten.

3. A small percentage of students earn an *Abitur* in *Gesamtschule* (comprehensive school), offered in some states as an alternative to the multiple pathways system.

4. The *Abitur* grade itself, however, does not affect student admission to university. By agreement among the states, a mere passing grade (for example, a 4 on a scale of 1 [best] to 6 [worst]) is sufficient to gain entry to any university in Germany in any discipline not subject to an enrollment limit. For students in humanities and social sciences—like the students in the current study—only a minimum passing grade is really necessary for them to enter university. Moreover, unlike most scholarship awards in U.S. colleges and universities, the financial aid offered by the government to German students is based entirely on the family's financial situation.

5. Descriptions of writing activities for each subject are nearly identical among the disciplinary guidelines within each state. Guidelines for German, history, and theology are the sources for the analysis that follows (theology is a major subject in *Gymnasium*). New versions of these guidelines have recently been issued, well after the period covered by this study.

6. Many interviews were conducted in English, and those are reproduced exactly as spoken, though the syntax in a few places shows that English is not the speaker's native language. Those interviews conducted in German (mostly in the Magdeburg area) were transcribed and translated by native speakers Nicola Dietzelt, Anja Reicherstorfer, and Rolf Swadzba. I have done the translations of published material myself.

7. *Professor Mamlock* won a national literary prize in the early years of the GDR. Set in Berlin in 1933, its hero is a Jewish doctor devoted to apolitical ideals of service to humanity who manages to evade Nazi persecution until he sacrifices his own freedom for a persecuted assistant. Required to acknowledge the new power of the Nazis, he shoots himself to avoid disgrace. As the play ends, his son and daughter have decided to fight the Nazis by joining the "new way" of communism.

8. This rule is currently under debate in federal and state governments, many academics and politicians arguing that it is high time to tighten up time requirements for degree completion.

9. At both Magdeburg and Münster, it is the students' responsibility to present this record to the university when they petition to take comprehensive examinations and write the thesis for the master's degree. They must present a verifying document for each credit they have received. Students keep these documents *(Leistungsnachweisen)* uneasily in file folders and desk drawers; they must appear at the testing office *(Prüfungsamt)* clutching a sheaf of documents attesting to all the credits they have earned, in order to prove their eligibility to take exams and write theses.

10. Though German students and faculty tend to translate *wissenschaftlich* as "scientific" in their English conversation, it is not actually associated with scientific work in the English-language sense of laboratory experimentation and the like. As Professor Gerd Brauer of Emory University says, "*wissenschaftlich* means 'academic,' not really 'scientific'—that would be *Naturwissenschaft*" (letter to David Foster, 4 April 1996).

11. Here are some titles: Axel Bänsch, *Wissenschaftliches Arbeiten*, 5th ed., Munich: R. Oldenbourg Verlag, 1996; Walter Krämer, *Wie Schreibe ich eine Seminar- , Examens- , und Diplomarbeit?* [How Do I Write a Seminar Paper, Examination Paper, or Degree Thesis?], Stuttgart: Gustav Fischer Verlag, 1992; Manuel R. Theisen, *Wissenschaftliches Arbeiten*: Technik-Methoden-Form, München: Verlag Franz Vahlen, 1991; Georg Rückriem, et al., *Die Technik Wissenschaftlichen Arbeitens,* 8th ed., Paderborn: Ferdinand Schoningh, 1994.

Works Cited

Anweiler, Oskar, et al., eds. "Deutschland." *Bildungssysteme in Europa*. Ed. Oscar Anweiler. Weinheim: Beltz, 1996. 31–56.

Bartholomae, David. "Inventing the University." *When a Writer Can't Write: Studies in Writer's Block and Other Composing-Process Problems.* Ed. M. Rose. New York: Guilford, 1985. 134–65.

Bereiter, Carl, and Marlene Scardamalia. *The Psychology of Written Composition.* Hillsdale, NJ: Erlbaum, 1987.

Bünting, Karl-Dieter. *Schreiben im Studium: Ein Trainingsprogram.* Berlin: Cornelsen Scriptor, 1996.

Cole, Michael, and Yrgo Engeström. "A Cultural-Historical Approach to Distributed Cognition." *Distributed Cognitions: Psychological and Educational Considerations.* Ed. Gavriel Salomon. Cambridge: Cambridge UP, 1993. 1–46.

Geisler, Cheryl. *Academic Literacy and the Nature of Expertise: Reading, Writing, and Knowing in Academic Philosophy.* Hillsdale, NJ: Erlbaum, 1994.

Golz, Reinhard, and Wolfgang Mayrhofer. *Education in Germany: An Overview of Developments in the Unification Process.* International Academy of Humanization of Education. Alberta, Can.: Alberta Learning, 2000.

Greene, Stuart. "Making Sense of My Own Ideas: The Problems of Authorship in a Beginning Writing Classroom." *Written Communication* 12 (1995): 186–218.

Kruse, Otto. *Keine Angst vor dem Leeren Blatt: Ohne Schreibblockaden durchs Studium.* 8th ed. Frankfurt: Campus Verlag, 2000.

Lave, Jean, and Etienne Wenger. *Situated Learning: Legitimate Peripheral Participation.* Cambridge: Cambridge UP, 1991.

Peterßen, Wilhelm H. *Wissenschaftliche(s) Arbeiten: Eine Einführung für Schüler und Studenten.* München: Ehrenwirth, 1987.

Prior, Paul A. *Writing/Disciplinarity: A Sociohistoric Account of Literate Activity in the Academy.* Mahwah, NJ: Erlbaum, 1998.

Rahmenrichtlinien: Gymnasium/FachGymnasium: Deutsch. Magdeburg: Kultusministerium des Landes Sachsen-Anhalt, 1994.

Richtlinien: Deutsch: Gymnasiale Oberstufe in Nordrhein-Westfalen. Düsseldorf: Schriftenreihe des Ministeriums für Schule und Weiterbildung, 1991.

Richtlinien: Geschichte: Gymnasiale Oberstufe in Nordrhein-Westfalen. Düsseldorf: Schriftenreihe des Ministeriums für Schule und Weiterbildung 1981.

Russell, David R. "Rethinking Genre in School and Society: An Activity Theory Analysis." *Written Communication* 14 (1997): 504–54.

von Werder, Lutz. *Wissenschaftliches Schreiben an Deutschen Universitäten*. HDZ-INFO 1994 Nr. 1, Alice-Salomon-Fachhochschule Berlin, 1994.

Westfälische Nachrichten, 6 Feb. 1998: 1.

CHAPTER FIVE

An Academic Writer in Kenya: The Transition from Secondary School to the University

MARY NYAMBURA MUCHIRI

Daystar University, Nairobi

The persistent interest in writing as an academic discipline in the United States and Canada has been evidenced by the development of a "composition industry" in those countries. The National Council of Teachers of English has promoted research on writing through its various journals. The Braddock Awards, for example, have also gone a long way in encouraging research on writing, as the 50th anniversary edition of *College Composition and Communication* reveals. As I and others have suggested, however, this interest in writing as a particular field of learning and teaching is limited outside the United States and Canada (Muchiri, Mulamba, Myers, and Ndoloi). In many countries, research in academic writing, rather than focusing on the writing development of all students, supports programs for students whose first language is not English. In Kenya, for example, academic writing is studied in applied linguistics or English-language-teaching departments under the general heading of English for Specific Purposes (ESP). As the name suggests, institutions that teach English under the heading ESP have a more limited view of their mission than English departments in the United States. Rather than offer a theory of composition or language use (except in discourse analysis courses), ESP tries to analyze the immediate needs of students, define an appropriate register of English for them, and suggest the most efficient ways of teaching English so that students can get on with their studies. This difference in approach is a result of the fact that while writing pedagogy in the

United States and Canada is based on the assumption that students are speakers of English as a first language (L1), those teaching English outside the United States have to deal with English as a second (L2) or foreign language (FL), as Tucker and Costello illustrate when they claim, "The United States is the only country where you can graduate from college without having studied a foreign language" (3).

In Kenya, English is the official language of instruction at university. Most students begin learning English in school and are expected to learn the skills of academic reading and writing in English during their school years. Kenya has an 8-4-4 educational system introduced in 1990, in which students attend eight years of primary education beginning at the age of six, four years of secondary education, and four years of undergraduate study for those who continue beyond the secondary level (see Figure 6). But the assumption that students can learn sufficient academic reading and writing skills in school to ensure a successful transition to university has become increasingly problematic. Under this new system, students have two years less of secondary school and one more year of university than they did under the previous system. Consequently, students have fewer years in which to develop adequate skills in written academic English. This lack of preparation in academic English creates difficulties especially for students in the first year at university, which is intended to serve as a foundation year for entering students. During this foundation year, students are supposed to be equipped with all the linguistic and study skills they need in order to cope with the rest of their university studies.

To help students develop academic writing skills once they arrive at university, the Communication Skills Project (COSP) was founded in the public universities of Kenya in the early 1990s. The project was funded by what was then the Overseas Development Administration of the British government. Departments of communication skills were established in all public universities in Kenya and charged with the responsibility of developing courses to bridge the gaps between the old and the new systems. One version of these courses is called English for Academic Purposes (EAP)—courses specifically intended to prepare students for academic writing at university. The courses referred to later in this

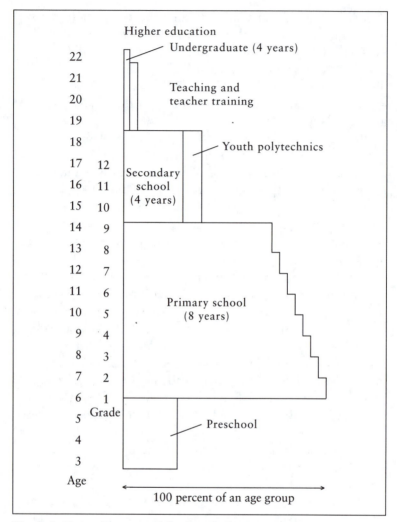

Figure 6. *Kenya: Structure of the formal education system.*

chapter are courses of this kind. Yet despite the introduction of these EAP courses in the first, general year of university to help students develop needed academic writing skills, most students do not receive adequate preparation in academic English. In a study of students entering Kenyatta University, where I was teaching in 1993, I found that because most students learn English in secondary school, and because under the new system students had fewer years of such schooling before university, the shortened years of English-language learning put most students at a clear disadvantage when they matriculated at university. They were generally less competent in academic English than those who had completed more years of the A-level under the old system.

I found, for example, that under the new system the General Paper previously written for A-level (the last two years of secondary schooling, ages seventeen to eighteen) was dropped in most EAP courses at university. This paper had played an important role in helping students learn the skills associated with academic English in the university. It was used to give students general practice in the writing of essays in academic English in all subjects. These essays were longer and required more student input than the compositions done earlier at the secondary school level. Other research has also shown that A-level students typically experience writing problems, especially during their first year at university. According to Drury, for example, "particular weaknesses lay in the field of study skills . . . [that is] . . . the inability to follow up library and reference materials, making notes from written sources, note-taking in lectures, presentations in tutorials" (122).

After the new educational system was established permitting fewer years in secondary school and thus less time for the development of academic English in school, Kenyan students began showing significant problems in making the transition to university as readers and writers of academic English. When the change to the new system first occurred, I and some colleagues determined that further research was required to assess the language proficiency levels of students entering university in the new system (Muchiri, Claessen, Rimbui, and Greenhalgh). With further input from COSP, a core course book for all public universities was developed (Bint, Barnett, Greenhalgh, and Robinson) that emphasized areas needing immediate development when students arrived at university:

1. library skills

2. study skills

3. reading and note-taking skills, and the interpretation of graphs

4. writing skills

This broad mandate for teaching both language and learning skills has proved to be a heavy burden for the EAP courses to bear. As I suggest later in this chapter, EAP courses have not been able to carry this burden satisfactorily for many students.

It should be noted, however, that the movement to establish separate communication and study skills departments did not affect the private universities such as Daystar, the university where I currently teach. The result has been that the Department of Language and Literature is expected to teach communication and study skills in addition to teaching English as a minor and a major subject. Moreover, Daystar admits students from all over the world, bringing in students who speak native languages such as Arabic and Amharic, as well as some U.S. students. This linguistic heterogeneity has forced my university to develop literacy skills courses analogous to the EAP courses of public universities so that students with diverse literacies can be given some developmental instruction in academic English as they enter university studies.

Since some students need remedial courses more than others, only those who fail a department placement test enroll for the courses. The test is modeled on the Test of English as a Foreign Language (TOEFL) but has proven particularly problematic for African students. It measures language skills, including listening, reading, and writing, in order to identify the right level of needed support for each student. Those students from countries where English is not used as the medium of instruction are not tested but instead automatically enrolled in a basic English as a second language (ESL) course for a semester; they are not allowed to take other courses, in order to give them time to develop a working knowledge of English. Those who produce satisfactory results of 500 points or above in the TOEFL are exempted from this remedial course. All students are required to take two general language courses, Advanced Reading and Advanced Writing, no matter what their majors. These courses, intended to help students develop their reading and writing abilities in academic English, are seldom adequate to students' needs. Thus most students from non-English-speaking countries struggle throughout their entire program of study in the university because they lack academic writing skills in English.

The rest of this chapter deals with the limitations of the EAP courses in helping students become academic writers and the social-cultural problems faced by teachers of writing. In addition, I elaborate on the concept of academic writing as opposed to other types of writing. Finally, I highlight specific problems faced by new Kenyan writers and suggest a possible way forward. The data for this essay come mainly from my personal experiences as a teacher of writing at both school and university in Kenya, and from research focused on the problems of language learning in multilingual educational settings.

Attitudes toward Writing in Kenya

Assumptions concerning why, what, and how people write vary widely from culture to culture. Some of the assumptions underlying Kenyans' perspectives on writing may be summarized as follows:

What is written is permanent. In work situations, one often hears words similar to the following: "Why did you have to write a memo? You could have discussed the matter with me." The implication is that a discussion would be forgotten quickly but a memo will remain permanently in the person's file, for better or worse. The same idea is expressed in many other ways. The main reason for writing a biography, for example, is to make sure the person will be remembered. So writing is seen as positive in that it makes a good record permanent, but it is also negatively perceived if the record is bad. This may explain the extensive use of proverbs in the oral African tradition since these apply generally rather than to specific individuals.

What is written is true. This assumption was prevalent in Kenya until recently. It sprang from the fact that writing is a recent phenomenon, Kenyan society being traditionally oral. One often heard such expressions as, "It is true, it was in the *Nation* [a local daily newspaper]." In student writing, this assumption manifests itself in the way students quote from books but do not question any of the views expressed because they assume that any statement printed in a book must be true. This is a major problem that teachers of writing in Kenya must address. A related problem is the idea that once an idea is written, it becomes public property. Students often quote long paragraphs without acknowledging the sources. The concept of plagiarism is foreign to many students.

What is written in English is worth more than what is written in local languages. This assumption has emerged because of the association of English with education. During the colonial period, only those who went to school knew how to read and write English. People learned how to write in local languages mainly for personal letters and records. Currently in Kenya most books and even newspapers and magazines are written in English. The widespread tendency to privilege English as the authoritative language of Kenya remains entrenched in Kenyan culture. Even a notable writer such as Ngugi wa Thiong'o, who has written such books as *Decolonizing the Mind* and *Matigari* in an effort to popularize local Kenyan languages, has not been able to change this attitude. It is a frequent saying even among the educated, "I have nothing to write about." What they really mean is that their ideas cannot easily be expressed in English.

It is very difficult to write in English. As a second, third, or fourth language for many Kenyans, English is not easily used for self-expression. When people are asked to write articles for our church magazine, for example, many excuse themselves by saying that they cannot express themselves well in English. If the same people are interviewed on the same topics, they have no problem expressing themselves as long as someone else writes the article.

Among university lecturers, the same problem manifests itself. A lecturer, for example, was returning a term paper to his student and informed him that his ideas "did not flow." The student wanted to know how he could make them flow, but the lecturer could not give a satisfactory answer because of his limited knowledge of writing skills and limited vocabulary in English. What he probably wanted to communicate to the student was that the paper lacked coherence due to the use of inappropriate sentence connectors and a misunderstanding of the structure of a paragraph. The lecturer's inability to articulate his ideas suggests the difficulties many instructors native to Kenya face in applying their limited command of academic English to pedagogical purposes.

Writing is creating. When one writes a poem, a play, or a novel, one is clearly perceived to be creating something new. What most students fail to understand is that an essay is also a creation of ideas and values through a writer's choice of words and style of writing. A good illustration of writing as creating may be seen in the popular Kenyan response to the main character in Thiong'o's *Matigari.* A few months after the book came out, many people were talking about him as if he were a real person. Rumors went around that politicians at one time demanded his arrest, only to be informed that he was a character in a book. In another act of creating through writing, the colonial powers claim to have "discovered" such places as Mount Kenya, probably meaning they were the first to put the name on a map, since the local people not only saw it daily but also regarded it as the home of their God, locally known as "Ngai."

The Influence of the Community on Academic Writing

The fact that peoples' attitude to writing may greatly enhance or hinder their success at school and university has been demonstrated in studies of community writing, such as those by Barton and Ivanic. In his chapter on the social nature of writing, Barton says that

> the social settings in which literacy occurs are particular to individual societies and have developed over time. Like other cultural activities, ways of being literate are passed on from generation to generation. They are reorganized and reinvented by each succeeding generation. We, therefore, also need to take a relativistic view where a historical perspective is included. . . . To take account of this, we need a view of literacy that allows change, a dynamic view of peoples constantly developing literacy rather than a static mode. . . . The position we take here is that school, work, and community are different domains of literacy and we

need to develop ways of talking about literacy in these different domains. (1–2)

I have found this insight into the connections between attitudes in Kenyan society and students' performances at school and university very important in my work as an evaluator of students' responses to examination prompts. Kenyan perspectives on literacy are reflected in both the attitude of the individual examiner and the practices of the wider society in which the institution is based. I have found, for example, that the concept of *harambee*, which means pulling together through contributing to other people's needs, is constantly exploited for examination purposes. In order to "survive" the examinations, a group of students will write notes on strips of paper known as "Mwakenya" (an underground political movement) or, more recently, "Chips," and pass them among themselves during the examination. They do not regard such an action as cheating but rather as helping one another. The examination system itself is so competitive that it does not encourage critical thinking, and students reproduce the teacher's notes because they fear failing the examination. Indeed, students are *expected* to take notes and reproduce them on examinations; they are not expected to contribute to knowledge during their studies. In the same way, university lecturers expect to be treated as "elders" and in most cases do not expect to be questioned by students about the validity of their knowledge. The individualistic competitiveness of the examination system thus conflicts with the African community way of life, the sense that all share in tasks affecting community members. The impact of *harambee* varies among different settings and groups. It has been exploited by some who claim they need money from friends to pay hospital fees, which have actually already been paid by their employer. Some give out money during *harambee* meetings as a way of controlling the group in need, while others ease their consciences by giving money to the local churches.

In their chapter on community writing and education, Ivanic and Moss distinguish between "imposed" and "self-generated" writing. By imposed writing, they mean "writing for which the style and range of allowable content is laid down for us by social institutions" (193). Self-imposed writing, on the other hand, means "writing that stems from our own needs, interests and purposes, in which we are free to adopt our own content and styles" (193). I believe most Kenyans are involved in imposed writing. Even letter writing in Kenya is not as common as in Western societies. It seems likely that self-generated writing is rare among Kenyans, but research in this area is needed. For students, learning to use the different forms of writing imposed by the Kenyan educational system is a key element of their transition from school to university.

From School Composition to University Essay

Kenyan students must learn an important distinction in Kenyan education between compositions and essays as they make the transition from school to university. This involves moving from brief narrative tasks to longer expository tasks, and from writing processes suitable for brief exam writing to processes suitable for longer essay writing, often researched.

A Student's Definition of Composition

To illustrate this distinction, I have used the words of my son Timothy, who was at home while I was writing this chapter. He had just finished writing his O-level examinations (the British General Certificate of Secondary Examination [GCSE] taken before the A-level course), so he had participated in writing compositions for the past four years in preparation for the examination. I asked him to write a brief explanation of what the word *composition* meant to him. This is what he wrote:

> A composition, from my point of view, is or could be, a **story** you have imagined or a real life account of the past or on the future. It is recording the events in point form or continuous writing, for example titles like, "My Summer Holiday" or "Modern Technology." This helps you to be imaginative in one topic and to have some information on the other, based on the facts and not assumptions. I would also say that a composition will also help in **summarizing** something you had read, thereby learning how to write things in brief.

A secondary school composition generally is for grammar and communication skills mainly the **basics,** for example punctuation, and correct standard English. When writing a composition and you for example, use figurative language you must explain the metaphor and then proceed with your story. A composition just shows the kind of a person or personality the writer is, on a very small scale, without a lot of research. The type of writing you are using could be expressive or informative or a kind of writing that influences the opinion of the examiner, like persuading him or her view of things. The tone which you use or your approach to a certain topic is also important, so is the audience that you are addressing. The type of sentences may be simple or complex, and this are arranged in paragraphs. You are restricted to write a total of between 350 and 600 words and to stick to the topic provided.

With an essay you are supposed to or advised to include quotes, comparisons for example the past and the present, what you hope to gain and how it is relevant to your topic, giving your own opinion or advantages and disadvantages, and then concluding. All these may be interpreted differently by different people, but with a composition you are advised to be brief, and to the point, so as not to go out of topic.

The words in bold suggest the main differences between compositions written by secondary school children and essays expected of university students in Kenya. The word *story* implies that the most common genre is the narrative. Students at secondary school are not normally expected to write expository or argument essays, for example. Most of the time they are expected to summarize information from texts or from their own experience and write short descriptive essays. They are provided with specific titles to write about. They may even discuss these titles as a whole class before being asked to write about them individually, a process normally referred to as "controlled composition."

The compositions are based on either facts known to the student or his or her own imagination. The writing should be correct with regard to the basics of grammar, spelling, and paragraphing. The student is not normally expected to do any research, except in cases such as oral literature, for which they are asked to find out information from members of their families about common stories and proverbs. Consequently, the length of the composition is normally restricted to between 350 and 600 words.

University Writing Tasks

At university, on the other hand, the term "composition" refers to short pieces of writing such as exercises for class assessment or responses to examination questions. Longer pieces of writing are referred to as "essays" or "term papers." For the undergraduate, the most frequent type of writing is the term paper. Other types of writing expected of undergraduates are laboratory or field reports, seminar presentations, and notes taken during lectures or made after reading library books. For students taking subjects such as communication or literature, poems, short stories, and newspaper articles may also be required. Most of the subject-specific skills are taught by lecturers in the disciplines, but teaching the basic skills for writing term papers is usually the responsibility of either the communication skills teachers or the English teachers.

In order to write good term papers, students must be able to cite other people's work without plagiarizing, what Timothy probably means by "include quotes." Kenyan students find this very difficult for two reasons. First, many find it strange to speak of ideas as "belonging" to someone. To them, once an idea is published it becomes public property. In a study I conducted among Daystar's academic staff in 1997, I found that plagiarism was the worst problem faculty had to deal with when marking term papers. Second, many students have difficulty distinguishing between various documentation styles and formats. Different lecturers tend to use different methods, thereby confusing students. Faculty in the English department, therefore, decided to expose the students to all the main methods, as described in Kate Turabian's *Manual for Writers*, but to caution them to use whatever system they choose consistently throughout a paper.

University students must also be able to write in other genres in addition to narrative, as Timothy suggests in referring to the tasks of comparisons and giving opinions. This is another area in which I have found Daystar students deficient. Students often confuse comparison with description, while accepting other peoples' opinions without criticism and often equating them with facts. In my earlier study at Kenyatta University, I found that students had similar problems when answering examination questions

(Muchiri, *Influence* 135). The following question, for example, posed difficulties for students:

> Compare and contrast the safety measures required in teaching swimming and athletics.

Here the contrast is signaled by the phrase "compare and contrast." This task seemed to present problems for students. Although they were asked to compare the safety measures in swimming and athletics, most of them described safety measures for swimming separately from those for athletics, without showing the relationship between the two. The problem may arise because students are not used to this type of writing at secondary school.

The Writing Process

Clouse enters a long-standing debate when she suggests that every academic writer, unlike the secondary composition writer, has to be concerned not just with the "product" of his or her writing, but with the writing process as well (63). She suggests that academic writers must be able to answer a series of questions as completely as possible when they plan and compose a piece of writing, addressing such matters as in what physical or social space to begin writing, how to organize ideas, whether to compose the piece in one sitting or in several, whether and how much to revise after the first draft, how to move ahead when stuck at a certain point, and how to shape the planning/composing process for best results. Students writing in secondary school in Kenya are generally not expected to concern themselves with these issues. Therefore, when they arrive at university, they do not have experience in the composing and revising processes represented by these questions. Yet many university lecturers assume that their students have learned the planning-composing-revising procedures implied by these questions and so do not help students until weaknesses in their term papers become clear.

A few examples may help illustrate specific problems that Kenyan students face in writing at university. Students find it very difficult, for example, to choose their own topics for term papers and then narrow them down, perhaps because they are used to being given topics to write about at the secondary level. Also, university students are expected to get their ideas from many sources and integrate them in a logical order. The challenge of synthesizing various authoritative voices in their own writing requires students to account for differing interpretations of the same issues, an idea that is introduced but not fully developed at secondary school. Students also have difficulty with logic and organization in their writing, and pitfalls in reasoning are sometimes not fully dealt with even at the university level.

In addition to mastering strategies for incorporating and citing authoritative sources, student writers at Kenyan universities must learn general conventions used in academic writing worldwide. They are expected, for example, to master formats for various types of essays such as narrative, expository, and argumentative. And they are expected to learn how to enter an ongoing scholarly conversation and establish their authority as writers by, in Bazerman's words, "placing themselves both within and against a discourse, or within competing discourses and working self-consciously to claim an interpretive project of their own, and that gives them their privilege to speak" (158). Bazerman assumes that the teacher of writing is always capable of leading the student into the world of research and debate. Unfortunately, this cannot occur if the teacher is not already in that world, and many Kenyan teachers are not.

Problems Faced by Emerging Kenyan Writers

Emerging writers in Kenya face a wide range of problems, which I analyze in terms of sociolinguistic challenges, sociocultural attitudes and values, and institutional constraints of teachers, schools, and management.

Sociolinguistic Challenges

Commenting on the sociolinguistic situation in Kenya, Love describes the Kenyan as being in the middle situation between native speaker and English-as-a-foreign-language speaker. In my own

study, I have noted that this middle situation has complex implications for teachers of academic English:

> The middle situation between native speakers and those speak-
> ing English as a Foreign Language (EFL) is problematic in that
> we are not dealing with students who, in general, have an inad-
> equate grasp of either the grammatical features or the vocabu-
> lary of English, especially in speaking, and so they tend to resent
> anything that might suggest that they are getting remedial En-
> glish. (Muchiri, *Communication* 72)

So despite students' mastery of English on the whole, both the
communication skills (CS) and subject specialist lecturers are
aware that there is an important mismatch between students'
perception of their own linguistic proficiency and their ability to
communicate successfully in academic contexts, especially in
writing.

The sociolinguistic situation is further complicated by the
fact that while English is mainly used in academic and other official domains, it is not prevalent in other areas of Kenyan life.
Kiswahili and more than forty mother tongues are also spoken,
especially in trade and at home. This means that all university
students must be able to speak at least three languages: English,
the medium of instruction at secondary and tertiary levels;
Kiswahili, the national language; and at least one mother tongue
specific to a student's native culture within Kenya. Students may
come to university speaking up to nine different languages. Moreover, there are few native speakers of English in rural schools
and more local, often untrained teachers at the secondary level.
These factors have contributed to a persistently low standard of
English instruction in the Kenyan system, as Drury describes:

> The senior Inspector of English Language wrote that there has
> been a widely expressed concern voiced by the public, govern-
> ment officials, teachers, university lecturers and others about a
> gradual decline in the standard of spoken and written English
> among our secondary school graduates . . . and simple surveys at
> the university college reveal the same problem, among first year
> undergraduates. (122)

Another major cause of the inadequacy of students' preparation in academic English has been the so-called communicative approach to the teaching of language. This method emphasizes fluency in speech over the ability to use grammatically correct expressions in writing. Although some teachers have now realized the importance of teaching grammatical structures, many students who went through the system are still suffering the consequences. The communicative approach, says Onguine, emphasizes

> contextualization through an eclectic approach. This means that from the context all the possible linguistic items are worked out and discussed. The context, therefore, serves as a frame of reference on which these items interplay to form meaningful and acceptable expressions. This approach generates communication both in writing and in speech. (v)

The result of this approach is that students are unable to understand how grammatical structures of the target language actually function. Consequently, Kenyan students are able to use grammatical features of English but without understanding how they work. They lack any analytical understanding of the bases of their own competence in English. Many students in my writing classes, for example, do not know what is meant by "parts of speech," although they use most of them correctly. Unfortunately, particularly for students training to be teachers, an analytic understanding of language elements is an important part of their literate mastery. It is vital that they understand grammatical structures so that they can explain why certain structures are correct or incorrect, and why idiomatic expressions in one language often cannot be literally rendered in a different language. Many students attempt literal translations from one language into another. It is common knowledge that speakers of certain Kenyan languages have specific problems when learning English sounds. A Meru student will tend to nasalize English sounds almost indiscriminately, whereas a Kikuyu student will confuse /l/ and /r/ sounds and a Luo will pronounce "sh" as /s/. A creative teacher will use these common difficulties as opportunities to explore the differences between the first and the second language rather than punish the students for the errors.

Another, related effect of the sociolinguistic situation in Kenya is "code mixing " or "code switching." According to Myers-Scotton, the two terms refer to the same phenomenon, that of "alterations of linguistic varieties within the same conversation" (3). She gives many examples from Nairobi and Harare, in Zimbabwe, to illustrate that "code switching exploits the socio-psychological attributes which languages use" (3). She goes on to identify three spheres of language usually involved in code-switching activity—home, neighborhood, and work:

> The executive secretary, with her sophisticated hair-style, becomes quite a different person when she goes home to become a mother and wife, tending children and cooking the evening meal. Not only does she exchange her Western dress for the indigenous "Kanga"—a length of brightly patterned cloth, but she also puts aside her fluent English and speaks her mother tongue with her family. (3)

Code switching, using more than one language simultaneously, is a way of life for most Kenyans, both in speech and in writing. One example from Myers-Scotton illustrates this:

> (Setting : A Nairobi office. Three young women from two ethnic groups (Luyia I, Luyia II, Luo) are conversing. Swahili is the main medium, with switches to English).

Luyia I.	Hello, guys. Shule zitafunguliwa lini? "Hello, guys. When will the schools be opened?"
Luyia II.	Na Kweli hata mimi si-ko sure lakini na-itakuwa week kesho (<u>week tomorrow</u>). "Well, even I am not sure, but I suspect it will be next week."
Luo.	Shule zi -ta open tarehe tatu mwezi wa tano. "Schools will open on <u>the third day of the fifth month </u>(3rd of May)."
Luyia II.	Nafikiri shule za primary na za secondary zitatangulia kufungua lakini colleges na polytechnics zitakua za mwisho kufunguliwa. "I think primary schools will be the first to open, but colleges and polytechnics will be the last to be opened." (5)

The underlined expressions are examples of literal translations that tend to be used in code switching and are sometimes transferred into written English. For example, a colleague tells of a secondary school student who came to her crying. When asked what the matter was, he said, "The students in my class are seeing for me." This is a literal translation from Kiswahili of "Wananionea," meaning they were accusing him falsely. So code switching may affect writing at both the lexical and grammatical levels. An exhaustive analysis of how code switching affects writing would be a useful area for future research in its application to writing development in multilingual educational systems such as Kenya's.

Unfortunately, if the writing teacher does not know the source language, it is difficult to help the students. The literal translation may be treated like other mistakes. No teacher will know all forty-plus Kenyan languages, of course, but if teachers are made sensitive enough during teacher training, they can identify such problems more easily and help the students to overcome them. With more and more untrained lecturers joining the teaching profession immediately after completing their university studies, this problem is likely to persist for a long time to come.

Sociocultural Attitudes and Values

As I suggested in the introduction, some Kenyan assumptions about writing are negative. Many students are not used to expressing themselves in writing, one possible reason being that Kenyan society tends to be repressive. Freedom of expression is the prerogative of only a few. The idea of keeping a personal journal is also foreign to many Kenyan students, unlike their U.S. counterparts, who tend to be more familiar with journaling. Only within the last four generations has writing been introduced to Kenyans, by the British colonial administrators. Moreover, bilingualism has on the whole been viewed as a disadvantage rather than an advantage. Until very recently, skills learned in one language and later transferred to the second have been described as "interference." Language teachers, and in fact most African educators, need Shorter's reminder that "what we are already determines—in part—what we perceive. Our creative imagination thus enlarges our experience of reality, and plays a role in all of our discoveries, those of science included" (18).

The negative values associated with African languages are the result of colonial education, wherein all worthwhile knowledge was attributed to the English language and Western/Christian values. Pupils in primary and secondary schools, for example, used to be punished for speaking their mother tongues anywhere on the school compound. Unfortunately, even thirty-six years after political independence the Kenyan mind has not been fully decolonized.

Moreover, a new kind of colonialism involving ideas as well as material things seems to have come into being. Knowledge is still vetted in the West despite apparent globalization:

> North American and European academics may be struck each day by how institutions of knowledge become more and more global in their reach. This change is particularly striking in composition research, as it achieves academic respectability, but it is true to different degrees in all fields. Journals, conferences, publishers, and research projects are international, linked by e-mail, photocopies, faxes, and airlines. But this apparent globalization is deceptive. Everyday academic work is still overwhelmingly determined by its national setting. The funding, the geography, the politics, the national ideology determine daily concerns like hours, class size, assessment, careers. And access to that global network of contacts is by no means equally apportioned. (Muchiri, Mulamba, Myers, and Ndoloi 194)

An example of this deceptive globalization is the tighter control that donor communities seem to be wielding over the recipient communities. Some time ago, for example, an international linguistic conference was due to be held in Kenya. It was canceled on the pretext that the local organizers were being "unreasonable." We later learned that the donor complained of too many "unknown" scholars being invited. The local organizers had argued that unless local scholars were invited on their home ground, they would never be known, since they were not usually invited to the international conferences held elsewhere, and when invited usually could not afford to go. The result of this negative influence has been that university lecturers in Kenya are often not exposed to research and so can hardly introduce their students to Bazerman's "ongoing conversation."

Some analysts of global development patterns predict that African countries such as Kenya will continue to be dominated economically and culturally by developed nations. Aseka, for example, argues that structural adjustment programs (SAPs) introduced by the World Bank are means of controlling African economies. Such programs are intended not only to prevent industrialization of African countries, says Aseka, but also to maintain their role as markets and sources of raw materials (1–3). Such policy fails to support, on a sustainable basis, one essential dimension of indigenous African capacities—knowledge.

Partly as a result of economic and cultural hegemony by developed countries, African scholars have received limited opportunities to contribute to global knowledge. The Kenyan government also seems to pay only lip service to research. All the talk about becoming an industrialized nation by the year 2020 does not result in government support in the form of research funds. Instead, most government funds are given to individuals in the form of bank loans that will not be repaid. Indeed, corruption has affected many academic institutions in Kenya. Many university lecturers, for example, retire poor because their pension money was embezzled by the "politically correct" people.

Institutional Problems

These problems can be divided into three categories: those related to teachers, to schools, and to management.

TEACHERS

In Kenyan universities, teachers are often untrained *as teachers*. Most are employed on the basis of their academic rather than professional qualifications. This means they are likely to use the methods that were used to teach them, most of which are often outdated. An additional problem is that they will have studied in different educational contexts and are therefore likely to introduce inappropriate teaching methods due to their lack of

awareness of their students' competencies and needs. The need
to help new teachers learn relevant teaching methodologies has
become apparent, but there are still too many untrained teachers
in all subjects. Lack of materials is one basic reason for this failure; introductions to effective teaching such as that by Gibbs and
Habeshaw need to be in wider distribution among new teachers.

Another major problem for teachers is the pay. Lecturers are
very poorly paid and so are forced to involve themselves with
moonlighting activities known as *Jua Kali* (hot sun) to make ends
meet. Research and writing for publication are not a priority for
most university faculty. If a publish-or-perish standard were to
be implemented, most lecturers would certainly perish. The weaknesses of the Kenyan economy can discourage even the most determined person. This chapter, for example, took much longer to
write than expected because it was impossible to use the computer during the day due to electricity rationing. After I completed the chapter, it took another month to send it by e-mail
because our computers are not powerful enough to send long
documents. Finally, a friend helped me send the chapter using a
multinational company's computer.

SCHOOLS

Kenyan university students come from varied cultural backgrounds, and secondary schools vary widely in quality. These
may be divided into three main categories: *harambee*, government, and private. *Harambee* schools are supported mainly by
parents and are the least equipped. Some provide only one textbook, which the teacher uses; students must rely on dictated notes.
There are no libraries nearby for most students, and some parents cannot afford even writing paper for their children or to pay
the salaries for trained teachers. Government schools, on the other
hand, may have minimum facilities and they may be allocated a
few trained teachers. They are also likely to be situated near a
national library or have access to a mobile library service. Parents pay partially subsidized fees, although fees are now generally on the increase as a result of the new government policy of
cost sharing, which spreads the cost of education between the

government and the recipient of the education. The private school is usually well equipped but expensive. It is likely to engage well-qualified teachers, when possible of European origin, and only a few students are assigned to each class so that each gets individual attention.

Though first-year university students may come from any of the three types of schools, most of them must take the same national examination, which prepares students for universities in Kenya. Some private school students take the Cambridge International Examination, which prepares them for British universities. It is important to remember that all students, not just the privileged, must be taught with respect. With varying backgrounds themselves, teachers not sensitive to students' needs may do harm by making assumptions about students without giving them the chance to prove themselves. Some students may despair, some may not be challenged enough, and others may become ashamed of their identity.

Yet giving students the preparation appropriate to their language needs and backgrounds is a complex challenge that does not allow for a universal solution. While the introduction of communication skills departments in public universities has helped the weaker student writers, those without many problems have regarded the courses as a waste of time. This negative attitude has led some students to overlook their own weaknesses as writers. For example, as an external examiner in some of these universities, I have run across students who assume they know everything and yet fail at easy tasks such as outlining an essay. They do not follow instructions and instead write the entire essay.

Moreover, English for Special Purposes courses are usually for one or two semesters only. As soon as these students finish the courses, they tend to forget what they have learned, except in the institutions where more advanced writing courses are integrated into the curriculum of second, third, and fourth years. This lack of continuity in writing development among different programs allows writing masteries gained in ESP courses to be lost in later semesters of study.

Some public and private universities have designed placement tests similar to TOEFL in order to discriminate between the weaker and stronger students in academic English. Depending on the results, the students are assigned to different courses that are deemed suitable for their specific needs. At Daystar, for example, those who fail the test are asked to take a remedial course in English grammar, while those who pass take a university course on advanced reading. Some are not allowed to take the test and are asked to take a basic course in English instead. These students come mainly from non-English-speaking countries where the medium of instruction may be another language such as French or Arabic.

While this diversity of offerings helps match students with appropriate courses in English, the writing and reading courses offered in the first year are not integrated into the rest of the curriculum. Students are often unable to write effective term papers in advanced courses in their second, third, and fourth years of university. In some public universities, such as Moi University, the students take a course every year as follows: Communication Skills (I), Communication Skills (II), Public Speaking Skills, Organizational Communication Skills, and Advanced Research and Writing Skills. These courses allow for a better integration of skills with the rest of the university programs and help students make progress in a variety of academic reading and writing skills.

Many students view English-language courses as extras that hinder them from pursuing their major subjects. This is especially true of science students and those not doing English as a major subject. Clearly, efforts to develop academic writing skills need to be integrated into all programs of study. University teachers in Kenya are also divided over the value of writing instruction across the curriculum. It is telling that many lecturers at Daystar, for example, regard content as their main focus in responding to term papers and consider writing skills such as grammar, spelling, and paragraphing as peripheral. Such an attitude encourages the view that form and content are different elements to be taught and learned separately. For this reason, as I suggest below, I believe it should be a crucial mission of Kenyan university faculty to develop ways of integrating writing development into the disciplines themselves as broadly as possible.

MANAGEMENT

Mismanagement of resources is the "curse of Africa" today, the result of selfish and self-perpetuating leaders. Nor has the education sector been spared. Many administrators are not interested in their people, the most important resource in any arena. The climate in academic institutions is demoralized, and despite many wonderful mission statements, very little is achieved. Managers are oppressive and the word *delegation* does not exist in their vocabularies; they rely on themselves or their assistant clones. No wonder the products of this educational system follow a similar path. Many students care more about good grades than about learning. And even good grades do not always help them find jobs; rather, who they know is what matters.

From this perspective, writing is not a real task but a way of getting the best grade possible, even if it means copying someone else's paper or using forged documents. At both Kenyatta and Daystar, I have had to deal with students who have copied other students' papers, and the reason is always the same: "Everyone does it: if I do not cheat, I shall fail while others get good grades from cheating." These students never consider how much they might learn through the process of writing, or how much they might benefit from the self-confidence of "knowing that they know." Many students, however, appreciate the value of writing. One student, for example, came to thank me for having been strict about making sure she had a draft of her paper. She said that although it was difficult for her, she had learned things, such as critiquing other peoples' ideas and coming up with her own views about issues, that she would not have experienced any other way.

A Way Forward

Clearly, the odds are stacked against student writers in Kenya. But while the general sociolinguistic situation cannot be changed, it can be studied in order to identify ways to help students develop as writers in schools and universities. I believe the greatest challenge for the teachers of writing in Kenya is to be aware of the uses of writing in their environment and to exploit this in their teaching methodology. This will require careful attention to cultural attitudes about writing that shape Kenyan students' development as writers. Ivanic and Moss suggest several general attitudes toward writing that can help Kenyan educators frame students' writing development within wider social and cultural settings. First, writing should be seen as part of a whole event and not an isolated activity; second, writing should be seen as purposeful, carrying out intentions embedded in the work and values of the community; third, writing should be evaluated not just as a measure of intelligence and achievement, but as an activity of communication and interaction. Kenyan teachers of writing must also recognize that there are different writing practices and conventions in different community and institutional settings, and that writing often involves collaboration and networking. These perspectives should be incorporated into school and university writing courses.

One way to achieve these objectives is to give students opportunities to write for different purposes and audiences. Students should also be encouraged, through collaboration between teachers and students, to publish in both local and international magazines and journals. As they revise drafts together, students will experience composing and revising activities in partnership with teachers and recognize the value of their own ideas as they are brought into play through the writing activities.

Teachers of writing must also understand the assumptions and values that students bring to their classes, developing strategies to deal with negative values and exploiting positive values. Reinforcing students' self-confidence will diminish the force of negative self-images created by colonialism. Teachers of writing must always bear in mind that they are working with multilinguals, and so must be sensitive to cultural values embedded in language attitudes and practices.

Money is difficult to come by in Kenya, a so-called Third World country. It is therefore a common complaint of both students and lecturers that they do not have enough teaching/learning facilities. Students at our university, for example, recently described their computer laboratory as an "archive." There are, however, resources available for language teaching that are not dependent on expensive technology, such as newspapers, magazines, and people. While computers are increasingly necessary in all areas of university education, teachers need to be aware of what can be done with what already exists. Myers-Scotton, for example, spent only a limited time in Nairobi and Harare working on her book on code switching, and all she needed was a simple tape recorder and her informants.

Thus teachers must develop a wider understanding of the nature of writing in Kenyan communities. If writing teachers were to look beyond their classrooms, they would discover new things about the processes and uses of writing in Kenyan life. I know of no studies of the forms of writing that Kenyans engage in outside of schools or college. Such research would help us understand what skills our students may bring from their families that may enhance or hinder their academic writing. Is writing a collaborative event among educated Kenyans, for example, as it often is for uneducated Kenyans? Uneducated parents in Kenya often use their school-going children to write letters to friends and complete various forms. Indeed, collaboration and sharing are implicit values in Kenyan culture generally. Do family literacy practices change as families' educational levels increase? Have changes in family literacy practices in recent years affected students' attitudes toward school writing? Recently my husband and I asked our son what he had learned about writing by helping us use our computers to produce our writing. He commented on the differences between my husband's writing style and mine, pointing out that we used different kinds of sentence structures. He also recognized that I try to blend ideas from many sources and use words that express feelings. He concluded that he hoped to do this when he goes to college. Our son's attitude may well reflect the aspirations of other student writers. It is crucial to explore further the assumptions that underlie Kenyans' views on literacy and particularly the roles that writing plays in students' development.

The question is, will the writing teacher be aware of the skills and desires that each student brings to class, and build on these? Teachers must let students express their assumptions, expectations, and desires about their own writing. Then the teacher will be able to start from the known and help students develop the writing capacities they need for success in their studies.

Unfortunately, too many university teachers—teaching three or more large classes—lack the time to respond appropriately to each student writer. This is where collaborative and interactive teaching practices may be useful. In my teaching methods classes at Kenyatta and Daystar Universities, for example, I helped my students produce a marking scheme and asked them to use it to respond to each other's work. As I went over the results, I found that when given the marking criteria, students responded carefully to each other's work, at times more strictly and thoroughly than I did. Through this interactive process, students learn from each other and realize that teachers are not the source of all knowledge. They become knowledge makers themselves, responsible for their own learning as well as that of their peers since they have to explain why they have awarded them a particular grade. Group projects offer another means of making students responsible for their own learning activities; students can be asked to collaborate on group writing tasks requiring interactive responsibility.

In an educational culture where the language of education is a second language for most students, translation exercises are very useful, though many teachers and students resist them. I believe that such exercises should be used even at advanced levels to help students realize that there are many cultural nuances in every language. Over the years of reading student texts, I have discovered that there is a persistent discrepancy between the speaker/writer's intention and the listener/reader's interpretation. It is helpful to remember, as Tucker and Costello suggest, that

> despite all the recent advances in computer technology, machines still produce, at best, rough translations that must be revised by humans. We alone can supply exact shades of meaning and a cultural context for each utterance. Failure to provide this context often results in comically unsuitable statements, as the creators of these advertising campaigns found out: Schweppes' Tonic Water was advertised in Italy as " Bathroom waters," " Come Alive with Pepsi" almost appeared in the Chinese version of *Readers' Digest* as "Pepsi Brings Your Ancestors Back from the Grave." (13)

It is also crucial to ensure that students perceive writing tasks as useful and appropriate to their needs. Writing tasks and prompts ought to be discipline specific insofar as possible so that students can see their relevance. If writing instruction is broadened to include writing activity across all disciplines, students will have opportunities to experience writing embedded in the learning activities specific to their studies. Team teaching should also be explored; communication skills lecturers could collaborate with lecturers from other departments. Communication skills lecturers would have to adapt their teaching practices to fit specific disciplinary needs, and instructors in the disciplines would be trained to incorporate writing tasks in the course work of their specialties.

Finally, the development of writing skills should be a goal not just for first-year students, but also for students throughout their studies at university. This can be done only if teachers in all disciplines see a relationship between what is said and how it is said. Language needs to be conceived as an activity embedded across all elements of the university curriculum. New teachers must be introduced to the value of writing as a major element of students' learning in all subjects if the value of writing as a way of knowing is to become a recognized element of Kenyan education.

Works Cited

Aseka, Eric Masinde. *Africa in the 21st Century.* Eldoret: Zapf Chancery, 1996.

Barton, David, and Roz Ivanic, eds. *Writing in the Community.* Vol. 6 of Written Comm. Annual. London: Sage, 1991.

Bazerman, Charles. *The Informed Writer: Using Sources in the Disciplines.* 2nd ed. Boston: Houghton, 1985.

Bint, Peter, Donald Barnett, Stuart M. Greenhalgh, and Paul Robinson. *A University Course in Academic Communication Skills Workbook.* Nairobi: Nairobi UP, 1990.

Clouse, Barbara. *The Student Writer: Editor and Critic.* 2nd ed. New York: McGraw-Hill, 1988.

Drury, James. "The Introduction of Service English Courses in ESL Tertiary Institutions." *Language Teaching Projects for the Third World. ELT Documents 116.* Ed. Christopher Brumfit. Oxford, UK: Pergamon, 1983.

Gibbs, Graham, and Trevor Habeshaw. *Preparing to Teach: An Introduction to Effective Teaching in Higher Education.* Bristol, UK: Technical Educational Services, 1989.

Ivanic, Roz, and Wendy Moss. "Bringing Community Writing Practices into Education." *Writing in the Community.* Ed. David Barton and Roz Ivanic. Vol. 6 of Written Comm. Annual. London: Sage, 1991.

Love, Alison. "Communication Skills in the ESL African Situation: The Need for a Strong Research Base." *Proceedings of the Conference on Academic Communication Skills in African Universities.* Council in Nairobi, July 1991.

Muchiri, Mary N. *Communication Skills: A Self Study Course for Universities and Colleges.* Nairobi: Longman, 1993.

———. *The Influence of Institutional Practices on Examinations: The Case of Kenyatta University.* Diss. Lancaster U, 1993

Muchiri, Mary N., A. Claessen, T. Rimbui, and S. Greenhalgh. *Evaluation of Efficiency in Communication Skills among Prospective University Entrants under the 8-4-4 System.* Kenyatta University, 1990.

Muchiri, Mary N., Nshindi G. Mulamba, Greg Myers, and Deoscorous B. Ndoloi. "Importing Composition: Teaching and Researching Academic Writing beyond North America." *College Composition and Communication* 46 (1995): 175–98.

Myers-Scotton, Carol. *Social Motivations for Code Switching: Evidence from Africa.* Oxford, UK: Clarendon, 1993.

Ngugi wa Thiong'o. *Decolonizing the Mind: The Politics of Language in African Literature.* Nairobi: EAEP LTD, 1981.

———. *Matigari.* Nairobi: EAEP LTD, 1987.

Oguine, Priscilla Ngozi. *Communicative Use of English.* Jos Nigeria: FAB Educational Books, 1990.

Shorter, Aylward. *Christianity and the African Imagination: After the African Synod: Resources for Inculturation.* Nairobi: Paulines Publications Africa, 1996.

Tucker, Amy, and Jacqueline Costello. *The Random House Writing Course for ESL Students*. New York: Random, 1985.

Whitely, W. H., ed. *Language in Kenya*. Nairobi: Oxford UP, 1974.

CHAPTER SIX

Roles under Construction: The Intersection of Writer Agency and Task Design in South Africa

SUELLEN SHAY AND ROB MOORE WITH ANTOINETTE CLOETE
University of Cape Town

We report on a study we conducted in a South African university, focusing on students coming to terms with the demands of university literacies for the first time. The study traces students as they make the transition from the demands of writing for school history to those of writing for history as a university discipline. As the study progressed, we were quickly confronted by a puzzle: although the course in question aimed to develop history writers in a particular way, the students persisted in producing texts quite at odds with this aim. The central question of the chapter is, "Why do students produce the texts they do?" We explore the complex interactions between curricular intent and learner response that give rise to varieties of student written performance. This exploration focuses on the writing and experiences of three students in order to construct an account of transitional literacies that holds powerful implications for curriculum practice.

The South African Context: Diversity and Transition

The themes of transition and diversity are central to this case study in the postapartheid South African context, and these are themes that play out across two dimensions. The first dimension is the transition of students from schooling to university, and the second dimension concerns the transitions underway in the

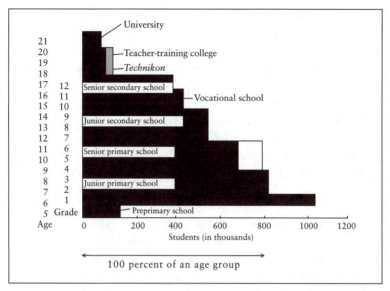

Figure 7. *South Africa: Structure of the formal education system.*

university itself as the student arrived there in the late 1990s. We look at each of these in turn. (See Figure 7 for the structure of the formal education system in South Africa.)

The learner's experience of the transition from schooling to university is still structured primarily by the racialized divisions of apartheid education. During the apartheid regime, the provision of state schooling was divided according to South Africa's various "race" groups, and these divisions were differently resourced. The four broad categories of apartheid's race ideology were White, Indian, Coloured, and African, and education was provided by different departments in descending priority. The result was severely underresourced schooling for African students (by far the majority) under the Department of Education and Training (DET) and for Coloured students under the Department of Education and Culture (DEC). High levels of political conflict and disruption in the township settings of these schools exacerbated the lack of resources. The combination of these factors, and the fact that African students learn through English as the medium of instruction rather than through their mother tongue, often results in these students having neither a sufficient conceptual foundation in their home language nor sufficient academic proficiency in English (similar to problems in Kenya noted by Muchiri in Chapter 5). This has serious implications for access to higher education and students' development as academic writers.

Although the transition out of apartheid has removed formal race barriers from access to schooling, the reality is that students who still attend—for example, those from former DET schools—are likely to be considerably less well prepared for entry to university than their counterparts in former white schools. The acuteness of these problems of access to higher education is borne out by that fact that in comparison to students in the "white" Department of National Education (DNR) schools in 1992, in which 42 percent of the age cohort achieved a matriculation exemption, only 10 percent of DET students received such exemption.[1] The "matric" is the secondary school leaving examination; it is a statutory minimum requirement for entry to university. For those who achieve matric exemption, further barriers are presented by the minimum matric points required for entry to some universities, particularly the professional faculties (e.g., commerce, medicine, law, and engineering). To counter some of these inequities, alternative admissions assessments have been introduced at the University of Cape Town (the academic language proficiency test noted later), including an extended piece of writing.

The transitions within the university milieu itself are complex and varied, depending on how institutions originated. The University of Cape Town (UCT) is South Africa's oldest university, and (like a few other English-language universities in South Africa) has its origins in European liberal traditions of the nineteenth century. Other universities were established to serve white Afrikaans-speaking communities and, since the 1950s, black communities.[2] Apartheid legislation attempted to exclude black students from white universities, efforts that met increasing resistance from the English liberal institutions in the final decades of apartheid rule. These developments saw the numbers of black students at UCT grow from a small handful in the early 1970s to nearly 50 percent of the student body in 1997, the year of the study reported in this chapter.[3] This case study is thus set in what was once a predominantly white, English-speaking institution that today seeks to cope with the twin transitionary pressures of (1) the changing political and demographic demands of postapartheid South Africa, and (2) the global shifts toward a more competitive, market-oriented higher education sector.

The South African education system follows a model of relatively early specialization, beginning in the last two years of secondary schooling (see Russell and Foster's introduction to this volume). South African universities generally follow the English model in which students begin discipline-specific curricula in their first year of study rather than following the U.S. model of an initial two years of formative general education. Institutions such as UCT, once accustomed to an overwhelmingly white and relatively well-prepared student body, have had to adjust to increasing numbers of black students of very differing levels of preparedness, many of whom may not speak English as a first language. Therefore first-year classes in the disciplines are likely to be made up of students with widely differing educational, linguistic, and social histories.

Like other institutions, UCT is attempting to position itself for greater competitiveness, reduced state funding, and a climate of increased accountability. As this case study was underway, the institution was engaged in multiple change exercises, including an across-the-board curriculum restructuring process that required academic staff to critically review their course offerings. Prominent among the review criteria was the new demand that curricula should equip students with "generic transferable skills" of relevance to the workplace (e.g., oral and written communication, critical thinking, and so forth). In the context of such comprehensive reviews of curriculum, it is appropriate that student performance comes under critical scrutiny in order to understand how individual performances are achieved in differing social contexts, and how curriculum can (or cannot) create the conditions for such performances. This chapter explores the transitional experiences of diverse students as they move into university and tries to account for the written performances they deliver in response to one of the new learning contexts they encounter there, a first-year history course—a context that is itself undergoing significant change.

Discourse and Agency in Tension

To answer the central question driving this study of transition—why do students produce the texts they do?—we construct an explanatory frame that places writer, text, and context in complex interaction, where ultimately the outcome is an "interplay of shaping forces" (Flower 43). We turn to an exploration of what this tension looks like in the day-to-day business of new students learning to write in their chosen disciplines. In the academic context, disciplines can be thought of as discourse communities. The discipline of history, for example, is constituted of all the practices in which scholars of history partake. Discourse provides a "social script" for "the way things are normally done," such as how to read, how to write, or how to behave in the staff room (Flower 20). Through the undergraduate curriculum, students are initiated to their "identity kit," i.e., "the appropriate costume and instructions on how to act, talk, and often write, so as to take on a particular social role that others will recognize" (Gee, 2nd ed. 127). They are told, largely through tacit forms of communication (e.g., course handbooks, prescribed readings, assignments), "If you want to study history, this is how we do it: this is how we think, this is how we act, these are our tools."

Gee, among others, introduces metaphors such as "insiders," "outsiders," and "colonized" (Gee, 1st ed. 155) to help us understand the challenges facing novice writers entering a new discipline. Though these metaphors are useful, they may conjure up the student as an agencyless individual wholly shaped by the demands of discourse rather than participants in their own shaping and the shaping of the university. In her study of the transition of first-year black South African students (a study located in the same institution as ours), Thesen finds limited support for the strong version of Gee's view of discourse—that one is an "insider," "colonized," or "outsider."[4] She writes,

> students are very aware of being in or out of discourses, but the problematic category is the middle one, "colonized," which suggests a lack of awareness of power relations. The interviews [with students] are coherent but often tentative accounts of emergent identity across different contexts in which students are clearly

agentive, making choices about where to merge and where to resist, assessing whether a strategy is working or not. (504)

She argues that in our attempts to understand students' complex transitional journeys into academe, we need to hold discourse, "the social envelope which creates 'insiders' and 'outsiders' in the educational process," in tension with "voice," that is, "the individual perspective which is often silent in large institutions" (494).

Much of our data supported the notion of students as insiders and outsiders to disciplinary discourses, but—consistent with Thesen's study—other parts of our data could not so easily be assimilated. We found evidence that suggested an act of resistance, a perplexing (for us) but conscious choice to ignore "scaffolded" approaches, a distancing, a scepticism. Rather than dismissing these students as inexplicable outliers, we explored these anomalous indications and discovered students who, like Thesen's, were "clearly agentive" (504).[5] Students emerged as meaning makers of their own texts, not simply having something to say but, throughout the production process, being consciously aware of (and often in control of) the myriad of choices they needed to make.

In order to explore further this "interplay of shaping forces" (Flower 43), we begin by drawing distinctions between the concepts of "agency," "role," and "voice." Agency is a configuration of personal commitments, confidence, and interests that are informed by the individual's particular discursive history.[6] In contrast, a role is a relatively generic, socially agreed-on pattern of behavior that individuals may be expected to enter and fulfill. These roles (which Kress refers to as subject positions) "describe and prescribe a range of actions, modes of thinking and being for an individual, compatible with the demands of a discourse" (*Linguistic* 37). Kress's particular interest (and a point to which we return in the conclusion) is the design of curricula, in particular how educational texts (e.g., textbooks, assessment tasks) construct particular roles for students.

But at the same time, we also recognize the power of individuals to constitute their own meaning making. Borrowing from Bakhtin, Flower argues that the construction of meaning for a text is an "on-going negotiation with the 'presence' of other voices" (98). These voices are not simply an inert addition of information but, rather, like talking heads, "voices that set goals, pose constraints, propose language, . . . voices of past experiences and present opportunity, . . . voices of reader's past, present and imagined" (67), linking the writer's current literate act with a myriad of previous conversations. Flower argues that the texts students construct are a provisional response to these voices, where the desired outcome (for both writer and reader) is a seamless web of meaning, a coherent account, a unified text.

As Herrington and Curtis put it, "learning is not a passive acculturation process but a negotiation where they [students] are actively considering how they would position themselves in relation to teacher and disciplinary expectations" (34). They argue that as we inhabit discourses we take on "particular orientations to the world" (Luke, qtd. in Herrington and Curtis 34). The extent to which students acquire these orientations depends on the fit (of these orientations) with their "private and personal sense of identities and values" (35). Herrington and Curtis coin the term "sponsoring discourse" to capture the notion that although students feel the force of discourse, they are not shaped in deterministic ways by disciplinary discourses. In fact, they select a sponsoring discourse, a selection prompted by their need to bring "their selves into their learning by linking private with public interests, self with others, personal with social identities" (375), and they conclude that "undergraduate education . . . should aim to foster, not frustrate, [this]" (375).

The explanatory frame for this study, then, focuses both on the discursive structures made available in the undergraduate roles of a discipline and on the distinctive forms of agency with which students fulfill (or resist) these roles.

Methodology

In view of our desire to hold social context and agency together in our explanatory framework, we felt that students' transitional experiences as learners/writers had to be explored within specific institutional contexts. These contexts are themselves often in transition as a result of pressures for change. In contrast to students in the U.S. system, South African students "plunge right in to the reading and writing of their major disciplines" (as Foster notes of German students, p. 193) with little explicit attention given to their development as writers. Therefore, to explore students' transitions as learners/writers, we had to focus on their writing within a disciplinary curriculum.

The choice of a first-year history course (coded HIS100W) for our research was a matter of convenience and expedience, since as researchers we already had a well-established relationship with the faculty in this course. The faculty included the course convenor (i.e., the professor) responsible for overall management of the course and much of the lecturing, and tutors who are postgraduate students in the department responsible for leading small weekly discussion groups (consisting of fifteen to twenty students).[7] The course was a two-semester course in which students attended three lectures and one tutorial a week.[8] Approximately 180 students were registered for the course in 1997, a third of whom were majoring in history and the rest taking the course as a prerequisite for another major. The course was assessed through four major essays (two per semester), a midyear test, and an end-of-year exam. The course convenor was open to our tracing students' development, assuming that this kind of research would be an asset to the department's ongoing curriculum development.

Since we wanted samples of preuniversity writing, our student sample began by identifying all students registered for HIS100W who had also written a preuniversity English-language proficiency test. This produced a group of thirty-three students who were then sent a letter explaining the project and inviting them to a meeting at which we presented the research project in greater detail. Out of the thirty-three students, fourteen agreed to participate in the project.

Each of these students was interviewed twice. The first interviews (open-ended and semistructured) were conducted in May 1997, immediately following the submission of their second essay that focused on the topic of slavery in colonial societies. The students were asked about (1) their experience of writing at school,

(2) their experience of writing since coming to UCT, and (3) their specific experience of writing the essay on slavery.

The second interviews were conducted in August, immediately following students' submission of their third essay. In the second round of interviews, we dug deeper into students' perceptions of themselves within their learning environment. We probed more abstract issues concerning their role as learners/writers and their perceptions of the various motives and intentions informing the tasks set by their lecturers. We focused specifically on their experience of writing the third essay, for which they were given more choices of topics and readings but less instructional support from the lecturer and tutors. We interviewed two of the history tutors, one because she lectured as well as tutored on the course and the other because she tutored many of our final group of students. We also interviewed a colleague doing research into literacy practices in ex-DET secondary schools.[9]

In addition to interview data, we collected samples of the students' writing. These included an essay from the English-language proficiency test, their second essay (the essay on slavery) and their third essay. For in-depth analysis, we focused almost exclusively on the slavery essay. In order to infer the roles students were enacting in the construction of their accounts, we began by exploring how students managed texts. As Russell and Foster note in the introduction to this volume, it is in the management of intertextuality that students negotiate identities of disciplinary apprenticeship. For example, what role do the readings (required and recommended) play in the construction of students' accounts? In order to answer this question, we looked at, for example, the number of readings referenced, which readings were selected and why, the total number of citations (i.e., footnotes) per essay, the number of citations per reading, and how the readings were cited. We also examined the organizational patterns that students adopted in the construction of their accounts. We looked at their introductions and conclusions, the number of comparative features per essay, the rationale informing the selection of comparative features, and the linguistic devices used to make the comparisons. We also looked at how the systems of slavery were described, especially the language used to describe the slaves and the colonizers. Once we had established some of the broad characteristics of the students' texts, we then used the interviews to explore the dynamics that played a role in constituting the texts.

Following the initial round of data collection, we arranged a work-in-progress report-back meeting with the HIS100W faculty. As a picture began to emerge from our data, we interviewed the convenor on two subsequent occasions in order to check our developing story. The three students who were ultimately selected for in-depth analysis were interviewed again in order to validate our emerging accounts of their stories.

Our study is exploratory and aims to map some of the complexity of the relationship between writer, text, and context. Specifically, we infer the roles made available to students through the history curriculum and try to understand how students interpreted these roles and to what extent they were able and willing to fulfill the roles presented to them by the essay on slavery. For future study, the insights generated from this exploratory study will need to be considered in the context of other history courses and other undergraduate curriculum sites.

Our chapter is divided into two parts. In the first part, we look at the way the HIS100W curriculum contributed to the constitution of a particular writer role. In the second part, we choose three students to illustrate the different ways students enacted this role in their responses and why. We conclude the chapter by examining how the revised 1998 course constructed different kinds of writer roles for students, and pointing to the implications for curriculum—the way learner roles are conceived and the forms of knowledge, agency, and identity that make these roles possible.

The Constitution of Writer Roles through Task

The content of the HIS100W course through 1997 was a comparative analysis of Atlantic societies. The rationale for this selection was that, by studying societies in comparison to one another, students would gain insight into the impact of different economic, political, and social dynamics on cultures. Through the course, they would come to "understand the world we live in and how that has come to be" and specifically that

> our own society has been very exceptional and very different. . . . South African history is often treated in isolation from the rest of the world, and yes, it is different but we want to understand what is different about it and how and why. (HIS100W convenor)

The faculty were aware that given the way school history is taught students might arrive at university with "single truth" accounts of history (HIS100W convenor) and the assumption that their role as learners and writers of history is simply to reproduce historical facts, such as "dates and the names of 'great men'" (Kapp, Personal interview).[10] The course therefore attempted in various ways to initiate students into a different kind of writer role. In contrast to the reproducer-writer role they were accustomed to in school, students were expected to play a far more active writer role—a movement from monologic knowledge telling (McCarthy Young and Leinhardt 29) to understanding the disciplinary field of history as a debate made up of multiple and contending narratives, a debate in which they too must participate.

The lecturing staff structured the course as a comparison between societies, assuming that students' exposure to the deeply contextualized nature of social processes would challenge students' notion of a single truth. By reading prescribed texts written by historians, students would witness for themselves how historians construct history—the methodologies they use and how their own positions contribute to their distinctive constructions. Through the essay assignments, students could practice these same historical methodological skills by constructing positions and arguments. Students would come to understand how they are "part of that process" (HIS100W convenor). Thus the aim of the course was to promote an awareness of the constructedness of historical accounts and to help students recognize that, as novice writers of history, they are managing and negotiating plural accounts of history. As they articulate and adjudicate multiple accounts, they are acquiring a historian's voice, enabling them to participate in the debates of historians.

This was the rationale of the carefully conceptualized unit of lectures, tutorial exercises, and an essay assignment on slavery in the Brazil and Cape colonies. The task (see Appendix 1 for the assignment handout) required students to do a comparative analysis of two colonial slavery societies. This comparative analysis involved three analytic steps. The first step, identifying the relevant features of slavery to be compared (e.g., origin of slaves, living conditions, manumission, etc), was done as a group exercise during a lecture (three weeks before the assignment due date), and students were given readings in preparation. The second step was to determine how the features identified in step 1 applied both in the Cape and in Brazil, noting the similarities and differences between the two colonies. Students were asked to complete this step in preparation for a tutorial discussion (a week before the essay due date). Again they were referred to relevant readings. The final step, the heart of the essay, required students to explain the similarities and differences between colonial slavery in Brazil and in the Cape. Students were expected to argue how, for example, the historical, economic, and political contexts of the two developing colonies influenced their respective slavery practices.

The students were given a course reader containing five of the key required readings, and they were referred to a number of additional references found in the short-loan section of the library. All the readings were secondary sources—interpretive accounts by expert historians of the slavery practices in either Brazil or the Cape. These secondary sources invited the reader into various historical debates. The key reading (Genovese), for example, steps into the debate at a metalevel, including a discussion of the comparative method, while another reading (Collins)[11] deconstructs a particular historical construction of Brazilian slavery. None of the readings makes explicit comparisons between Brazil and the Cape.

Our study revealed, however, that the assignment required students to construct an analytic account for which they had neither the requisite methodological nor theoretical resources. In the absence of these, the task (as understood by the students) defaulted to the single-truth kind of essay writing characteristic of schooling; in order to fulfill this task, students could only resort to the discursive resources available to them.

It seems that in responding to the essay prompt, students were confronted with a conflict (what Kress calls "discursive difference," in that the curricular discourse projects conflicting roles [*Linguistic* 12]). On the one hand, the discipline of history values and advocates a particular kind of role—historians as interpretive agents in the process of constructing historical accounts. This role was modeled in many tacit ways through the lectures, readings, and tutorial tasks (as discussed earlier). On the other hand, the comparative task effectively constructed for students a different kind of writer role—the role of selecting from preconstructed authoritative accounts (i.e., secondary sources) in order to produce a single-truth account.

From the vantage point of hindsight, the convenor problematized the HIS100W course, identifying a gap between the intended aim of the course and what was actually achieved:

> I think the problem we were finding was that although we thought we were challenging the notion of a single truth—of course, that is really what our main aim should be in a first-year history course, and getting students to think about how knowledge is constructed and how they are part of that process—it almost was coming in by default, if we were lucky. It wasn't really at the top of the agenda.

As the convenor critiqued his own slavery assignment, he noted a number of issues that inadvertently cast students into a particular writer's role, what he refers to as "information retriever." Despite the carefully scaffolded process the students were taken through, he acknowledged that

> in essence, [the] assignment last year, I think ended up as being more of an information retrieval exercise than anything else. It was an "okay, we know we have got to look at slavery, we know that there are different aspects of slavery that we can look at and compare, now where the heck do I find new information on manumission in Brazil in all this material?" You know, I am not sure that that really achieved the function of seeing . . . the process of constructing history. But also I am not sure [it achieved]

much in understanding the nature of the two societies. Sometimes it did, sometimes it didn't—it was almost by accident, I feel.

Students' Responses

In this section, we discuss how students interpreted the ambivalent roles available to them in this context, and the extent to which they were able and willing to fulfill the roles (and try out the voices) presented to them by the slavery assignment. Our analysis weaves together both students' texts (i.e., their essay on slavery) and their interviews about themselves as learners and writers. We also took account of the views of other participants in the literate act (e.g., tutors and the course convenor). What we discovered was that although students were indeed retrieving information, they were not simply reproducing it in rote fashion, as some described of their school writing. Within the limited range of roles open to them, they were making choices informed by their own sense of agency. In order to illustrate this complex interplay between curriculum/task and personal agency, we offer the stories of three students negotiating this particular task.

Buti

Buti comes from a working-class, Zulu-speaking African home in a township outside a small town in the Mpumalanga Province. He is the first of his family to attend university. Buti's account of his school writing experiences is consistent with those of other students who came through the DET matriculation authority (for "African" schools). According to Buti, very little in his prior school literacy practices prepared him for any writer role other than reproducing information in rote fashion from authoritative sources, usually the teacher and sometimes a textbook. In reference to writing at school, Buti recounts:

Actually, the chance I had of writing was only in history. The other subjects I was doing, we didn't have much writing. . . . [E]ven in history, it was just you had to give the facts as they are, it's the only thing we were required to do there. . . . [T]he teacher wrote the notes as they are, what we are required to do is just to take them as they are and we reproduced them.[12]

Before coming to UCT, Buti had never heard of academic argument or the practice of referencing and citation. Although we want to be careful not to homogenize the DET experience, our interviews revealed a consistently bleak account of the writing opportunities offered to students who traversed the DET system, in contrast to the accounts of those who came from either private schools or better-resourced education departments catering to students. When asked about the writer role he played at school compared to that expected of him at university, Buti was acutely aware that there is a difference, which he immediately pinpointed: "I think one has to play a very important role, especially tertiary compared to school." In contrast to school, where the teacher "gave us everything, . . . here [at university] you need to bring your own information, your own ideas along." Buti elaborated on aspects of this "very important role," which strongly resembles that of an active, agentive writer—he spoke of students as "interpret[ers] of the contents," as "coming with [their] own understanding." He noted that students may not "feel the same about the topic." The interviewer asked him to explain what he meant.

> Ja, well I think firstly, especially in the Industrial Revolution [a reference to the third essay topic], it is not something which was, can I say, effective [beneficial?] to everyone, so it did harm to others and it brought some changes to others, so . . . there will be a division, there will be an argument about this—some will say "no it brought change" and some say "no it didn't." . . . I mean, are all students going to argue the same thing or are they . . . going to differ, how are they going to differ and if they argue, for why—what makes the difference?

Not only does Buti articulate student writers as having motivated differences of opinion, but he also demonstrates an awareness that writers "construct" history because of their "different perspectives."

It emerged in the interviews that Buti likes history (in contrast to some of his other subjects) because history "does give one a room or space to write—you don't have to confine to a sort of one book or just to a text, you can go out from the text and bring out your own knowledge and your own evaluations about things." When the interviewer asked Buti to elaborate on this notion of "a room or space to write," he continued:

> Your own judgement, your own evaluation, you can differ with some of the points that are being made by the authors. Just say no, well if, maybe Karl Marx says this, it was like this and this and this. Well, according to my understanding it should have been this and this and this. . . . Why? You know, all those things . . . . So well in history writing I found there is room of doing that.

In the interviews, Buti described a role in which he appears to have invested himself with the authority to criticize, make judgments, and differ with the authors, even Karl Marx. Where does an understanding of this writer's role come from? Kapp suggests that such an understanding may be intuitive, based on students' experiences as black South Africans of the stark contrast between "history in the textbook" and history informed by oral sources and their own lived experiences. Of her own schooling experience, she recounts, "it was very much accepted that the history you were taught at school is not the history you should believe." It is also possible that having nearly completed one semester of university (at the time of the interview), Buti was aware that an active, critical stance is part of the academic writer's "identity kit" (Gee, 2nd ed. 127).

How does the writer's role Buti articulates get enacted in the actual process of writing? Our analysis reveals inconsistencies between the role that Buti advocates in the interview—that of an authoritative interpreter and evaluator of the content—and the one he actually enacts in his written text. The following extract consists of the first five opening paragraphs and the conclusion of Buti's slavery essay. The first issue Buti addresses is the origin of the slaves; that is, the colonizers' use of indigenous versus "imported" peoples for their labor supply (see the essay prompt in Appendix 1). The numbers in parentheses indicate Buti's footnotes:

This assignment is going to argue about the nature of slavery in Brazil and the Cape. However, there are similarities and differences between these two colonies. Therefore, the profound aim of this argument is to look into the causes of this similarities and differences that existed between the two colonies in seventeenth and eighteenth centuries. Firstly, a very brief historical reason of why slaves were used as form of labour in the colonies shall be discuss.

The trading system between Indians and the Portuguese led to Indian enslavement. The Portuguese wanted people to work for them in the sugar mills. They first start to use Indians who were not suitable to perform the work because of physical weakness. Portuguese decided to venture into slave trade from Western Africa, Angola and Guana. Slaves were coming direct from Africa with the exchange of trade commodities such as iron and copper with the local chiefs.

In the Cape most slave were coming from West Africa, East Africa, Mozambique and Madgascar with the exchange of guns and ammunition with local rulers for providing them enough security for their kingdoms. (1) In Brazil slaves worked on sugar plantation which was discovered by the Portuguese in Pernambuco, Bahia, and Rio de Janerio. Again the discovery of tobacco and gold in Mina.

Gerais increased the necessity of labor force to work in the mines and in the tobacco plantations. (2) On the contrary, the Cape slaves workers performed various work such as cultivation of the grain field, making wine. The woman performed domestic work such as looking after children of their masters. (3) The slave also kept livestock of their masters which has been seized to local people such as Khoi who were farmers, they also milked the cows. (4)

The preference of using foreign slaves in Brazil and in the Cape was that in Brazil the aborigenes who were Indian people were physical weak to work in plantation and because their nationality and their place they could escape easily. The same problem occured in the Cape the Dutch did not prefer the local people who were the Khoi and the San. The reason was that they know the geographical position of the Cape they easily escaped and dissappeared in the open terrain. (5)

· · · · ·

[conclusion] The slaves played a very important role in shaping the economy of Brazil and in Cape. Although there were differences between these two societies there were minor similarities. The differences were caused by the different trade production between Brazil and the Cape.

In contrast to the authoritative role that Buti advocates in the interview, in his essay he has enacted an "information retrieval" role. His 900-word essay (eight handwritten pages) consists of a discussion of eleven different features of slavery (e.g., origins of slaves, food, relations between master and slaves), with one paragraph discussing the feature in one colony and another paragraph comparing/contrasting this feature in the other colony. The rationale for the selection of these features is not clear. The discussion draws heavily from three readings, which he has cited a total of twenty-eight times. Interestingly, not one of Buti's twenty-eight citations refers to the authors of the sources (saying, for example, "according to de Queiros"). Buti has not cited positions, views, or interpretations that various historians hold, but rather what he perceives to be historical facts. This is not surprising given his school experience of history writing and given that the task itself caused students by default to be assemblers of "content" in the construction of a single-truth account.

The most striking characteristic of Buti's essay is that it in fact contains no convincing account of the different origins of slavery. Buti fails to construct an explanation for the similarities and differences between the two slave-holding societies, although he clearly understood that this was the requirement of the task. He confirmed this in the interview. When the interviewer asked him whether he had found the essay topic difficult to understand, he responded:

> No, I think that this was explained, that what was important with the question was not to give the differences and similarities, but what was important was you had to say how [it] was different, I mean why there were differences and all those things.

His text shows traces of his awareness of the requirement; for example, in the introduction he promisingly declares, "the profound aim of this argument is to look into the *causes* of this similarities and differences" (emphasis added). Attempts at explanation are peppered throughout the essay; for example, the fact that the Khoi and San could easily escape is given as a reason why the Dutch did not "prefer the local people." In his conclusion, he makes a final attempt to offer an economic explanation for the similarities and differences, but little in the essay supports this conclusion. Ultimately, the essay remains a feature-by-feature comparison of slavery practices in the two societies, with no sustained explanatory argument. Buti was also deeply conscious of his failure:

> [T]he essay was very confusing to me. I didn't know the exact way of answering the question, however, I have tried some ways which will confine me to the question. But I am pessimistic that I have done what I am suppose to.[13]

As we delved into Buti's text and listened to his own account of his process, we discovered that although he was indeed retrieving information, he was not simply reproducing it in rote fashion as he said he had in his school writing. Within the role constructed for him by the task, he was negotiating a range of complex choices—what Flower refers to as "voices" (67). Buti appears to be negotiating three different voices: (1) the authoritative voices of the texts versus his own views, (2) the voice of comparison, and (3) a voice articulating a discourse of a naturalized economic order.[14] An exploration of these sites of negotiation provides insight into Buti's attempts to exert his own constrained agency, albeit unsuccessfully.

In one site, the voices of the authoritative texts and warnings against plagiarism compete with Buti's novice historian voice, making his presence as author and constructor of his own text barely visible. In an interview, Buti gives insight into the power of these authoritative voices and the difficulties of negotiating successful resolution. He articulates an acute sense of how his own personal interests and investment have been compromised, and he expresses a common dilemma that novice academic writers often experience—how to authoritatively assert their own voices in relation to the authority of the canon:

> Then another thing which gives me a problem in so far as referencing is concerned especially in the slavery essay, you find that there are different authors who wrote about the same thing so

we read different books so now the problem is how can you integrate all those ideas to form a single idea? So you find that it's confusing—because sometimes you have to put your own views, so you don't know how to put them because sometimes the tutor would ask you about the view and the evidence of that view so it's becoming confusing because I can try to give an evidence of my argument so find that I'm using another author's ideas so it's becoming confusing so by that way I can fall into the trap of plagiarism. . . . I'm confused on which . . . of the ideas of the author are you supposed to reference because sometimes I find that all my writing, they are derived from the authors' writing so it's a bit confusing.

In reference to his first history essay, Buti says this:

> BUTI: So I remember during the first essay I referenced almost all the words so it was terrible.
> INTERVIEWER: So you had half a hundred references!
> BUTI: Ja! Because I didn't know nothing!

Although the history curriculum advocates an authoritative role students are to enact (i.e., "you have to put your own views"), in the act of writing Buti became confused: "you don't know how to put them." At the risk of falling "into the trap of plagiarism," he resorted to the "author's ideas," only to find that "all my writing [was] derived from the author's writing."

Acknowledging that disciplining students to refer to authorities in their field is one way of bringing students into an academic world, Angélil-Carter argues that the practice of referencing and citation and the monitoring of plagiarism may strip students of their own authority. In a study conducted at UCT, she quotes a lecturer from an undergraduate social science course:

> I would suspect that if you asked students to write, if you like, a political biography or autobiography in week 1, it would be far more rich, unique, significant, really significant, profound, than if we asked them to do the same exercise in the third or fourth quarter. I think that we actually start to numb them intellectually. . . . [W]hat we do is we take their authority away, I think. We devalidate them, we say to them, hold on, there are real authorities out there [that] you need to come to grips with . . . but implicitly, we are saying, you don't qualify as a thinker, you don't

qualify as an intellect, you don't qualify as somebody whom we really take seriously, I mean, until you've engaged with the lights of the discipline.(76)[15]

Angélil-Carter demonstrates through her analysis of students' texts and interviews that the practice of referencing and the policing of plagiarism can shut out other sources of students' knowledge (76). We argue, however, that it is not the practice of referencing itself that affects students' agency as writers. Rather, it is the roles that the task of referencing sets up for students that may inadvertently invest them with or divest them of authority. Referencing is embedded within a larger set of practices that constitute students' roles as writers within disciplines. In these roles, students may learn to recognize themselves and thus develop a sense of investment and appropriate authority.

Another instruction that helps constitute Buti's role as a writer is embedded in the academic essay's convention of comparison. Buti was introduced to this convention in a supplementary tutorial in which students were taught an organizational style (as well as the linguistic conventions) for a comparative essay; for example, "In Brazil, slaves . . . . On the contrary, the Cape slaves . . . ." Buti describes the difficulties that the demands of this voice pose for him:

> Another problem in so far as this essay's concerned, I didn't have a clear idea of how am I going to answer it because they're saying that we have to give similarities and dissimilarities. What is important is to give why are there some differences and similarities so now the problem came to me—if now I have to give some similarities, how am I going to give the similarities or am I going to give similarities on the one page and say this are the similarities and this are the differences? So I was totally confused about the structure of this essay and how to present the argument.

Traces of the voice of comparative essay conventions are seen throughout Buti's essay. What seems to compel Buti is the requirement to make comparisons, find relevant information, and structure it convincingly. What is needed, however, is a rationale for the comparisons, a principled disciplinary basis from which he can construct his own comparative account.

But instead of a clearly articulated historical method, we hear another voice emerging from Buti's language, a voice speaking of a naturalized economic order in which slavery is a natural, commonsense practice. In Buti's uncritical depiction, the responsibility for slavery is attributed to economic systems and events (e.g., "the trading system . . . led to Indian enslavement, or "the discovery of tobacco and gold . . . increased the necessity of labor force"). The colonizers are depicted as neutral agents within larger economic systems (for example, "the Portuguese wanted people to work for them," "they first start to use Indians," then "decided to venture into . . . Africa," and "the Dutch did not prefer the local people"). The slaves themselves appear agencyless except in relation to the work they must perform. The indigenous Indian population originally enslaved by the Portuguese is described as "not suitable . . . because of physical weakness," presumably a reference to the diseases that decimated much of the Indian population. This same reason is given in paragraph 5 and, according to Buti, also accounts for why, in addition to the fact that the locals could easily escape, the Dutch did not "prefer the local people." The reference Buti cites is a general discussion of slave resistance and not a reference to the Khoi, who were never enslaved.

We asked the convenor where this voice might be coming from, a voice that seems to suspend any critical, moral judgment of the practices of slavery. The convenor speculated that it is an imitation of the academic voice that students encounter in the readings and lectures, where the emphasis is on the need for neutrality—"the removal of explicit value-judgments from academic writing." Two weeks before turning in the assignment, the students had had what the convenor referred to as "the moral judgment tutorial." He recounts:

> The main message that comes through very strong from that tutorial is that, of course there are going to be issues of moral judgment, but we shouldn't allow that to obscure our understanding of historical processes . . . what we are saying about historical studies, and one of the key themes of the course is that we are trying to understand how people thought and behaved and reacted in a particular historical situation, so we keep stressing

that there is a danger of imposing our late twentieth-century views on another society.

Having acknowledged the potentially strong influence of this "message" on the construction of students' accounts, he acknowledged the dilemma this influence might pose for students like Buti. On the one hand, they are asked for their own opinions, but in reality "we want [their] opinions about a historical process, [not] about moral issues"—for example, the way slaves were treated. Thus, because Buti's personal moral and political voice is disallowed, he resorts to a register of academic neutrality not sufficiently informed by historical method (and perhaps linguistic proficiency) to adequately compare the differing accounts of slavery offered by the readings.

To summarize our discussion of Buti, we return to our original question: Why do students produce the texts they do? Two major points have emerged from our discussion. First, we have shown how Buti is disabled from the active, agentive role he knows is required of him. We have argued that the incongruity between Buti's grasp of his writer's role and the role he is able to enact lies in the discursive conflict posed by the course curriculum. On the one hand, the discipline values a particular kind of role—historians as agents in the process of constructing history. On the other hand, a different kind of role is inadvertently constructed for students in the assignment's comparative task—that of selecting from preconstructed authoritative accounts in order to produce a single-truth account. When confronted with the authoritative voices of the canon, Buti does not know how to assert his own authority. The novice historian's voice ostensibly requires a form of agency from the learner ("your own views"), but the curriculum is silent about how students can develop this agency in relation to the authoritative canon. In the face of this, we argue, Buti resorts to constructing an "authorless" text about a naturalized world. The outcome is a text that bears little evidence of Buti's understanding of himself as a meaning-making agent in the discipline of history.

Second, Buti fails to produce a convincing account of the similarities and differences between the colonies engaging in slavery because he lacks the interpretive framework needed to move from the second analytical step (i.e., making the comparisons) to the third (i.e., identifying a disciplinary basis for the comparisons). About the cognitive demands of the comparisons, the convenor noted: "Really, the comparative approach is tricky—it's not an easy exercise, for any of us." About the readings, he noted that students may easily have become "so overwhelmed with the information and trying to absorb that information" that they then failed to deal with the real substantive issues, which include how social processes construct history.

Daniel

Daniel comes from a middle-class, English-speaking, Coloured home in which several extended family members (uncles) had attended UCT. He attended a historically white school in the southern suburbs of Cape Town.[16] He describes a relatively rich school literacy environment in which an English teacher features prominently as a stimulator of creativity. What emerges in the interviews is Daniel's interest in history: "I used to get A's for history at school and it was my favourite subject and I used to go overboard for projects, like for the Vietnam War I did this whole thing with visual images, information, and I got a cassette, it was like a multimedia experience for the teacher." His decision to major in history at UCT arose from a "work shadow" experience, in which he followed a history lecturer at UCT around for a day. Although he has all the potential to succeed at university, at the time of his second interview Daniel was clearly disaffected with his history course, and his grades had progressively declined. He comments about the work shadow experience, "I said 'this is nice,' but when I got to history [at UCT], I said, 'this is not passionate enough, man.' They're not getting excited about what's happening and how people relate to history, it's like 'how can you prove this fact?'" Halfway through his first year, he had decided to change his major from history to social anthropology. We asked Daniel's tutor about him, and she admitted to being puzzled:

Daniel . . . has great potential—very enthusiastic student—he is always at his tutorials, always participates, always has something to say, comes up with some really good insights in the tutorials . . . but [he] doesn't follow through in the written work. His written work is weak and untidy and slapdash.

As with Buti, we wanted to gain insight into how Daniel interpreted the writer's roles constructed for him by the tasks required in the slavery assignment, and the extent to which he was able and willing to fulfill these roles. As we examined his texts and listened to his account of himself as writer and learner, we discovered inconsistencies. Despite the fact that Daniel had the confidence and ability, his essay lacks any personal authorial investment. The following extract consists of Daniel's introduction, his fourth and fifth paragraphs (where Daniel compares the roles that slaves played in the respective colonial societies), and his conclusion (see the essay prompt in Appendix 1). The numbers in parentheses indicate Daniel's footnotes:

This essay will compare slavery in Brazil and the Cape during the 17th and 18th centuries and, by drawing on the works from Genovese, Rout, Bethal, Armstrong and Collins, provide explanations for the similarities and differences which arise during this comparission.

. . . . .

[paragraph 4] The respective economies of Brazil and the Cape were also vitally important in determining the role of slaves. In Brazil, slaves were first used on the early sugar plantations (engenhoes) of Bahaia and Pernambuco (10) and later on coffee plantations in Bessouras and San Paulo (11). When gold was discovered in Central Brazil a mining industry was born which necessitated much labour (12) and therefore slaves were also used in, and constituted a high percentage of, the total population of many mining towns (e.g. Salvador and Recife) where they were employed in various capacities besides mining such as hunting, fishing and food cultivation or in more specifically urban jobs, such as transporters, municipality workers, boatmen and so on (13). It can be seen that although the economy of Brazil dictated that some slaves be skilled in certain areas e.g. those slaves who worked as kettlemen in the mill house or even as slave masters

(14), most of the work which the Brazillian economy required was simply labour intensive, and needed a much less skilled individual who was therefore expendable and of less value to his owner.

[paragraph 5] The Cape economy was different to that of Brazil because it did not "develop a monoculture system dependent upon an external market and based on large-scale production units" (15). The farms in the Cape although having some specialization (wine and grain farming) were much smaller and therefore less labour intensive (16). The pastoral farmers depended even less on slave labour (17), and most of the slaves were employed in the western districts where they were needed as domestic servants and artisans (18). Slaves were further used for wet nursing their master's children, as craftsmen (19), as ox drivers during the ploughing season (20), shepards, and other specialized jobs. We can see that because these slaves possessed skills which the colonists needed they were more highly valued than their Brazilian counterparts and were therefore less easily replaced.

. . . . .

[conclusion] In conclusion we can see that the various similarities and differences in slavery which occured between the Cape and Brazil were the product of various economic, cultural and topographical factors which determined the nature of these respective societies.

Like Buti, Daniel has produced a 900-word essay (three and one-half typewritten pages). Although his bibliography contains five references (the five required readings in the course reader), he has drawn from only two of them. Out of a total of thirty-seven citations, seventeen are from one reading, from which he has drawn information on Brazil, and eighteen are from the other reading in support of the Cape. This excerpt illustrates his extensive use of the readings, paragraphs 4 and 5 showing approximately one citation per sentence and sometimes more. Like Buti, except for a listing in the introduction, Daniel's essay never mentions the authors of the texts he is drawing from. Again, it is a single account without any suggestion that the "facts" he draws on are interpretations by various historians in support of their own accounts.

Daniel, however, is aware that there are multiple accounts.

Noting that he, unlike many other students, had included the Genovese reading in his bibliography, the interviewer asks Daniel about his use of Genovese:

> The only reason I put it down is because I read it. I didn't actually use it because I found that he's talking about—that was very confusing because he's talking about the different planes [levels?] in which you analyze the way in which slaves were treated. . . . I thought I had to apply what he was saying to what all the other writers were saying. . . . That would've taken me a month to do!

Daniel is acutely aware that the Genovese article is modeling the analytical voice he is expected to perform as a writer. But he is also aware that he does not have the resources (particularly the time) to incorporate Genovese into this construction. He chooses instead to "cut him [Genovese] off totally" in favor of a single account that he knows he can manage.

Unlike Buti, Daniel is able to construct a clear account of the different origins of slavery. In contrast to Buti's eleven comparative features, Daniel has selected four. When asked how he made his selection, he admits, "I was pressed for time; I took the first four things and cut off the rest." In paragraph 4, Daniel introduces his discussion of slaves in the two colonies with an explanatory sentence, "The respective economies of Brazil and the Cape were also vitally important in determining the role of slaves." He then supports his argument in the Brazil context. In paragraph 5, he indicates a contrast with the Cape, which had a different economy. He concludes this paragraph by saying that the Cape slaves were more highly skilled than their Brazilian counterparts given the different economies of the two colonies. This is apparently Daniel's own interpretation—the emerging voice of the novice historian.

Like Buti's, Daniel's account presents the practice of slavery uncritically, attributing agency throughout the paragraphs to a seemingly naturalized economic order in such statements as "[t]he respective economies . . . were . . . vitally important in determining the role of slaves," "a mining industry was born which necessitated much labour," and "the economy of Brazil dictated that some slaves be skilled." Slaves, on the other hand, are "used" or "employed." In the Brazilian context (paragraph 4), the slave is described as "expendable and of less value to his owner." In contrast, the Cape slave was "more highly valued . . . [and] less easily replaced" (paragraph 5). Instead of masters and slaves, Daniel could just as easily have been writing about farmers and cattle. As with Buti, Daniel's voice appears to represent his understanding of a neutralized, academic way of writing.

What also struck us about Daniel's account was that, like Buti, his own presence as the author is barely visible. In his introduction, Daniel has followed novice academic writers' common practice of restating the topic.[17] The overall effect of this generic introduction is to mask Daniel's agency as writer. He fails to position himself as an author with something unique to contribute to the discussion—this introduction could have been written by anyone. Similarly, his conclusion lacks any personal investment. He has fulfilled the assignment as best he can given the particular time constraints under which he was operating. He confesses in the interview, "I'm just in a frenzy when I do it and I just do this, do that—I mean that's why I'm very unsure, because you know it [the essay] could be brilliant or it could be totally, you know, not what they wanted." Daniel lacks a disciplinary basis from which to evaluate the choices he makes in tackling the task.

The ultimate effect of Daniel's text is a disinvested and bland account of two societies practicing slavery. How do we explain this? Our analysis of Buti indicated a student struggling to marshal the necessary authority to bring the multitude of conflicting voices into alignment. What about Daniel? Is this simply a case of a capable student "with great potential" who is unmotivated or disinterested? Tempting as this conclusion was, we had caught a glimpse of a different Daniel in our conversations with him.

When the interviewer asks Daniel to compare his learner role at school ("where the point of learning was to get out of high school") with his role at university, Daniel clearly articulates the intrinsic motivations and personal investment he brings to his university learner role:

> [Here] I have a responsibility in the sense that what I learn I have to remember it, I have to apply it to my life, it has to mean something to me so I'm not learning for the sake of just getting a degree. I'm learning in order to benefit myself in the future in order to be a member of society or an adult citizen.

When the interviewer probes for an example of how what Daniel is learning "has to mean something," Daniel draws from another course he is currently enrolled in—social anthropology. In this learning context, Daniel finds continuity between the course and his own interests ("as a kid I was interested in other cultures"). Through this course, he has experienced and been empowered by the development of a social consciousness ("I'm not as blind or ignorant as I was before because anthro teaches you to look at the world in a totally different way and it makes you more of a force to be reckoned with, because you can't be oppressed anymore"). Social anthropology has empowered Daniel by giving him an interpretive framework (an "academic view," as he calls it) through which to view his world. This academic view enables him to see the forces that underlie social practices. For example:

> Say I had my friends over at my house and they invite me to a *braai* (barbecue) or something, you take that for granted, but anthro forces you to analyze it and actually ask yourself, what's actually going on here? . . . It gives you a discipline in which to explore those things in a more structured way.

In contrast to Daniel's experience of history, in the context of social anthropology we get a glimpse of Daniel as a student who is deeply invested in the analysis of his world. This role is not new to him (he admits that he asked these kinds of questions before), but for Daniel social anthropology provides him with an intellectual framework for his social analysis.

In our interview with Daniel, we investigated the implications of this academic view for his role as a writer. Daniel knows that what he calls this "anthropological style of writing" requires detachment and distancing. No longer is it appropriate to simply "pick out the facts"; this role involves "observing," "not stating the obvious thing," but "taking a step back." For Daniel this means that "basically you have to look at other people's arguments; you can't say anything about your own views. . . . I mean, everything you say, you have to reference it." He appears to recognize a conflict between a particular writer's role, which requires an invested agency, and the detachment of personal agency (his "own views"), which many academic tasks seem to him to require. This conflict suggests the dilemma that students perceive between the requirement to advance their own opinions and the need to construct systematic arguments through disciplinary method.

When this seeming conflict between detachment and investment was explored in the context of the essay on slavery, Daniel confirmed the convenor's hunch that the nature of the comparative task ultimately constructed a particular kind of information-retrieving role.

> INTERVIEWER: Did you feel that you were able to take that . . . kind of "step back"?
>
> DANIEL: In a sense, in a sense yes I did, but . . . in a sense I didn't really have to step back because he [Collins] was doing that in the essay [Collins's article], so in a sense it was like picking out the facts, right, but because his essay did that, I was able to just pick out the facts from his essay, because he himself did that in that essay, you understand what I'm saying?

By the second interview, Daniel seemed to be increasingly frustrated as a writer and disenchanted with the HIS100W course. On the one hand, Daniel appreciated the importance of learning the discourse:

> If we're studying anthro and you're going to have to write papers and thesis and stuff which other anthropologists can read, so you need a structure which we can all relate to, a certain standard of writing which will enable us to convey what we learnt to other anthropologists in America, Britain. . . . That's the only way we're going to communicate properly.

But Daniel was also sensitive to what seemed to him an artificial exercise, something that first-year students do: you write essays as "proof that you're taking in what's being said. . . . They [the lecturers] need something they can show the external examiner."[18] It's not "real life," he continued, it's not "dynamic." Daniel hankers after a learner role "where you can show also more individuality in a sense, show your opinion more strongly"—a role that foregrounds his agency and identity in meaning making.

Later, the interviewer asked about the assessment practices that Daniel is critiquing:

INTERVIEWER: Something's lacking—something isn't being tapped?

DANIEL: Ja, your understanding of what you're learning, of the process of history.

Daniel does not perceive the slavery assignment or the course as a whole as giving him the opportunity to display the mode of inquiry he feels should typify history. He sees it instead as a dispassionate and perfunctory exercise of finding the information and organizing it acceptably. For Daniel this is not what history is about: "It's not passionate enough. . . . They're not doing stuff that I want to do, man. If I had to continue with my studies and get my doctorate, once I'm a historian, I wouldn't do this." Daniel cannot recognize himself in the role constructed for him in this task, and thus the agency with which he fulfills this role is disinvested.

Yeki

Yeki comes from a middle-class African home where both Sotho and Xhosa are spoken. Although he lives in an African township situated on the outskirts of Stellenbosch, his family is well off in comparison to his neighbors. His mother is a nurse, his father a professor at a nearby university. Yeki's motivation for his studies arises out of desire to "improve the quality of life in my community." He writes of his neighborhood:

> The area which I live in has also had an effect on my life, because living in a densely populated area has exposed me to various issues which effect the community as a whole. Crime, poverty, violence and unemployment had been constant occurings. You would find that these tend to have a deep effect on me in the sense that watching people struggle has also made me want to achieve more in life and university so that I can go back to my community and try to improve the quality of life in my community. What has also affected me are the prejudices within the community when it comes to me and my family with regards to the fortunate situation of having a car, a house and not going to bed

hungry always. People tend to label you as being "well-off" and you will be the target of their frustrations and for reasons unknown to you, someone whom you've never even met before will hate you.[19]

Yeki attended a DET township school. Contrary to his parents' desire that he apply to attend a historically white school (when this became possible in the early nineties), he was determined to remain at the school in his community. Here he felt a sense of "solidarity," of rootededness—socially, culturally, and politically:

> Political awareness was something which I never thought about because I was always protected by my parents as a child against racial prejudice which was happening. It was only at high school when I came to realize what people called "freedom songs" were all about. . . . There were numerous boycotts, rallies and riots which I found myself involved [in]. . . . I also came to realise that what I was fighting for was not only for resources that were never given to us as school pupils but also for my fellow black men's rights as individuals against a system which viewed one race as being inferior and subordinate to the other.

It is clear from Yeki's account that his preuniversity literacy experiences were relatively rich: he had educated parents and a university-educated older brother, and was editor of the school newspaper. Yet, by his account, this richness is no credit to his formal schooling. His description of his school literacy opportunities resonates with those of Buti and other ex-DET students. Before university he had no experience of writing outside of the genre of class tests, where he was expected to "give back the facts," although some personal experience could be drawn on as examples. He had never had any experience of referencing, argument, or bibliography. His school had a library where he did some independent research, but this was not expected of him. This initiative got mixed reviews: one teacher encouraged him, another warned him that he should "stay within the boundaries" of the task. Like all the students we interviewed, Yeki felt that his school writing experiences did "not in any way" prepare him for what was expected at university.

Yeki recounts his first realization of a new role and a different set of expectations at university: he went to his lectures and
"the instructor only put up a few points on the OHP [overhead
projector]" and then "referred to a lot of books and journals in
short loan. . . . Then I knew things were different." He was going
to have to discover things for himself. At university he had to
"read, make some assessments, and select the relevant parts":

> I'm on my own [at university] because I have to be more respon-
> sible, whereas at high school I could sit back and the teacher
> would come in and help me with whatever needed to be done,
> whereas here I have to take the initiative and actually start things,
> and to a certain extent it's more about responsibility and taking
> charge of your life.

Yeki hoped to read law at UCT if his first-year grades were good
enough; otherwise he would continue with history and politics,
which he found interesting but very demanding. Obviously, he
had come to university for a degree, but "I think the self-devel-
opment within the degree is what I'm looking for."

As in our analysis of Buti's and Daniel's written texts and
personal accounts, we attempted to infer from Yeki's responses
how he interpreted the writer's role constructed for him by the
tasks required in the slavery assignment. In Yeki's essay, we found
visible traces of his authorial self. Unlike Buti and Daniel, Yeki
appears to be both able and willing to construct an authoritative
account. What follows is an extract consisting of Yeki's first two
paragraphs and conclusion from his slavery essay. He also begins
his essay with a discussion of the colonizers' use of indigenous
versus "imported" peoples for their labor supply (see the essay
prompt in Appendix 1). The numbers in parentheses indicate
Yeki's footnotes:

> [paragraph 1] Colonial slavery which can be defined as the coer-
> cive exploitation of workers, usually regarded of inferior race, to
> achieve the productive ends for those who own them. Colonial
> slavery had a significant impact in shaping slave societies, as re-
> gards to their status in the foreign regions in which they found
> themselves. In this essay we shall be making a comparative analysis
> between the nature of slavery in Colonial Brazil and the Cape

Colony during the seventeenth and eighteenth centuries and also try to account for the similarities and differences which we shall be looking at.

[paragraph 2] Similarities can first be noted that during the early 17th century both the Cape and Brazilian colonies relied on external labour for their different economic needs. (1) Being emergent colonies with development in prospect, they had to rely constantly on skilled and unskilled labour from outside the colonies. This was a result of the fact that when they tried to enslave the indigenous people of the lands they had invaded they encountered difficulties. This is evident in the case of Brazil where the colonists had problems with the Indians as regards to labour (2). The colonists in the Cape however could not enslave the indigenous Khoi tribe, because they were dependent on them in the first years of their stay in the Cape (3). Differences occur as to where the slaves of the two colonies originated from.

· · · · ·

(conclusion) The similarities and the dissimilarities pointed above as regards to the nature of colonial slavery, should have implications, that perhaps in light of our present world, especially South Africa's past history, it is essential for historians when they study, where discriminatory policies come from. They should first start looking at the natures in which society was based during the colonial slavery era.

Yeki's essay is longer than the others—1,600 words (nine and one-half handwritten pages). His thirty-five citations are drawn fairly evenly from seven different readings, several of which he retrieved from short loan. Like Buti and Daniel, Yeki has constructed from the readings a single-truth account without any trace of the constructedness of history (i.e., there is no mention in his essay of authors' interpretations or contending positions).

Also like Buti and Daniel, however, Yeki is not unaware that there are multiple accounts. Like Buti, Yeki wrestles with a conflict between the authoritative voices of these contending accounts and his own voice. He articulates the problem as "trying to find your own argument." This problem emerges in the context of a discussion about "different authors saying different things about the same subject and unfortunately I want to choose. . . . You end up getting really lost." Yeki understands that "people can't have the same opinion on historical events—there are different sources that they can use and from there they make their own arguments based on the sources which may be primary sources or secondary sources." But he finds differing opinions confusing because "unfortunately, I want to choose—if I take this author, why?" Yeki hankers for a principled basis from which to adjudicate multiple, contending accounts—a position from which his voice can speak.

And yet, unlike the other two writers, this single-truth account is nonetheless Yeki's account. His presence as author and constructor of his account is clear from the opening sentence of his essay: "Colonial slavery . . . can be defined as the coercive exploitation of workers, usually regarded of inferior race, to achieve the productive ends for those who own them." There is a clear continuity between Yeki's autobiographical self (recall his autobiographical piece in which he refers to "a system [apartheid] which viewed one race as being inferior") and the reference in his essay to slaves as "usually regarded of inferior race." This sense of continuity between self and task can be seen again in Yeki's conclusion, where he makes a link between the colonial slavery practices and discriminatory policies in South Africa today. Yeki's understanding of his own history drives his analysis and provides a rationale for his account. Here the convenor's intention behind the task has been fulfilled: by studying other societies, Yeki has gained an appreciation of the way events of the past have shaped present society.

Unlike Buti and Daniel's "naturalized" accounts, Yeki's essay is oriented toward the view that economic relationships entail differential levels of power. He writes later in the essay, "where there is slavery, there is always a profit to be made, and where there is a profit to be made, there is always exploitation involved in achieving the desired profits." Also later in the essay, he describes the economic tension as a "struggle for supremacy between Brazil and the West Indies, with the unfortunate victim being the slave." Yeki's account, unlike Daniel's, asserts the exploitative consequences of power for the powerless. Yeki is so compelled to make his argument that the comparative task is at times overshadowed. Recall, for example, Daniel's apt argument that different economies produced different roles for slaves in the two colonies. Yeki takes a different stance altogether:

Although the two colonies were based on different economies at different scales, working conditions for slaves on both colonies, be it the large sugar plantation of Brazil or the small pastoral or wine farms of the Cape, were relatively hard and dangerous. This is especially true in the case of the rural areas where slaves toiled hard during the harvest periods, where work seemed unending, with little time to rest or eat.

Again, recall the reasons Buti gives to explain why the colonizers "did not prefer the local people"—their physical weakness and their knowledge of the terrain. Yeki argues differently, saying that "when they [the colonizers] tried to enslave the indigenous people of the lands they had invaded, they encountered difficulties." Yeki chooses not to elaborate on these difficulties, however. The point he seems to want to emphasize is that the indigenous people were not merely passive victims but, rather, resistant agents. He then drives this point further in his reference to the Cape—"the colonists could not enslave the indigenous Khoi tribe, because they were dependent on them."

At the time of the interview, immediately after he had handed in the essay, Yeki was not happy with it. Personal circumstances had prevented him from spending as much time as he would have liked. He felt that he had never really got to the core task of the essay, which was to account for the reasons behind the similarities and differences. Despite his insecurity, however, he produced a convincing, authoritative account. His tutor commented on the essay: "Yeki: well done—thorough, in-depth analysis with a very good synthesis of all the relevant points. Your own voice and opinions come through well in your essay."[20] In an interview later in the year, this same tutor commented about Yeki, "He has great insight—okay, he can assimilate the work and then bring his own voice and opinions into the work and that is very unusual in first year. That's what pushes an essay up into a first and he did that very well in his [third] essay."

By the time he wrote his third essay, Yeki's confidence in himself as a writer had been bolstered. For the third essay, the students were given a choice of topics. Yeki's choice of African responses to imperialism was motivated by his political interest in Africa. With reference to the topic, Yeki recounts:

> Well, it's a little bit closer to home, it's within Africa and I found I could understand it more in a political context because there are some parts of South Africa that were affected by imperialism .... If you read my conclusion there, I think it more or less to a certain extent my own views came out there, that's why I also had an interest in the topic, because the other topics, I could summarize, but in that one my own voice came through.

Unlike Buti, whose agency is subverted, or Daniel, who consciously chooses to disinvest his agency, Yeki stands out to us (and to his tutor) as an exceptional student. Drawing on the strongly politicized frames of reference available from his family and his involvement in student politics, Yeki asserts a coherent and authoritative account. His agency as writer is clearly visible as he links his personal history with the academic task at hand. Why should this be so "very unusual" in first-year student writing?

Conclusion

We return to our central question: why do students produce the texts they do? We also consider the conditions that will best enable students to produce successful texts—that is, those that provide a "provisional resolution" (Flower 67) to the conflicting voices of past and present by means of a confident disciplinary agency. These conditions are illustrated in the context of the revised 1998 HIS100W curriculum.

What emerges from our three accounts is a profile of students who are able to articulate an authoritative academic writer's role. As novice historians, they are conscious that, given the constructedness of history, they are expected to interpret and evaluate texts in a critical manner. And yet, in the context of the slavery essay, we discover our students enacting three versions of a different role, characterized by the retrieval of information in the production of single-truth accounts of history.

This role is consonant with school writer roles. We have also argued that, despite its very different intention, the HIS100W curriculum was complicit in constructing this role for students. The HIS100W course presented students with conflicting roles.

The discipline of history values historians as agents constructing accounts of history through their interpretation of multiple and contending narratives. In failing to provide students with adequate disciplinary resources to tackle a complex argument, however, the tasks required in the slavery assignment placed students in a different kind of writer's role—that of selecting from preconstructed authoritative accounts (i.e., secondary sources) in order to produce a single-truth account.

Our analysis shows students resolving this conflict in different ways. We noted that in university, students are not simply producing texts in rote fashion (as they often do in school writer roles), but instead are involved in the negotiation of a multitude of voices from past and present contexts. Although with different degrees of adeptness, Buti and Daniel both adopt a discourse invested in a naturalized economic order. Buti draws on more limited academic resources (given his prior schooling and relatively weaker English-language proficiency) that prevent him from successfully resolving the conflict. He lacks both the resources and confidence to project a coherent and authoritative voice. As a result, his agency is masked in his text. Daniel has both confidence and discursive resources and produces a moderately successful text, but he is not interested in complying with the role he feels the history course has constructed for him. He disinvests himself from the history course, choosing instead to invest himself in other curricular sites where he feels invited to participate as an agentive meaning maker. Yeki, like Buti, also experiences conflict between his own voice and the authoritative voices of the canon, expressing anxieties about "losing himself." Yeki, however, has access to resources that Buti does not have. Yeki draws on a voice constructed out of political turbulence arising from the transition from apartheid to a postapartheid era. Yeki is both able and willing to project this voice in the construction of a coherent and authoritative account.

Based on the insights gained from this research as well as the developments in the course after our research, we believe that disciplinary roles must be explicitly foregrounded to enable students to produce successful texts. In constructing roles for learners, academic staff must take a long-term view of the social roles and social futures envisaged for learners. Kress argues that a curriculum is a design for the future; "it represents, explicitly or implicitly, an image, a vision of what kind of human being is envisaged here, and, by further implication, what kind of society is imagined and projected in the curriculum" (*Making Signs* 20).

These social roles and social futures must be incorporated into assessment tasks constructed by curriculum designers. Moreover, designers must provide instructional support (or scaffolding) that models appropriate roles and voices for students and gives them the opportunity to rehearse these new roles in a nonthreatening learning environment. The convenor of HIS100W said in an interview that it was precisely these concerns that contributed to a radical revision of the HIS100W course. This revision resulted in a curriculum that constituted students' roles as historians in a more explicit and intentional way. This outcome is the result of a shift from an academic socialization orientation to an academic literacies orientation (see Russell and Foster's introductory chapter), recognizing writing as integral to the discipline and requiring teachers to draw students' attention to the features of disciplinary discourse.

While our study was being conducted in 1997, internal and external pressures led to a substantial revision of the 1997 HIS100W course.[21] Perhaps the most significant of these pressures was the university's policy imperative that undergraduate programs pay more attention to the kinds of graduates the institution wished to produce. The university had embarked on a major curriculum transformation that required all curriculum designers to consider what kinds of literacy practices graduates needed in order to succeed at diverse societal roles. For the history faculty, this meant a consideration of which skills of working as a historian were needed for the problems likely to face students in diverse and changing employment sectors. As the convenor put it:

> I'm thinking in terms of dealing with preconceptions, thinking about how prevalent viewpoints come about, . . . thinking about stereotyping, thinking about what are the dominant kinds of ideas about how society operates and how are those widespread; where do they come from, how do we deal with them and challenge them, because they need to be challenged.

The convenor elaborated with examples of future graduate roles the history program might anticipate: for example, public communicators (such as journalists or broadcasters) who have to sift through a range of information to construct and communicate a particular account, or members of the business community who have to assess people's arguments, determine factors contributing to a particular decision, then arrive at a personally informed opinion that they can communicate to others. In summary, "what this comes down to [is] dealing with a large body of information in a critical, aware way and being able to produce something oneself out of that, which is applicable to a particular situation and communicable in that situation" (HIS100W convenor).

Having explicitly articulated the historian roles in civic society, history faculty turned to the remaining challenge of considering how such roles could be represented, constituted, and enacted at various levels of the undergraduate curriculum. One change they made was to break down the assignments (i.e., the essays) into miniassignments focused on different skills historians need, such as giving students a controversial reading and asking them to write an opposing argument. In another shift in course design, students were made more conscious of sources—where they came from and how and why they were written. The convenor recounts, "So rather than giving them a reading list of historians who have already worked through the material, it was getting them to, in effect, go back to the raw material and construct something themselves."

The revised slavery assignment (see Appendix 2) gave the students the opportunity to work with primary sources (for example, a traveler's eyewitness account of a Cape auction sale of a slave family in the eighteenth century, or extracts from the testimony of a runaway slave at his trial). Given the requirement to work with primary sources, the most apparent role available to students was that of an interpretive "constructor." The option to reproduce from authoritative constructions (secondary sources) was not readily available to students. According to the convenor, "we wanted them to make their own argument from this material, and of course they had to because they had nothing to fall back on." Hence the task positioned students as constructors of their own meaning making:

> So what I am really saying is . . . these small pieces of work were the building blocks of getting to an understanding of how history is produced, why it's produced in different ways, but also most importantly of all, they [the students] are producing it—we are all producing it. (HIS100W convenor)[22]

The convenor's account reveals his confidence that the new course helped constitute a different kind of writer's role for the majority of the class in 1998.[23] Evidence supporting this new role included students' increased enthusiasm and engagement, which the convenor had not experienced before: "A momentum was building up, and after a few weeks of the course, certainly around the middle of it, students were putting forward proposals and ideas themselves of how they could use material and what they could do with it, . . . which is tremendously exciting." He also noted a growing sense of confidence and authority amongst students, particularly in comparison with students' earlier difficulties in disagreeing with or arguing against authoritative sources, in particular himself ("Collins"). He commented, "This year they've been countering me quite happily and that's fine."

Finally, the convenor noted that students appeared to be referencing in more meaningful ways. In contrast to students' attitudes in the past—"'Why should we [reference] because you know that we have got it from this book anyway'—this time students did referencing because they wanted to show they had used this court case—the purpose of referencing was then coming through more." In addition, the problem of plagiarism "fell away" because

> there was nothing to plagiarize this time! It wasn't the sort of material they could plagiarize— what was happening was, many of them were very opposed to the kinds of arguments that were being made by these eighteenth-century writers, and so, far from wanting to copy what was said, they were actually wanting to argue with them! Which was great. That was the whole purpose.

The convenor noted that eventually students would have to deal with secondary sources, a requirement in their second-year history courses. The expectation was that since students had already constructed an interpretive account from multiple primary sources, they would be well positioned to deal with secondary sources as interpretive accounts of history, which are constructed through the processes of historical method and informed by a range of theoretical resources.

In summary, we understand that there are at least two broad components to the apprentice historian's task: first, the interpretive task, reading from primary sources, and second, the adjudicative task, appraising and responding to secondary sources. Both tasks are conducted from a particular interpretive position. There are two stages in the construction of an apprentice historian's voice as it evolves, building on this interpretive base: first, achieving the understanding that historical accounts are interpretive representations, and as such are contextual and ideologically informed constructions; second, an apprenticeship in the theoretical frames of reference informing the application of historical methods. Central to putting these resources into operation is a sense of self as an agentive participant in the disciplinary community, one who has an evolving discursive identity.

The contrast between the 1997 and 1998 curricula offers a number of important pedagogical insights. Clearly, the ways in which tasks are designed and mediated play an important role in developing students who are able and willing to be active members of their disciplinary discourse communities. Key to understanding how a curriculum and its activities succeed or fail in their intent is disciplinary experts' awareness of their own epistemologies, value systems, and orientations. These critical components of disciplinary agency may be tacit or invisible, or inadvertently obscured by a preoccupation with content or form. Understanding, and making visible and available, the wellspring of intellectual agency (as the convenor in this study did so well) may be as important as the knowledge bases and skills of disciplinary curricula. This is central to the academic literacies orientation identified by Russell and Foster in the introduction to this volume.

As noted earlier, this is an exploratory study of the construction of writers' roles within one particular course, students' interpretation and enactment of these roles, and the extent to which they are willing or able to invest their agency as they negotiate a myriad of voices in producing coherent, meaningful texts. The insights we have gained, particularly from the students and the convenor, need to be pursued further in the context of the emerging undergraduate program, as well as in other contexts. Our exploration thus far suggests great complexity in the interplay of shaping forces constituting writers and their texts. An understanding of such complexity and how it is configured in individual contexts should be a key resource as we design curricula for diverse and changing social futures.

Appendix 1

Slavery Assignment 1997

HIS100W: Assignment 2
Essay Topic

How do you account for the similarities and differences between colonial slavery in Brazil and the Cape in the seventeenth and eighteenth centuries?

This question requires you to compare the nature of slavery in two of the colonial societies we are studying in this part of the course.

In your reading for this assignment you will need to:

1. identify the characteristics of slavery in each colony;

2. decide what differences there were between these characteristics;

3. explain why these differences occurred.

Appendix 2

Slavery Assignment 1998

HIS100W: Assignment 2

This assignment is about Cape slavery. You are required to read material written by historians, as well as a range of primary sources on the topic.

You should demonstrate in your answer:

1. your ability to evaluate the arguments of historians of Cape slavery

2. your ability to evaluate and use primary course materials

3. your ability to develop your own arguments on the topic, backed up with examples from the primary sources

Choose one of the following questions for your assignment:

1. "Physical coersion . . . provides little in the way of explaining how slavery worked at the Cape" (Shell). Do you agree?

2. How gendered was the experience of Cape slaves?

3. What types of resistance occurred among Cape slaves? Explain why these types of resistance predominated over other types?

Notes

1. Though these figures are dated, the percentages have not changed much over the past decade.

2. Unless otherwise noted, our usage of the term "black" is inclusive of African, Coloured, and Indian people.

3. The first year student intake in 1997 was White (49 percent), African (28 percent), Coloured (15 percent), and Indian (8 percent).

4. It is interesting to note that this strong version of the role of discourse is absent from Gee's second edition.

5. "Scaffolded" pedagogy refers to curriculum design that attempts to support the learner through the learning process according to the learner's needs; initially the learner receives a great deal of support, but this support is gradually removed as the learner becomes more independent.

6. Discursive history refers to all the ways of speaking, writing/drawing, and listening that an individual has acquired as a result of his or her particular social-cultural upbringing. See, for example, Kress's study *(Making Signs and Making Subjects),* which shows how children from different sociocultural backgrounds (an English child and a Nigerian child) would have very different ways of hearing, interpreting, and depicting the fairy tale *Snow White and the Seven Dwarfs.*

7. In the South African system, undergraduate classes are lectured to by full-time senior academics. The course convenor does most of the lecturing but may share the lecturing load with other colleagues.

8. The South African academic year begins in February, with the first semester running from February to June and the second semester running from July to October.

9. In 1999, Kapp conducted observations of five history classrooms in two separate ex-DET secondary schools in townships outside of Cape Town ("Politics"). Data from her interview served to support the ex-DET students' accounts, as well as to provide more insight into the teaching of history in secondary schools. Although the classrooms she observed are not the ones attended by our students, we would argue that teaching practices across DET schools are fairly uniform in their poor quality and that (sadly) little has changed in the past few years.

10. Bam and Visser (18) cite studies conducted on South African history school textbooks from the past two decades, noting a trend of history syllabi that do not reflect history as a social process.

11. This reading was authored by the course convenor. "Collins" is a pseudonym.

12. Kapp's research confirms Buti's (and other ex-DET students') account. She reports that essentially the teacher tells the students what they need to know (knowledge strongly influenced by the examination) and then writes the facts on the board. Students are instructed to copy the board notes. Students then revise these facts the following day through a series of "one right answer"-type questions. They are then tested on these facts in an exam essay. One teacher Kapp observed told the students, "Thirty points for thirty facts."

13. This comment is an extract from an evaluation sheet that students were asked to submit with the essay.

14. "Naturalized" is used in the Fairclough sense, whereby discourse can make things appear to be natural, normal, and common sense, when in fact they are not so at all.

15. It is important to note that this lecturer came from another first-year course in a neighboring department—a course Buti was taking, albeit a few years after Angélil-Carter's research was conducted.

16. In the early 1990s, before the official dismantling of apartheid education, many historically White schools were "open" to limited numbers of African and Coloured students.

17. McCarthy Young and Leinhardt refer to this as "vacuous rearrangements" of the essay topic (54).

18. In the South African system, examinations are graded internally (i.e., by faculty responsible for the course), but the grades are moderated by external examiners (i.e., faculty from a history department at another university) whose role is to ensure the maintenance of standards across the discipline.

19. These quotations are excerpts from the first written (although unmarked) assignment required of the HIS100W students. The assignment asked, "What are the most important factors which have influenced your life? Explain why they are significant and how they affected your life." Unfortunately, Yeki was the only student in our sample whose essay we managed to collect.

20. Because Yeki was so pleased with his essay mark, he brought it to us, allowing us to see his tutor's comments. This is the only essay for which we saw feedback given by the markers/tutors.

21. Although insights were fed back to the history staff in 1997 as the study progressed, our research was only one of a number of catalysts exerting pressure for curriculum change.

22. This is supported by McCarthy Young and Leinhardt whose study also points to the importance of instruction that "enhanc[es] intentionality and clarity about those features of historical writing that are expected, intended, modeled, scaffolded, taught and valued." They also advocate students writing from primary documents in order to help students "learn that history involves controversy and uncertainty, [and] to learn how to synthesize information from multiple perspectives" (60).

23. The convenor also noted, however, that a number of curricular conditions contributed to the enhanced learner/writer roles in the 1998 course. These included multimedia materials on referencing and fewer students, which enabled students to participate more actively throughout the course. Another interesting shift was to focus the entire course on Africa so that some of the alienation students experienced in 1997 because of the unfamiliarity of material was absent in 1998.

Works Cited

Angélil-Carter, Shelley. *Stolen Language? Plagiarism in Writing*. New York: Longman, 2000.

Bakhtin, M. M. *The Dialogic Imagination: Four Essays.* Trans. Caryl Emerson and Michael Holquist. Austin: U of Texas P, 1981.

Bam, June, and Pippa Visser. *A New History for a New South Africa.* Cape Town: Kagiso, 1996.

Fairclough, Norman. *Discourse and Social Change.* Cambridge, UK: Polity, 1992.

Flower, Linda. *The Construction of Negotiated Meaning: A Social Cognitive Theory of Writing.* Carbondale: Southern Illinois UP, 1994.

Gee, James Paul. *Social Linguistics and Literacies: Ideology in Discourses.* 1st ed. London: Falmer, 1990.

———. *Social Linguistics and Literacies: Ideology in Discourses.* 2nd ed. London: Taylor & Francis, 1996.

Herrington, Anne J., and Marcia Curtis. *Persons in Process: Four Stories of Writing and Personal Development in College.* Urbana, IL: NCTE, 2000.

Kapp, Rochelle. Personal interview with Suellen Shay. 6 July 1998.

———. "The Politics of English: A Study of Classroom Discourse in a Township School." M.A. thesis. U of Cape Town, 2002 (expected).

Kress, Gunther. *Linguistic Processes in Sociocultural Practice.* 2nd ed. Oxford: Oxford UP, 1989.

———. *Making Signs and Making Subjects: The English Curriculum and Social Futures.* Inaugural lecture. Institute of Education, University of London, 2 Mar. 1995.

McCarthy Young, Kathleen, and Gaea Leinhardt. "Writing from Primary Documents: A Way of Knowing in History." *Written Composition* 15.1 (1998): 25–68.

Thesen, Lucia. "Voices, Discourse, and Transition: In Search of New Categories in EAP." *TESOL Quarterly* 31 (1997): 487–511.

CONCLUSION

DAVID FOSTER
Drake University

DAVID R. RUSSELL
Iowa State University

The essays in this volume describe a wide range of national traditions that shape student writing in myriad ways. In fact, it's tempting to concede that writing is too deeply situated within each educational culture to make any sensible comparisons possible, and leave it at that. How, for example, could one compare the influence of the school-leaving examinations in China—with their exquisitely formal codes—with those in France, Germany, or England, where exams are grueling tests of early disciplinary mastery, far more demanding than those most U.S. high school seniors face? Or how could the roles of student writers in radically restructured systems such as those of Kenya and South Africa be usefully compared with the historically conditioned subjectivities of student writers entering the universities of Europe and Britain? Perhaps we could be forgiven if we took the easy way out, acknowledged the obvious about cultural difference, and bowed ourselves off.

We could do that—but we'd lose a great opportunity. In this final section, we'd like to address several important issues, including the connections between students' agency as writers and institutional/systemic expectations, the growing impact of social transformation on students' transitions from school to university, and some major contrasts between the U.S. system and the systems discussed in this collection in relation to the place and functions of writing. We want to avoid any generalizations that might blur or disguise the deep differences in systems and cultures among the countries represented in this book. But we do believe that some illuminating comparisons and contrasts can be made as we reflect on the national systems described in these chapters. To begin with, each of the six represented countries, unlike the United States, requires extensive, high-stakes written examinations that determine whether and where students enter the postsecondary system. Learning to produce carefully structured essays under heavy time pressure is crucial to the success of students seeking university admission. The power of these exams over the shape of the entire educational system and students' lives demands that secondary school curricula be organized around them, creating what we termed in the introduction a "washback" of effects on curricula and students. But the widespread custom of early specialization also demands that students select their major disciplines while still in high school, or no later than when they apply to university. Unlike American students, those in most other systems must participate in disciplinary activities from the beginning of their university studies. Once in their disciplinary communities at university, students discover they must master a variety of written forms and genres to participate in disciplinary discourses.

At the heart of this transition for student learners/writers is the question of agency. Sociologist Anthony Giddens defines agency as the capacity "to exercise some sort of power" to "make a difference in the world," demonstrating "purposiveness" and "reflexivity" (3). For student learners/writers, the term implies both the power of individual action and, as John Trimbur suggests, participation "in organizational or institutional goals and practices," so that they "*join* their productive labors to that of the institution and social structures they live within" (286–87). Students gaining university admission by writing acceptable examinations are by definition successful agents of school learning and writing practices. But in the transition to university, they must also begin mastering the roles and discursive practices identified with membership in disciplinary and institutional communities. The shift from school test writing to disciplinary writing in university is a source of both challenge and dissonance for students in most of the systems represented here. With the remarkable exception of France, students are often dismayed at the degree to which school writing fails to prepare them for university work. Such dissonance offers an excellent vantage point for comparing the tensions embedded in changing institutional expectations.

Expectations and Students' Agency as Writers

These tensions are apparent in the contrast between what institutions and teachers expect of student writers and how students perceive themselves. In several systems, for example, secondary schooling encourages universalized value judgments and "objective" personal opinions in argumentation, while universities demand the submission of personal viewpoints to the assimilation of disciplinary voices that reflect the constructed nature of knowledge. This rhetorical shift causes great difficulty for students in most national systems, raising an important question: how do students confident in their mastery of secondary writing genres—especially extended written examinations—cope with the challenges of the different generic and rhetorical demands of university writing? This question has two fundamental parts:

1. What kinds of agency are required for success by student learners/writers in this transition?

2. How, and how well, do institutions and systems nurture this agency?

Perhaps the best way to begin making comparisons is to contrast the educational systems of France and China, whose students have very different experiences of the transition from school to university as learners/writers. Students in both systems must take extensive written examinations to gain access to university study. The successful ones encounter very different transitions as writers from school to university. The transition seems least difficult for French student writers because there is so much continuity in writing between the levels—writing roles and forms are virtually the same at university as they are in school. In China, on the other hand, students encounter a clear shift of focus as they pass from the universal form of the entrance examination essay to the diverse requirements of disciplinary writing. According to Xiao-ming Li, Chinese students must accommodate to writing that is totally different from the examination forms they were trained to write in high school. Though the Chinese educational system is undergoing rapid change as more students seek admission to university, it remains committed to a national examination as the gatekeeper of university access. The impact of this examination on the school curricula and the students is profound but very different in these two systems.

At the heart of this extensive examination in China is the composition section. As Li depicts it, this section carries decisive power far exceeding its official weight in the total examination. That is because it can be readily assessed by exam readers who are themselves invested in its sponsoring traditions. In its complex structure and moral focus, it reflects both the "eight-legged essay" of the Imperial Civil Service Examination and the *sanwen,* another traditional form. Though the Civil Service exam itself has long since been replaced by an entrance examination adapted to current disciplinary needs, the composition task remains, evidence of the power of a genre to preserve itself amid change. Chinese students must practice this form intensively because of its outsized importance on the exam, though they are aware that its tone and rhetorical stance have little relevance to writing in the disciplines at university. Students see such tasks as limiting, with "the point of view . . . already decided" by the tone of the assignment, Li quotes one student as saying (Chapter 1, p. 76). Not surprisingly, Li's research reveals students' desire for systemic change, particularly a lessening of moral and ideological emphasis in school compositions and in the exam composition's "unalterable mould" for text structure. Yet, interestingly, Chinese students do not perceive the traditions of school and exam writing in a particularly negative light. Indeed, they credit school writing as useful preparation for the "syntax" and "organization" needed for successful university writing. Systemic dislocation doesn't necessarily interfere with students' development as writers when they enter a new learning environment. As Mary

Scott reminds us in Chapter 2, what Vygotsky calls the "zone of proximal development"—the interactive potential of individual readiness and environmental stimulus—is what drives students' growth as learners/writers. Two related findings in these chapters seem clear: first, students' adaptability is crucial in their transition to university as learners/writers, and second, adaptability is nourished by a mix of freedom and motive embedded in the institutional and disciplinary spaces of their environments.

In France, as in China, the school leaving examination requires mastery of specific forms of writing thoroughly rehearsed in the upper secondary levels. As in China, students in France expect to be judged on their mastery of well-practiced forms. But unlike in China, these forms in France are tightly linked to university study, providing strong continuity between school and university writing. As Christiane Donahue demonstrates, upper secondary students passing the BAC (*baccalauréat* examination) are viewed as entering their first cycle of university, where they will use the same forms of writing they have practiced in upper secondary school: "From the *lycée* on, the exam system encourages autonomous writers who learn to . . . associate [writing assignments] with preordained structures" that they must be able to "produce . . . without revision, without peer review, without a teacher's intervention" in their university studies (Chapter 3, p. 147). Through their enabling familiarity with scholastic/academic forms, French students are endowed with agentive control over their writing by the linked character of the French system. The dissonance experienced by students entering university in other national systems is minimized for French students by this linkage.

But as Donahue shows, students working with well-practiced formal structures of school writing cannot simply transport them unchanged into university discourse. Students must adapt familiar forms to what Cheryl Geisler calls the "problem spaces" of domain knowledge and its rhetorical demands in the complex arenas of disciplinary discourse. In her essay, Donahue's exemplary writer finds it necessary to resist and subvert familiar structures when they constrain his viewpoint. He modulates his point of view through several voices, from the impersonal "one" through the collective "we" to—occasionally—an "I," as he seeks to express his own rhetorical agency without directly violating rules forbidding the "personal" in argumentation. His construction of an "imagined reader" and his elaboration of "hypothetical examples" are further adaptations of school forms for university discourse—in this case an essay in a first-year French literature course. How does he learn these strategies when writing is not directly taught either in school or university? Donahue makes it clear that the French system assumes students' abilities to reshape school forms for more complex purposes at university. She speculates that the challenge of "course content itself" calls out students' developing agency as writers, another instance of the school-university transition functioning as a zone of proximal development. Readiness to adapt is crucial, while systemic opportunity nurtures adaptability. Students' freedom to develop self-activating power can only emerge within available institutional and disciplinary spaces. The control over the essay form exhibited by Donahue's student suggests how the system "works" for students able to read and respond to its expectations.

The development of students' agency as writers has much to do, then, with how systemic expectations are communicated and how students are motivated to respond. What of students who do not successfully read institutional and disciplinary expectations, or who find them confusing or contradictory? Mary Scott's analysis of essays in first-year English university literature courses demonstrates the contradictory signals students receive as writers when they make the transition from A-level (upper secondary) studies to university. Students come to the "unsettling realization that what they learned in the past has become mysteriously inappropriate" (Chapter 2, p. 90). In their last years of secondary study, they practice textual analysis using abstract third-person voice (much as French students are taught) and invoking general moral values as grounds for judgment. In their introductory literature courses at university, however, they are required to consider how texts make meaning and how individual texts exemplify theoretical interpretive stances. As Scott shows, school students master those analytic approaches that, at university, contemporary interpretive practices call into question. To succeed in university literary study, they must reexamine and problematize the very strategies they have been taught to trust. If they do not develop adaptive agency as writers, reading and re-sponding to the new expectations embedded in the discourse of university literary study, they will not succeed. Scott illustrates the importance of opening institutional spaces and providing structural stimulus for this adaptation. Writing tasks, she says, should be framed as "motivated signs" emerging from particular histories and social contexts. She suggests designing writing tasks as spaces for "self-reflexivity," which can bring out the cultural positioning underlying specific acts of writing and reading.

The studies of developing nations' educational systems in this volume demonstrate the crucial importance of system expecta-tions and roles for student writers in the transition to university. As Suellen Shay and Rob Moore demonstrate, South African stu-dent writers experience a major shift of expectations in this tran-sition. In their study of three students in a first-year history course, Shay and Moore track the ways in which students' roles as writ-ers in school are challenged in writing about history at univer-sity. Rehearsed in the textbook-and-teacher-centered "single truth" approach to history, students "had neither the requisite methodological nor theoretical resources" (Chapter 6, p. 283) to enact the roles of university history study. Though the students grasped the idea of history as constructed and contested, most could not shape the rhetorical authority needed to convey that perspective in an essay. Rather than imposing a controlling voice on a synthesis of contested viewpoints, students could only ana-lyze an issue from an impersonal, single-truth perspective. Only one student in the study was able to synthesize competing voices through a controlling personal viewpoint in his essay. Shay and Moore speculate that this student's adaptive agency in historical discourse arises from his family history and involvement in stu-dent politics. He was positioned by means of his personal lit-eracy background to read and act on systemic expectations. His adaptive agency as a learner/writer in history is not explained by schooling; if it were, the other students would have shown equal competence. Rather, it arises from the wider social and cultural contexts of his life—further evidence that literacy is more socio-cultural activity than schooled skill. Shay and Moore's tracking of revisions in the history program shows a keen awareness of the importance of systemic expectations in motivating students' agency as writers. Course planners sought to "articulate the historian roles in civic society" in order to signal expectations to students about the roles expected of them as writers in the history curriculum. Thus students' roles as writers are shaped by the complex interaction between system expectations, personal circumstances, and the wider cultural and political forces at play in their literacy environments.

Academic Literacies and Social Transformation

Setting expectations for the literacies of students coming to universities in postcolonial nations is both crucial and difficult. That is clear from both Shay and Moore's study and Muchiri's description of the difficulties Kenyan students have with academic writing at university. Both systems have emerged from a colonial past and retain European and British patterns. English is the language of instruction in both systems but not the native language for the majority of students. Two of Shay and Moore's three students learned English as a second, school-based language, as did most of the students in Muchiri's courses. The dominance of English as the language of education creates significant dissonance for Kenyan students entering university, as Muchiri indicates, for several reasons. Their literacies are acquired amid a complicated mix of first- and second-language contexts, making the transfer of literacy skills from family and social activity to educational contexts a complex and difficult process. As Muchiri notes, her students' school English is often insufficient for university-level academic discourse, requiring developmental instruction that delays students' entry into disciplinary communities and their discourses. Code switching among languages interferes with students' fluency as writers of academic English. And, like South African students, Kenyan students have difficulty developing the authority as writers necessary to cite contested viewpoints in disciplinary writing, in part because discerning ownership of verbal artifacts is new to Kenyan culture. Moreover, Kenyan students, inculcated with a deep sense of community, resist the individually competitive practices necessary for success in examinations.

The system changes proposed by Shay and Moore and Muchiri go directly to the issue of how students' roles as learners/writers may be shaped by institutional expectations in systems under transformation. Shay and Moore propose that educators "take a long-term view of the social roles and social futures envisaged" for students and shape institutional structures to support these roles (Chapter 6, pp. 309–10). In close agreement, Muchiri also emphasizes the need for educators to "develop a wider understanding of the nature of writing in Kenyan communities" (Chapter 5, p. 267) to better understand relationships between family and social literacy patterns and school/university literacies. Muchiri's and Shay and Moore's concerns are rooted in their commitment to wider access to educational opportunity among the peoples and cultures of their countries. Only if teachers and institutions enable and motivate students' adaptive potential, urges Muchiri, can educational systems shape students' agency as writers: "Teachers must let students express their assumptions . . . and desires about their own writing. Then the teacher will be able to start from the known and help students develop the writing capacities they need for success" (Chapter 5, pp. 267–68).

All the educational systems described in this collection are coping with the costs of enhanced social equity, in the form of broadened educational access and the resulting strain on resources. The numbers of students moving into the academic school tracks and on to university has sharply increased in most European systems, as Donahue notes about France, for example. That trend is especially visible in Germany where the number of students entering the *Gymnasium*-university (academic) track has nearly tripled in the last three decades since 1970 (Führ 24). Despite the long-standing "dual system" of vocational education and on-the-job training for students not in the academic track, more and more German students have sought selection for the academic path, believing it more promising than the job-specific focus of non-academic education. As a result, the *Gymnasien* enroll many more students needing preparation for study in the disciplines, in turn compelling university programs to accommodate a wider range of student backgrounds than in earlier decades. Thus, despite the tradition of early disciplinary specialization in *Gymnasium*, greater numbers of students are coming to university with a less consistent range of experience in the discourses of their disciplines.

To be sure, systemic motivation for student writers is built into Germany's educational system, but it comes at a cost to students making the transition to university as learners/writers. Students are persistently reminded that all writing, in class or outside class, long or short, must be taken as a measure of *Abitur* readiness, a gauge of future success. As in the other systems covered in this volume, the washback from the examinations—their impact on the ways writing is taught and practiced in the upper secondary school years—has a strong impact on students' transition to university. The autonomy inherent in German university study can be disturbing for students accustomed to the intensive classroom presence and feedback associated with exam-oriented school writing. As in other systems, the determinative power of the leaving examinations in Germany shapes and constrains school preparation and sets the stage for the displacements of the transition to university. While examinations are still important for academic success at university, the equal importance of independent seminar research and writing in the disciplines requires the additional mastery of authorial roles quite different from those of school examinations. This discovery generates a dissonance for German students similar to that analyzed by Scott in England and Shay and Moore in South Africa, as students struggle to shape new rhetorical authority in assimilating and synthesizing competing disciplinary voices and sources in extended writing projects. Indeed, as more students from different backgrounds and preparations enter university literacy environments, the variability embedded in social difference and access that affects students throughout their schooling becomes an increasing challenge for university planning and pedagogy.

Cross-National Perspectives: Comparisons with the U.S. System

There are several significant contrasts between the national systems discussed in these chapters and the U.S. system, affecting the place and functions of writing. To begin with, as we pointed out in the introduction, educational processes in most of the systems are strongly centralized, whereas education in the United States is profoundly dispersed and decentralized. As these studies show, the centralized pattern strongly influences the roles of writing in most systems. The leaving examinations and university matriculation processes in China, England, and France, for example, are centrally controlled by national governments. The extended written examinations that qualify students for university and influence assignment to universities are administered by national ministries and agencies whose goal is to standardize— and thus, in their view, equalize—the testing and admissions of all students seeking entry to academic higher education. In Germany and South Africa, these processes are moderately centralized. In Germany, university admission is controlled by national policies, but the leaving examinations are administered by state and local educational authorities who retain control over the content and standards of assessment. In South Africa, examinations are both set and marked at the regional rather than national level, with education officials in the different provinces controlling the process. In all these systems, writing is a fundamental element of educational tradition and philosophy, essential to the learning feedback given and the access decisions made at crucial points in students' learning progress.

Extended written examinations for assessment and selection are as marginal to the U.S. educational system as they are central to most other systems. In the systems examined in this book, the merciless repetition of various forms of timed writing in school— hours at a sitting, days at a time—prepares students for successful selection to university and for successful exam writing at university. That is why passing the *baccalauréat* examination (BAC) is the defining event of French students' careers. They find that the same forms and strategies of examination writing that brought them success in school help them greatly in university examinations. Passing the university entrance examination is an equally crucial step for Chinese students heading for university; by the time they reach the point of writing the examination, they have been intensively rehearsed and prepared in the forms of writing needed for success on the examination. German students discover that their preparation in extended written examinations is crucial for success in lecture courses (equal in importance to seminars in most programs) and in the progress-assessing exams they must take in many disciplines to move into advanced levels of study.

The writing U.S. students do in high school, on the other hand (and many schools require a lot of writing), plays only a marginal role in postsecondary admissions, and an equally small role in giving feedback to students about their readiness for disciplinary study or even general education course work or general writing instruction at college or university. U.S. students are often tested, to be sure, but not through extended writing in tests that count. Multiple-choice tests are the primary bases for access decisions in the United States: the SAT, ACT, GRE, MEDCAT, LSAT, GMAT—all the familiar exam acronyms for U.S. students—require little or no writing. To be sure, the ACT and SAT exams have short writing components, usually optional and having little impact on admissions decisions. And Advanced Placement courses available in some high schools do require nationally evaluated curriculum-based written examinations if students want college credit for them, but their rigor and intensity vary widely among schools and teachers.[1] Moreover, students need take the extended written exams only if they want postsecondary credit for their AP courses, and many students do not need or want such credit. Even when AP credits are awarded, they are not usually essential to admissions decisions, as are the leaving examinations in other systems. Further, in about half of U.S. states, short written tests intended to measure writing competence itself are required—so-called "literacy" or "exit" tests for high school students (and some for college/university students also)—for graduation.[2] But unlike the tests in other national systems, these writing samples are not intended to measure students' knowledge. They are not culminations of repeated writing experiences in particular areas of study. Rather, as a result of Americans' mistrust of secondary education, they are intended to assess basic competencies, so that students can be declared graduated and can apply for college or university. Political pressures and competition for funds have made such exit tests and the writing samples included in them necessary for schools' survival.

Thus, while extended curriculum-based written examinations play a central role in the systems examined in this book, such exams have only a marginal role in most U.S. students' educational access, existing only as end-of-course tests for most. It's not that U.S. students don't write in their school studies. Indeed, U.S. schoolteachers typically read and respond often to student writing in most humanities and social science disciplines. The difference is that U.S. students' writing outcomes are dispersed and personal rather than centralized and decisive, a matter of individual grades and credits rather than crucial performances for qualification and postsecondary admission. U.S. school and university students finish their papers, get their course grades, and go on to the next semester; their writing is parceled into their course work and expresses itself in their grade point averages.[3] The same can be said for student writing in colleges and universities. For the most part, when U.S. students leave school or university their writing carries meaning only as personal archives in folders and boxes. It typically does not gain them university access, disciplinary entry, or access to further graduate or professional training. Writing thus plays a far smaller role in the articulation between secondary and higher education than in the other systems represented here.

The extensive preparation for leaving examinations in the upper secondary years of most systems fulfills another important function for students in those systems. Because many of them concentrate their university studies on subjects and disciplines they have begun studying for their leaving exams, these exams function as a direct link to their university work, enabling students to begin university study as experienced apprentices in chosen disciplines. In this regard, the U.S. educational system creates a fundamental disconnect between secondary competencies and university-level readiness. This lack of connection is embedded in the U.S. tradition of deferring disciplinary choices and emphasizing general studies in early postsecondary semesters. U.S. undergraduates are assumed by the system both to lack the needed agency as learners/writers to enter disciplinary discourses, and to be unable to handle the autonomy that disciplinary community membership requires. It is this assumption of unreadiness that most distinguishes U.S. college first-year students from first-year university students in other national systems. It is this assumption that controls learning/writing expectations set by teachers and institutions, which for U.S. students means the task of proving "basic academic literacy"—a construct seriously questioned by many faculty—before taking up the challenges of apprenticeship in specific communities. Part of the apparent imbalance in preparedness between U.S. students and those in many other systems is the extra (thirteenth) year of study at the upper secondary level of many systems, during which students prepare intensively for their leaving examinations. U.S. students, coming to university a year sooner than students in many other systems, must often expend a year or more of intellectual energy in general writing courses that lead into no particular learning/writing community and that challenge students with no particular disciplinary goals or discourse practices.

Thus, for U.S. students, the linkage between high school and university study is more contingent and unpredictable than for students in other systems precisely because U.S. students do not experience the intense disciplinary focus that underlies the transition to university in these systems. At issue here is the pervasive diffuseness of expectations and requirements among both U.S. schools and U.S. postsecondary institutions. Once again the lack of articulation between secondary and postsecondary levels in relation to the functions of writing is evident in the U.S. system. Writing requirements are too local and variable among U.S. postsecondary institutions to permit schools to adequately prepare students for particular programs, even if schools have the desire and the resources to attempt such connections. It is conventional in U.S. educational culture to valorize this centrifugal tendency and prize it as the power of U.S. democracy in action. Differences across districts and states among teachers and administrators do, however, make U.S. secondary outcomes inconsistent and unpredictable from a national perspective. As a result, the learning/writing preparations that U.S. high school graduates bring to universities will vary widely from student to student and school to school. And because a great many U.S. students entering university have not chosen their major disciplines, any connection between writing in high school and writing in early semesters of university is circumstantial and unpredictable for many students. Students may be able to select preferred disciplines in first-year writing-across-the-curriculum (WAC) courses—but only if they know their preferences, and many don't. Certainly, this deferral of disciplinary focus offers students the clear advantage of time and systemic flexibility in deciding what study commitments to make. This openness in the choice-rich, flexible U.S. system allows students to investigate a range of disciplines and their discourses with a tolerance impossible in the more discipline-focused school-to-university transitions of other systems. Yet this openness carries a price: systemic uncertainty and unpredictability for U.S. students encountering new disciplines as they make their way through the early semesters of postsecondary study.

In most nations, students' early investment in disciplinary discourse draws them into disciplinary-community apprenticeships far sooner than is possible for most U.S. students. This contrast manifests itself in two complementary ways. The U.S. system is in one sense moving toward the European model. Writing in the disciplines is receiving more emphasis. First-year general writing instruction—traditional freshman comp—has yielded to discipline-based WAC courses on many campuses, and instructors in many disciplines have developed more writing-oriented pedagogy in their courses. To be sure, general composition instruction is alive and well in many institutions, but it has become more inclusive in its focus under pressure from critics arguing that a "universal academic discourse" outside particular disciplines is a will-o'-the-wisp students ought not to be chasing. There is an equally clear movement in other national systems, however, toward the U.S. college and university tendency to give institutional attention to individual students' development as writers. In this regard, the more centralized organization of U.S. colleges and universities themselves (as opposed to the *decentralization* of the larger U.S. system) is the significant factor, as cross-disciplinary units for writing development can be organized to reach out to student writers in all disciplines. Because of the autonomous, discipline-centered organization of universities in many other national systems, efforts to help students develop as writers are localized within—and vary widely among—individual disciplines and programs. But as the chapters in this volume make clear, institutional awareness of the need to address students' development as academic writers is growing. Muchiri's call for "writing embedded in the learning activities," Shay and Moore's emphasis on clarifying students' learner/writer roles through curriculum redesign, and Donahue's account of the coming of writing workshops and group collaboration to French classrooms suggest growing awareness of the need for institutional attention to students' individual writing development.

Because the transition from secondary school to university is vital to system articulation in all nations, it must be at the center of attention in evaluating the success of national educational systems. Do the differences described in the previous paragraph mean that U.S. students are less competent as writers or less literate than those in other national systems? This is an easy question to ask but a problematic one to attempt to answer. As we suggest in the following section, making specific cross-national comparisons will require careful, fully situated inquiry that is responsive to intellectual, cultural, and social traditions. And the matter of agency for student learners/writers is crucial in this judgment. The inquiries suggest issues important to all educational systems as they formulate goals and practices related to students' transition from secondary to postsecondary educational levels. Differences in the way each system addresses these issues can illuminate the roles student literacy plays in each nation's concept of education.

The Need for Broad-Based Research

These studies support the view that students' writing is profoundly situated within the educational, social, and political traditions of individual national systems. The traditions underlying each system shape the place of writing in social and political goals, which are expressed through educational access policies and in school and university curricula. In addition, the personal meanings of these goals for students are signified in the roles they play as learners/writers confronting new forms of institutional accommodation, work orientation, and self-awareness in the transition from school to university. What these studies particularly reveal is how deeply a student's writing is embedded both in the institutional elements of the learning/writing environment and in the forms and practices of academic discourse communities. There is a clear need for more context-sensitive study of the development of students' agency as writers within these environments. The complexity of these contextual elements argues for a holistic approach as the best way to capture the interplay among system goals and expectations, institutional and curricular structures, faculty-student relations, time and space structures, and discourse activities.

Contextual elements, both local and systemic, are especially important to address in studies of students' transition from school to university as writers. Most writing research has tended to focus on writing at a particular level of school or university, rather than on the transition itself. Yet because in most national systems this transition is the point of sharpest change for students as writers, it deserves broad study. Students' difficulties in early semesters of university study often arise from their attempts to adapt writing attitudes and practices successful at the upper secondary level to the challenges of postsecondary writing. Decentralization of structural planning among regional and local authorities— particularly in the United States—makes it difficult to study the effect of this transition on students because of differences in expectations and practices between the levels. That is why specific, focused attention to this transition as it is situated in particular systems and settings is so important in a broader research perspective. Only through such study can the rich texture of students' developing academic literacies be understood.

We conclude by proposing several categories of further study that incorporate these issues and the approaches to them taken by studies in this collection. As we said in the introduction, we want to encourage teachers and policymakers at all levels to rethink relationships between national and local institutions and to identify ways to rearticulate writing development between schools and universities. We propose the following kinds of study as ways of achieving this rearticulation:

1. *Studies of the effects of emphasizing examination writing as the primary writing activity at the upper secondary level.* Social pressure for increased access to university and the corresponding need for an efficient assessment system have pushed many systems toward ever-greater reliance on gatekeeping examinations. What are the effects of this process on students' development as learners/writers? Studies in this collection report some curricular "crowding out" and alienation in students' attitudes toward writing. We think it is essential to give broad research scrutiny to these effects as they influence the adaptive process by which students identify and make changes in rhetorical stances, personal composing practices, and their institutional roles as learners/ writers, and to institutional and curricular measures that can nurture this adaptivity. Well-situated studies both within and across national systems could be revealing. For example, working within a system that does not emphasize extended written examinations, U.S. students may experience this adaptive process differently—in terms of attitudes, roles, and writing practices—from students in examination-based systems. Such differences could help us understand what elements of students' writing development are shared across cultures and what features are specific to certain institutions and their sponsoring systems.

2. *Studies of the impact of early disciplinary specialization in the upper secondary years.* Such studies could explore how students perceive and shape their roles as apprentices in specific disciplinary communities, how they experience relations between experienced and inexperienced community members, and how they set about learning discourse practices in disciplinary activity. It would be particularly useful to explore how students in some systems enter disciplines at the upper secondary level, and how this early disciplinary access influences the development of writing roles and practices as students make the transition to university. Again, U.S. students enter disciplinary specialties later than students in most other nations; cross-national studies could illuminate how this difference influences students' development as learners/writers.

3. Studies of the influence of changing expectations on student learners/writers in the transition to university, and the changing forms of authority students must acquire as writers in this transition. The ways in which institutions and disciplinary communities communicate their expectations, and the ways in which students read and respond to them, are not often directly scrutinized. Expectations about writing goals and practices usually lurk as tacit knowledge in institutions and disciplines. In most systems, students encounter them embedded in disciplinary discourse and curricular structures and activities. Some disciplines foreground writing expectations for apprentice learners/writers; others clarify them mainly through praxis. A better understanding of the impact of embedded expectations on learners/writers can help shape pedagogical assumptions and practices related to students' writing.

4. Studies of the effects of changing social and material settings on students' attitudes and practices as writers in the transition to university. At upper secondary levels in most systems, cohesion is created through shared backgrounds, frequent classroom interactions, and tightly regulated time and space constraints. This cohesion gives way at university to individual autonomy, dispersed academic units and resources, and diffuse time/space configurations. What are the effects of these changes on students' self-perceptions, social roles, and learning/writing practices? What forms of material and social authority must students develop to work successfully within the more diverse learning/writing environments of university? Again, well-situated studies both within and across national systems could illuminate these issues.

5. Studies of university support for student writers. More institutions around the world are focusing on student writers' needs, establishing student support units such as writing centers, and giving systematic attention to inexperienced writers, but as the studies in this volume suggest, the need is widespread. The institutional models of writing centers found in the United Kingdom and the United States have gained attention in some of the systems discussed here, particularly those of Germany and South Africa. More attention needs to be given to such support for student learners/writers, particularly in systems with underserved populations or with diverse national languages. Such studies would need to examine how mutual interests could be developed among decentralized and autonomous disciplinary units, leading to allocations of needed resources across disciplines and programs.

These suggestions, of course, represent only some of the ways writing development could be studied within and across systems. Indeed, it is likely that research on writing in the transition from secondary to higher education will grow rapidly as nations expand their education systems, reaching out to students from traditionally underrepresented groups. In recent years, global conferences on learning/writing issues have brought teachers and policymakers from many nations together to develop shared perspectives on learning/writing issues. Educators in some European countries, for example, have begun to respond to this need by forming the European Association for the Teaching of Academic Writing (EATAW), which has emerged in response to the continent-wide growth of support units involved in improving students' writing. And the National Council of Teachers of English (United States) and the National Association for the Teaching of English (United Kingdom) have sponsored several international conferences entitled "Global Conversations on Language and Literacy."[4]

It is important to continue cross-national dialogue and collaboration about student writers and writing in order to elicit common concerns and shared needs between systems and institutions. This collection is intended to encourage such dialogue between readers everywhere and bring increased attention to the importance of writing in the work of learning.

Notes

1. Roughly 750,000 matriculating students took one or more AP exams in 2000. See the ETS-AP Web site for numbers: http://www.college board.org/ap/index.html.

2. See the table on "States that require students to pass an assessment with a minimum score to graduate," Educational Commission of the States, 2000: www.ecs.org/clearinghouse/15/52/1552.htm.

3. A number of postsecondary institutions use portfolio evaluation to assess student writing progress, but such attention to students' cumulative writing history does not have determinative public implications in the way that extended written examinations do in most other educational systems. See *Assessment of Writing: Politics, Policies, Practices*, ed. Edward M. White, William D. Lutz, and Sandra Kamusikiri, New York: MLA, 1996.

4. EATAW's main goal is "the exchange of teaching and tutoring methods and strategies, and their theoretical and organizatorial framework." Research on secondary-higher education articulation through writing is an integral part of the effort. The NCTE/NATE conferences are co-sponsored by the National Writing Project (United States) and the U.S. Department of Defense Dependents School, and focus on the teaching of English in different cultures.

Works Cited

European Association for the Teaching of Academic Writing. <http://www.hum.ku.dk/formidling/eataw/>, 2001.

Führ, Christoph. *The German Education System since 1945*. Ed. Iván Tapîa. Trans. Vera Heidingsfeld and Timothy Nevill. Bonn: Inter Nationes, 1997.

Geisler, Cheryl. *Academic Literacy and the Nature of Expertise: Reading, Writing, and Knowing in Academic Philosophy*. Hillsdale, NJ: Erlbaum, 1994.

Giddens, Anthony. *The Constitution of Society: Outline of the Theory of Structuration*. Berkeley: U of California P, 1984.

National Association for the Teaching of English. <http://www.nate.org.uk/top.html>, 2002.

National Council of Teachers of English. <http://www.ncte.org/>, 2001.

Trimbur, John. "Agency and the Death of the Author: A Partial Defense of Modernism." *Journal of Composition* 20 (2000): 283–98.

INDEX

EDITORS

David Foster is professor of English at Drake University in Des Moines, Iowa, where he teaches writing, literacy studies, discourse theory, and literature courses. He is the author of *A Primer for Writing Teachers* as well as chapters in several edited collections and articles on writing, rhetoric, and literature in such journals as *College Composition and Communication, JAC, Rhetorica, Journal of English and Germanic Philology, PLL: Papers on Language and Literature,* and others. Foster is currently engaged in a long-term study of cross-national differences in students' development as writers, focusing primarily on contrasts between U.S. and German contexts.

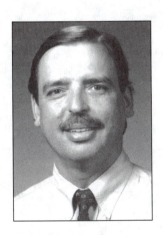

David R. Russell is professor of English at Iowa State University in Ames, Iowa, teaching in the Ph.D. program in rhetoric and professional communication. His book *Writing in the Academic Disciplines, 1870–1990: A Curricular History* examines the history of U.S. writing instruction outside of composition courses. He has published many articles on writing across the curriculum and co-edited *Landmark Essays on Writing Across the Curriculum* and a special issue of *Mind, Culture, and Activity* on writing research. Russell has given many workshops and lectures on WAC, nationally and internationally, and he was the first Knight Visiting Scholar in Writing at Cornell University. He has also published articles on assessment in international context and served as consultant to the NCTE/IRE English Language Arts Standards Project.

CONTRIBUTORS

Antoinette Cloete is a postgraduate student at the University of Capetown doing research in the area of language policy. At the time of the study, she was a consultant in the University of Capetown's Writing Centre.

Christiane Donahue is assistant professor of English and director of middle-year writing at Northeastern University in Boston. She recently received her Ph.D. from the University of Paris-René Descartes with *les félicitations du jury* (highest distinction). Donahue teaches undergraduate courses in writing and graduate courses in composition and linguistics, presents frequently at CCCC and NCTE/NATE Global Conversations on Language and Literacy conferences, and spends her summers working with teachers and researchers in France.

Xiao-ming Li was born and raised in the People's Republic of China, and her first language is Chinese. She is associate professor of English at Long Island University, Brooklyn Campus, where she teaches ESL writing, rhetoric and composition theory, and Asian and Asian American literature. Her major publication is *"Good Writing" in Cross-Cultural Context*. Li has also contributed to anthologies, newspapers, and reference books for English teachers in China, and translated stories of Chinese myths.

Rob Moore is senior lecturer in the Centre for Higher Education Development at the University of Cape Town in South Africa. He is also joint coordinator (with Suellen Shay) of UCT's Writing Centre. His work now focuses on professional development initiatives with faculty, and his current research interests include the implementation of national curriculum restructuring policies.

Mary Nyambura Muchiri is professor of English at Daystar University in Nairobi, Kenya, where she teaches courses in writing. Her dissertation was a study of the role of examination questions in an institutional culture. She authored *Communications Skills: A Study Course for Universities and Colleges* and has published in journals such as *College Composition and Communication*. Muchiri has also served as dean of the Faculty of Arts at Daystar University.

Mary Scott is director of the Centre for Academic and Professional Literacy Studies at the Institute of Education, University of London. The center undertakes research that can feed into practice in school, university, or workplace settings. She also runs an M.A. program in the learning and teaching of English. Scott began her career teaching English in secondary schools and for the past ten years has taught English at the undergraduate and postgraduate levels. She has published a number of articles on the teaching of English and academic writing and is currently working on a book offering new perspectives on the writer in the text.

Suellen Shay is senior lecturer in the Centre for Higher Education Development at the University of Cape Town in South Africa. She currently convenes a postgraduate program in higher education studies primarily targeting academics who seek professional development in their role as educators. Her research interests focus on the social dimensions of assessment practice.

This book was typeset in Sabon by Electronic Imaging.
Typefaces used on the cover include Albertus MT and
Univers Condensed Bold.
The book was printed on 50-lb. Husky Offset
by IPC Communications.

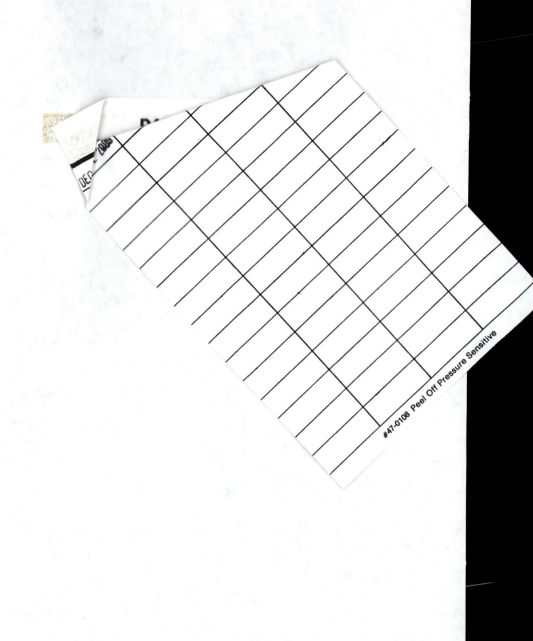

#47-0108 Peel Off Pressure Sensitive